Culture in Psychology

Culture in Psychology breaks new ground by attempting to understand the complexity and specificity of cultural identities today. It rejects the idea that western culture is a standard, or that any culture is homogeneous and stable. Equally, it rejects the notion that culture is a mechanism that enhances reproductive fitness.

Instead, it alerts psychologists to the many forms of 'foreignness' that research should address and to alliances psychology can make with other disciplines such as anthropology, feminism and psychoanalysis.

Part I explores the origins of the new 'cultural psychology' in social change movements, in fields such as ethnography and cultural studies, and as a response to evolutionary psychology. Part II looks at how people create and sustain the meanings of social categories of 'class', gender, 'race' and ethnicity, while Part III examines the interaction between written and visual representations in popular culture and everyday lived culture. Part IV examines the idiosyncratic significance cultural forms have for individuals and their unconscious meanings.

Written by internationally renowned researchers, *Culture in Psychology* will be of great appeal to students and researchers of psychology, cultural studies, psychoanalysis and gender.

Corinne Squire is Senior Lecturer in Psychosocial Studies at the University of East London.

Culture in Psychology

**Edited by
Corinne Squire**

London and Philadelphia

First published 2000 by Routledge
11 New Fetter Lane, London EC4P 4EE

Simultaneously published in the USA and Canada
by Taylor & Francis, Inc.
325 Chestnut Street, Suite 800, Philadelphia, PA 19106

Routledge is an imprint of the Taylor & Francis Group

© 2000 Selection and editorial matter Corinne Squire;
individual chapters, the contributors

Typeset in Times by Keystroke, Jacaranda Lodge, Wolverhampton
Printed and bound in Great Britain by Biddles Ltd, Guildford and King's Lynn

British Library Cataloguing in Publication Data
A catalogue record for this book is available from the British Library

Library of Congress Cataloging in Publication Data
A catalogue record for this book has been requested

ISBN 0–415–21703–2 (hbk)
ISBN 0–415–24354–8 (pbk)

Contents

Notes on contributors

Bipasha Ahmed is presently a lecturer in social psychology at the School of Social Sciences, University of Greenwich. She obtained her Ph.D. on 'The social construction of identities and intergroup experiences: the case of second generation Bangladeshis in Britain' from the University of Sheffield in 1997.

Erika Apfelbaum is Director of Research in GEDISST (Groupe de Recherche sur la Division Sexuelle et Sociale de Travail), CNRS (Centre National de Recherche Scientifique), Paris. Her research interests are in game theory applied to the social psychology of conflict; social and liberation movements, in particular feminism; equal opportunities; women's empowerment and women in power structures; power relations in knowledge institutions; the history and psycho-sociology of the social sciences; the memory of the Shoah/Holocaust, and identities and culture.

Susannah J. Browne is a health psychologist specialising in women's health and oncology. She is based in the Psychology Department of University College London where she is completing a Ph.D. on premenstrual syndrome and illness perception.

Shelley Day Sclater is a Reader in psycho-social studies at the University of East London, Leverhulme Research Fellow at Lucy Cavendish College, Cambridge and codirector of UEL's Centre for Narrative Research in the Social Sciences. Recent publications include *Divorce: A Psychosocial Study* (Ashgate, 1999); *Undercurrents of Divorce* (edited with Christine Piper, Dartmouth, 1999) and *What is a Parent? A Socio-Legal Analysis* (edited with Andrew Bainham and Martin Richards, Hart, 1999). Current research interests include family law, surrogacy, narrative methods, and the applicability of psychoanalytic concepts in social research.

Michelle Fine is Professor of psychology at the City University of New York Graduate Center and Senior Consultant at the Philadelphia Schools Collaborative. Her recent publications include *Charting Urban School Reform: Reflections on Public High Schools in the Midst of Change* (1994), *Beyond Silenced Voices: Class, Race and Gender in American Schools* (with Lois Weis, 1992), *Disruptive Voices: The Transgressive Possibilities of Feminist Research*

(1992) and *Framing Dropouts: Notes on the Politics of an Urban School* (1991). In addition, she works nationally as a consultant to parents' groups, community groups and teacher unions, and provides courtroom expert testimony. In 1994 she was awarded the Janet Helms Distinguished Scholar Award.

Stephen Frosh is Professor of psychology at Birkbeck College, University of London, and Consultant Clinical Psychologist and Vice Dean of the Tavistock Clinic, London. He is the author of many papers on psychoanalysis, psycho-therapy and social processes, and of several books, including *For and Against Psychoanalysis* (Routledge, 1997), *Sexual Difference* (Routledge, 1994), *Identity Crisis* (Macmillan, 1991) and *The Politics of Psychoanalysis* (Macmillan, 1987).

Rosalind Gill is a lecturer in gender theory at the London School of Economics. She is interested in questions about the politics of cultural representations, and new media and technologies. Her publications include *The Gender Technology Relation* (with Keith Grint; Taylor & Francis, 1995) and *Gender, Media Representation and Cultural Politics* (Polity Press, in press).

Christine Griffin is Senior Lecturer in social psychology at the University of Birmingham, UK. From 1979 to 1982 she worked at the Centre for Contemporary Cultural Studies, Birmingham University, on a three-year study of the move from school to the job market for young working-class women. Her main research interests are young people's experiences, and representations of youth and adolescence in the academic and popular domains; sexuality and gender relations, including constructions of masculinity; and the use of qualitative methods in critical feminist psychology. She has published widely in these and related areas, and is the author of *Typical Girls?* (Routledge & Kegan Paul, 1985) and *Representations of Youth* (Polity Press, 1993).

Karen Henwood is a psychologist who now works in the School of Health Policy and Practice at the University of East Anglia. She has research interests in culture, gender and difference, health and environment, and qualitative research methods. In her published work she has reported on an empirical investigation into adult mother–daughter relationships, reflected upon teaching the subject of 'race' in psychology (with Ann Phoenix), analysed gender and moral positionings in talk (with Ellen Sieg), and commented on various perspectives and methods in qualitative research (with Nick Pidgeon). She also edited the volume *Standpoints and Differences: Essays on the Practice of Feminist Psychology*, with Chris Griffin and Ann Phoenix (Sage, 1998). Recently she has completed projects on 'qualitative research and clinical psychology', 'masculinities and the body', and 'the role of forestry in modern Welsh culture and life'. She is Chair of the British Psychological Society Psychology of Women Section.

Myra Hunter is Head of clinical health psychology, St Thomas' Hospital, London and Senior Lecturer with Guys', King's and St Thomas' Medical Schools. She has worked for over twenty years with women in both research and clinical capacities, and has published widely on women's health issues including menopause and midlife, reproduction and gynaecology.

Carl McLean has a Masters degree in media and communications from Goldsmiths' College, University of London. He is currently working as a research assistant on a project called 'Mapping the psychologies of men', based at the University of Wales, Bangor, and the London School of Economics. He is also working on a Ph.D. on masculine identities.

Rabia Malik is a visiting lecturer at the University of East London and a researcher at the Marlborough Family Studies Institute. She completed a Ph.D. on experiences and concepts of depression in Pakistanis and British people of Pakistani origin. She is currently researching the efficacy and meanings of family therapy.

Harriette Marshall is a Reader at Staffordshire University. Her research interests are rooted in critical social psychology and the relationship between psychology and social inequities. Her recent publications have concentrated on the social construction of youth, with a particular concern with ways in which ethnic, gender and sexual diversities pose challenges to traditional psychological conceptualisations of young people.

Rob Pattman wrote his Ph.D., based on ethnographic research, on gender, identity and sex education in postcolonial Zimbabwe. For the past three years he has been working as a research officer at Birkbeck College, London University, with Stephen Frosh and Ann Phoenix, investigating the ways London boys construct their identities.

Ann Phoenix is Reader in psychology at The Open University. Her publications include *Young Mothers?* (Polity Press, 1991), *Black, White or Mixed Race? Race and Racism in the Lives of Young People* (with Barbara Tizard; Routledge, 1993), *Shifting Identities Shifting Racisms* (ed., with Kum-Kum Bhavnani; Sage, 1994), and *Standpoints and Differences* (ed., with Karen Henwood and Christine Griffin; Sage, 1998).

Lynne Segal is Anniversary Professor of psychology and the humanities at Birkbeck College, University of London. She is the author of *Is the Future Female? Troubled Thoughts on Contemporary Feminism* (Virago Press, 1987; 2nd edn, 1994), *Slow Motion: Changing Masculinities, Changing Men* (Virago Press, 1990; 2nd edn, Rutgers University Press and Virago Press, 1997), *Sex Exposed: Feminism and the Pornography Debate* (ed., with Mary MacIntosh; Virago Press and Rutgers University Press, 1992), *Straight Sex: The Politics of Pleasure* (Virago Press and California University Press, 1994), *New Sexual Agendas* (Macmillan and New York University Press, 1997) and *Why Feminism?* (Polity Press, 1999).

Corinne Squire is Senior Lecturer in psycho-social studies at the University of East London and codirector of UEL's Centre for Narrative Research in the Social

Sciences. Her books include *Women and AIDS* (Sage, 1993), *Morality USA* (Minnesota University Press, 1998, with Ellen Friedman) and *Lines of Narrative* (with Molly Andrews, Shelley Day Sclater and Amal Treacher; Routledge, 2000). She is currently researching and writing about HIV and citizenship.

Abigail Stewart is Professor of psychology and women's studies at the University of Michigan, where she also heads the Institute for Research on Women and Gender. She was educated at Wesleyan University (BA), London School of Economics (M.Sc. in social psychology) and Harvard University (Ph.D. in psychology and social relations). She studies the intersection of social and individual history in women's lives. Her recent publications include *Separating Together* (Westview, 1997) and several articles on the psychology of middle age for contemporary women.

Jane Ussher is Associate Professor in the Centre for Critical Psychology at the University of Western Sydney, Nepean, Australia. Her books include *The Psychology of the Female Body* (Routledge, 1989); *The Psychology of Women's Health and Health Care* (Macmillan, 1992); *Gender Issues in Clinical Psychology* (Routledge, 1992); *Psychological Perspectives on Sexual Problems* (Routledge, 1993); *Women's Madness: Misogyny or Mental Illness?* (Prentice Hall, 1991); *Body Talk: The Material and Discursive Regulation of Sexuality, Madness and Reproduction* (Routledge, 1997); *Fantasies of Femininity: Reframing the Boundaries of Sex* (1997; Penguin and Rutgers), and *Women's Health: Contemporary International Perspectives* (BPS Books, 2000).

Valerie Walkerdine is Foundation Professor of critical psychology at the University of Western Sydney, Australia. Among her books are *Daddy's Girls* (Macmillan, 1997), *Changing the Subject* (2nd edn, with Julian Henriques, Wendy Hollway, Cathy Urwin and Couze Venn; Routledge, 1998), *Counting Girls Out* (2nd edn, Falmer, 1998) and *Poststructuralism, Psychology and the Media* (with Lisa Blackman; Macmillan, 1999). She also directed the film *Didn't She Do Well* (1992).

Anne Woollett is a Professor in the Psychology Department of the University of East London. Her research interests are in the area of family formation and the experiences of family life of children and young people, mothers and fathers, and changes in family relationships resulting from separation, divorce and remarriage. With Ann Phoenix and Eva Lloyd she edited *Mothers: Meanings, Practices and Ideologies* (Sage, 1991) and with David White *Families: A Context for Development* (1992). Her research is conducted largely with families living in the inner city, and includes women whose families originated in the Indian subcontinent. She is a member of the Editorial Board of the *Journal of Reproductive and Infant Psychology*, and *Feminism and Psychology: An International Journal*. She is guest editing a *Feminism and Psychology* Special Issue on Reproduction with Mary Boyle.

Candida Yates is a lecturer in psycho-social studies at the University of East

London. Her research interests include the psychoanalytic sociology of the emotions, and the construction of sexual difference in consumer culture. She is currently completing her doctoral thesis on the formations of male jealousy in late modernity.

Alyssa Zucker is a recent graduate of the University of Michigan, where she received a doctorate in personality psychology and a graduate certificate in women's studies. She is currently a postdoctoral scholar in the Gender and Mental Health Program at the University of Michigan. Her research interests span a number of areas in political psychology, including feminist identity development, social change movements and processes of politicisation.

Acknowledgements

I would like to thank all the contributors to this book for their creative and hard work, often under considerable time pressure, their stimulating engagement with the issues in the book, and their encouragement. Molly Andrews and Wendy Hollway provided valuable early contributions to the project. The audience at the 'Culture in Psychology' symposium of the 1997 European Congress of Psychology in Dublin also gave us helpful feedback. At Psychology Press, Alison Dixon, Imogen Burch and Rachel Brazil have been sympathetic and skilful guides through the process of book production. Many thanks, too, to Chila Kumari Burman for permission to use the front cover image of Kamla Vati and Bhajan Singh Burman.

Part I

Reconfiguring psychology and culture

Introduction

Corinne Squire

Interest in cultural phenomena, and in work that takes a cultural perspective, is growing within psychology (Cole, 1996; Shweder, 1991; Unger and Sanchez-Hucles, 1993; the journal *Culture and Psychology*). This developing framework, exemplified in the chapters that follow, no longer takes western culture as standard, or grounds itself in mainstream western psychology (Woollett *et al.*, 1994). Nor does it aim, like contemporary evolutionary psychology, to turn the study of culture into biological 'big science' (Plotkin, 1998: 223). Instead, it tries to address the specific characteristics of different aspects of culture. This work breaks with the notion of 'cultures' as the fixed properties of stable groups (Clifford and Marcus, 1986). It seeks to understand the complexity of identities and identifications as they cut across established cultural categories. Such work shifts concern with cultural differences from the margins to the centre. It alerts us to the many forms of 'foreignness' that psychological research should be addressing (MacPherson and Fine, 1995), and to the potential alliances between them (Unger, 1999) – as well as to the intractable, 'outsider' nature of such differences (Unger, 1999: 61). In this work, culture is something that is cultivated (Mercer, 1994), made or done; it is not a noun but a verb (Unger, 1999: 60).[1] And so culture can happen anywhere, breaching conventional boundaries between 'high' and 'low' culture. A psychology of culture can itself appear in unlikely places. Some of the most startling and innovative moments in the chapters that follow are when contributors recount instances not just of cultural creativity or resistance, but of cultural theory, in the words or actions of research participants.

To live in a culture and to be lived by it is also to 'make choices, distinguish, differentiate, evaluate' (Derrida, 1995: 4). Research participants and researchers alike are cultural performers and cultural critics at the same time.

In order to examine this new 'cultural psychology' in more detail, I will consider briefly the contexts in which it has arisen.

Defining and studying culture within psychology

Defining culture has been, for psychologists and other academics, a project intimately related to studying it. Culture, Matthew Arnold famously said, is 'the best which has been thought and said in the world' (in Williams, 1958: 124). Today, psychological and other writers on culture still often refer to Arnold's definition, if only to rule it out (Kuper, 1999; Shweder, 1999). Generally, however, psychologists lean towards a less hierarchical, more anthropological under-standing. They look at culture as traditional and communicated meanings and practices, and focus on how these meanings and practices are lived individually, how they affect identities and subjectivities (Griffin, Chapter 1, this volume). Yet psychology has rarely taken the 'emic' anthropological approach of immersing itself in cultures and studying their internal structures. Instead, 'cultural' psychology has classically been 'cross-cultural' psychology, studying culture comparatively.

The cross-cultural, 'etic' approach assumes that there are some universal prop-erties of culture, despite difficulties in defining and measuring them, and that they derive from common perceptual, cognitive and emotional structures (Triandis and Berry, 1980). It tries to relate its comparative study of cultural groups to these underlying factors. The approach tends to assume a cultural hierarchy in its choices of what to compare between which groups. Sometimes the hierarchy looks unnervingly like that of Arnold: everyone has culture, but some have better culture than others. In Chapter 10 (this volume), Rabia Malik makes a detailed critique of these tendencies while reviewing cross-cultural studies of the emotions. As she points out, this work focuses on emotions named and recognised in the west, like 'depression'; it uses methods developed by western psychology to study the same phenomena in non-western cultures; it values western individualised psychological addresses to emotional problems and it treats emotions the west sees as 'good', as universal signs of mental health. Malik's own study displays some of the fallacies of this approach. The notions of depression and the word itself are inadequate to her indigenous Pakistani and first-generation British Pakistani interviewees' descriptions of transitive, social distress. They prefer social and religious remedies to personal and health-professional ones, and they understand distress itself as a normal rather than an aberrant part of psychic life.[2] As Malik says, these findings show the severe limitations that cross-cultural psychological research now encounters.

While traditional psychological research on culture sometimes investigates 'emic', qualitative differences between cultures, it tends even then to hierarchise these differences by treating them within an 'acculturation' framework that assumes a teleological progression from marginal to dominant, usually western culture. Alternatively, such research often describes 'other' cultures in its own, western terms without paying sufficient attention to the linguistic and conceptual translation problems involved. This framework also assumes that while individuals may adopt different cultures or aspects of different cultures, 'cultures' themselves are fairly stable entities (Marshall and Woollett, Chapter 8, this volume). Malik's study, again, displays some of the problems with this approach. Of her interviewees, even those who had spent most of their lives in Britain described mental and physical health in terms clearly related to holistic, South Asian Ayurveda and Unani Tibb medical concepts. These concepts seemed to be not defensive but helpful, even to British Pakistanis who were well able to access western psychiatric concepts of depression.

Cultural psychology is increasingly aware of the problems of western-centred methods and theories, such as the notion of 'acculturation', and of the need to recognise the specific characteristics of different cultures without subsuming them under existing and familiar conceptual frames. Some work still ends up reinstating the older tradition's biases and hierarchies, though in subtler ways. Yet as Christine Griffin concludes in her evaluation of this work in Chapter 1, some researchers have made more radical criticisms of the tradition, and construct a quite different version of 'cultural' psychology (see also Marshall and Woollett, Chapter 8, this volume). The limitations of the older tradition have been only some of the factors guiding this transformation. For the writers in this volume, perhaps the most powerful impetus has come from social change movements, and it is to their influence that I now turn.

The impact of social change movements

Feminism and complexity

Rhoda Unger and Janice Sanchez-Hucles (1993), editors of the Special Issue on Culture of the US-based journal *Psychology of Women Quarterly*, place their consideration of culture in the context of the psychology of gender, and more specifically of feminist work in psychology. Feminism, they say, is one of the interests through which, since the 1970s, psychology has integrated concerns with social justice into its search for knowledge, understanding and interventions. They argue, too, that a focus on culture allows psychology to take on the complexity of feminist analyses: to address not just gender differences and similarities but the nature of gender itself. For gender is socially constructed yet deeply felt, relatively stable yet a 'flickering' consciousness (Riley, 1988: 96), defining us but modulated by other social factors and by cultural representations.

In many of the chapters that follow, such complex feminist voices make themselves heard – in Jane Ussher and her co-writers' theorisation of women's accounts of premenstrual and non-menstrual bodies, for example, as instances of mainstream discourses of femininity (Chapter 6). Like the discourses, the women's accounts polarise between private irrationality, and idealised public control and success. Ros Gill and her co-authors, through listening to men talking about advertising images of men's bodies, explore the multiplicity and changeability of discourses of masculinity, as well as masculinity's contemporary convergence, through its visualisation and objectification, with discourses of femininity (Chapter 7). And through their qualitative and quantitative studies of how girls and women in the United States approach cultural sameness and difference, Michelle Fine and her colleagues produce a complex map of how white respondents 'white out' differences, and how feminism can promote the recognition of differences, particularly racialised differences, and can preserve a sense of political possibility (Chapter 4).

Sexuality, gender and performance

Feminist contributions to psychology have always been implicated with critiques of dominant discourses of sexuality. Contemporary versions of this work, emphasising the ubiquitous yet flexible interconnections of sexuality and gender and insisting that performances of them occur everywhere, all of the time, are having powerful effects on cultural psychology (Butler, 1993, 1997), as many of the chapters in this volume demonstrate. Ussher and her co-writers, for example, discuss the premenstrual body's transgression of a normative femininity defined by its heterosexual relationships with men, as well as relationships with children, friends and at work. Gill and her co-authors explore the erotising of men's bodies within consumer culture: heterosexual-identified men start to recognise, and often reject, the desirability, in both senses, of these bodies. More generally, Christine Griffin's emphasis on the *practice* of culture, which is taken up by other contributors, draws in part on analyses of culture as performance in recent work on sexuality and gender (Butler, 1993).

Class, power and change

Other social justice movements have also been important in generating new forms of cultural psychology. Arnold's meritocratic notion of culture failed when confronted with the English working class, which appeared to him, in Raymond Williams' phrase, as a 'magnified image of the Rough' (1958: 134), culture's feared Other. Mainstream psychology's rather similar fear and neglect of class Others has given rise to a long-standing critical tradition influenced by liberal and socialist thinking. This tradition has emphasised the independent existence and non-pathological functioning of class Others, and has made innovations in research methods, often in qualitative research (Brown, 1973). This critical-psychological tradition has also incorporated some postmodern political thinking, notably Foucault's analysis of discourses as forms of power (Henriques *et al.*, 1998); Parker, 1992; Rose, 1996; Walkerdine, 1997). And Foucauldian analyses have perhaps the most impact for psychologists when they are applied to culture, since it is cultural phenomena that are most likely to disappear when approached either quantitatively or through 'personal experience'. In Chapter 3 by Frosh and his co-writers on young white British men's discourses of 'race' and racism, the men's speech is analysed not as a quantitative indicator of their behaviour, or as a guide to their personal feelings, but as a sign of the cultural resources available to them, resources that are importantly determined by class as well as by gendered, historical and racialised positionings: a 'whirlpool of forces' (p. 57). In such work, 'culture' loses its comfortable independence from politics, and the inevitable involvement of cultural psychology in cultural change becomes explicit.

'Race', hybridity and creativity

Implicated with social change movements focused on class, sexuality and gender, are initiatives directed against racism and towards pluralist cultural formations within which 'minority' cultures can be sustained. Such initiatives are crucial to any reformulation of cultural psychology, partly because of the traditional equation of 'culture' with 'race' (Kuper, 1999), but more importantly because cultural formations in the west are always traversed by racialised identities and differences. Much psychological work around 'race' has addressed omissions and prejudices in research and practice. However, considerable effort has also gone into examining the nature and effects of racialised culture, as for instance in the work that began with Kenneth and Mamie Clark's influential studies of black children's preference for white dolls in the later 1930s (Clark and Clark, 1947) or, in the 1980s, Stephen Reicher's (1984) much-cited portrayals of the St Paul's (Bristol) uprising as a racially plural, politically engaged social system rather than the irrational black riot pictured in the popular media and predicted by mainstream crowd research. Today, in conditions of multiple diaspora, increasing transnational migration and moves towards both localisation and 'globalisation', antiracist initiatives coexist in psychology with sophisticated analyses of what Paul Gilroy calls the 'lived profane differences within cultures' (1993: 1)[3] and the hybridising negotiations and struggles between them (Bhabha, 1994; Bhachu, 1997). Such analyses appear, for example, in Malik's careful charting of 'distress' in British and indigenous Pakistani interviewees in relation to both western and South Asian concepts of health and illness; Fine and her co-writers' descriptions of 'race', ethnicity and gender as flexible categories and feminism as a lens that makes whiteness invisible but politics visible, and Frosh and his co-authors' account of a white British masculinity defined in uneasy relation to the Othered masculinities associated with black British men of African Caribbean and Asian descent – historically and socially particular varieties of 'blackness'.

Bipasha Ahmed (Chapter 5) focuses on a topic psychology has neglected, the effects of racism, but refuses, like her interviewees, second-generation Bangladeshis, to turn racism's subjects into either victims or self-deluding deniers of racism. If these young middle-class interviewees assert that racism is both less than it was, and more ineradicably subtle, she argues, this is both because they will not let it structure their lives, and because they recognise that their experiences as young middle-class British Asians are quite distinct from those of their parents or their working-class Asian contemporaries. Harriette Marshall and Anne Woollett present a hopeful, though modest prototype of hybridity in an account of their 'Changing youth' research on young women's and men's transitions to adulthood (Chapter 8). They analyse the video diary of a 15-year-old Asian woman, Kavita, looking at the varieties of 'raced', gendered and other religious, historical and everyday lived cultures on display. In this case, representations drawn from Hinduism, Madonna, Frida Kahlo, antiracism, a contemporary Hindu youth movement and the young woman's mother's life all appear within an apparently straightforward and singular self-presentation. Moving further away from particularity, Erika Apfelbaum (Chapter 11) explores the conditions of uprooted-ness and unfamiliarity that increasingly break up our cultural lives, geographically but also through language, history, work and values. She argues that the trans-lations such fractures require are difficult but potentially creative, and that we can still pursue a limited but concrete universality across cultural dispersion.

In the Conclusion to this book, Valerie Walkerdine deploys the term 'hybridity' to describe the contributions, and applauds their emphasis on cultural survival and expression at the expense of more obviously political, 'resistant' aspects of culture. It would be a mistake to see cultural moments such as Kavita's multiple video images of herself, or the ambiguous self-positioning of Ahmed's interviewees, bracketed off from racism though still touched by it, as weightless and insub-stantial, part of the cloud of ideology that Marxists used to argue obscured the reality of material, economic relations. Nor are such moments 'mere' enter-tainment or escapism, as they would appear in dominant liberal discourses of culture as an unpolitical realm, only aesthetically contentious. Arnold's own idea of culture was of something that must be struggled for and won at the level of the state (Said, 1984; Williams, 1958). Such struggles can have regressive effects (Jacobs, 2000). Here, though, they include moments of critical, oppositional 'individual consciousness' (Said, 1984: 14): the new articulations of identity emerging from Kavita's video, or Ahmed's interviewees' understanding of currently developing forms of cultural difference, or the brief queering of hetero-sexual men's lives described by Gill and her co-writers, or the white girls and women in Fine and her co-authors' studies who preserve, through feminism, the possibility of political alliance and change.

A focus on culture may be a depoliticising force within psychology, a 'substitute for religion' (Williams, 1958: 134);[4] or it may be a form of action. A relativist, 'culturalist' concern with lived differences in cultures may fail to analyse them either theoretically or politically (Spivak, 1996), and may overestimate their value. In the chapters that follow, however, cultural psychology is a kind of culture-making in itself – as indeed all psychology is, only here the endeavour is self-conscious and reflective. Such an endeavour does not preclude theory, but it does also make psychologists aware that their research participants are themselves producers of culture, and sometimes theorists of it too (Spivak, 1996). As Peter Wollen puts it, 'creativity always comes from beneath, it always finds an unexpected and indirect path and it always makes use of what it can scavenge by night' (1993: 209–10).

Disciplinary intersections

Social change movements are not the only factors in the emergence of new kinds of cultural psychology. Related disciplines – sociology, anthropology and cultural studies – have had their own effects. While psychologists in general, as Unger and Sanchez-Hucles (1993) say, ignore variables belonging to these disciplines, in the realm of cultural psychology this neglect is difficult to sustain. The chapters in this book signal a marked shift in psychology's relations with other disciplines.

The debt to anthropology: reflexivity, reality and history

Many of the chapters owe a debt to work in anthropology, a discipline that has a long history of debate with psychology over culture. A productive early moment in that collaboration occurred with the plan of Edward Sapir in the 1930s to produce a really 'social' psychology of how mind is constituted in and 'thought through' culture and history (Sapir, 1994: 72; see also Shweder, 1991). Psychology tends to ignore the history and cultural meanings of symbols and to reduce culture to personality, Sapir claims, but it also pays attention to idiosyncratic events that anthropologists ignore. A 'science of man' could result from the expansion of either field: 'the anthropologist . . . needs only to trespass a little on the untilled acres of psychology, the psychiatrist to poach a few of the uneaten apples of anthropology's Golden Bough' (1994: 203). Recently there has been a lot of poaching. Psychology has gained considerably from critical anthropological work on the difficulties of emic research written in the observer's own colonising language (Clifford, 1988), on the disunity of subjectivities, on historical change in cultural formations, and on relativism and the need to address the different forms of reality that are registered culturally (Shweder, 1991: 53–4). In this volume, for example, Griffin proposes an ethnography inflected by these critical concerns, and capable of bringing an anthropological sensitivity to the structuring of everyday practices into cultural psychology. Reflexively, Frosh and his colleagues point out how their interview research itself constructs as well as records discourses of masculinity. Ahmed, Malik and Apfelbaum all address the problem of cultural relativism, Ahmed and Malik by adopting a social constructionism that insists on the reality of 'racism' and 'distress' respectively, despite the multiple ways in which they are organised, expressed and interpreted (Parker, 1992); Apfelbaum by proposing a limited universalism that gives some structure to the many varieties of uprootedness she describes.

Between psychology and sociology: culture as structure, discourse and activity

Perhaps the new cultural psychology's more obvious disciplinary connection is with sociology. The chapters in this book all demonstrate a strong awareness of the structural factors with which sociology is concerned. Unger and Sanchez-Hucles (1993) believe that a consideration of culture mediates between 'social constructionist' approaches focused on such factors, and 'essentialist' approaches that locate determining factors inside individuals. Certainly the work in this book avoids such sterile polarity. Yates and Sclater (Chapter 9), for instance, produce a highly 'psychological' account of people's relation to culture when they use the ideas of the psychoanalyst Donald Winnicott to understand the deep emotional resonances of genetically modified (GM) foods; yet they also emphasise the variable and changeable emotional meanings of popular culture. Frosh and his co-writers avoid reducing white boys' racist talk to psychopathology or explaining it through social disadvantage; instead they map the complex of culturally available discourse the boys draw on.

Such careful attention to a specific cultural matrix, in this case that of language, is also characteristic of contemporary sociology. Indeed, the exploration of patterns of discourse in talk is now an area of work shared between sociology and psychology. But the authors here are concerned not just with language but also with the functioning of culture, with what is done as well as what is said. This pre-occupation owes much to Raymond Williams, who tried to dissolve Arnold's fetishisation of culture as knowledge through an address to culture as process (1958: 134), and the work of Stuart Hall and the Centre for Contemporary Cultural Studies (1980), which developed a highly influential sociology of culture, a socially aware ethnography that pays attention to the fluidity of cultural formations and to the broad strata of popular culture as well as to the intricate patterns of everyday life. This influence is clearest in Griffin's proposal for such ethnography to be used more in the psychological study of culture, and her demonstration of its value in youth research, which, when focused on behavioural responses or on language, tends to overlook many elements of youth-cultural production and consumption. The influence appears also in Fine and her co-writers' first, ethnographic study of how racialised and gender differences are managed in talk and behaviour in a high school classroom, and in Marshall and Woollett's emphasis on Kavita's self-presentation, integrating words, music, visual images, clothes and other objects, and produced in collaboration with the researcher, in her own home. More generally, the writers in this volume all treat talk as action as well as structure: as one of the materials for doing culture, not simply a guide to culture's shape.

Learning from cultural studies: culture as text, banality and desire

The developing genre of cultural psychology also has more surprising connections with literary, historical and cultural studies. Walkerdine, in the Conclusion, sees these links as the defining feature of the work in this book. They enable the contributors to pay attention to the rhetorical structuring of writing, visual images and cultural practice – a realm that, as Griffin (Chapter 1) points out, is usually neglected even in sociologically influenced work. Usually, psychological research on culture tries to find its psychological meanings. Consumer psychology, for example, is interested in how advertising, goods and services work on audiences and markets, who is susceptible to which messages, and what product meets whose 'needs'. But here the cultural texts themselves become objects of study, part of a style 'politics'. Frosh and his co-writers address the revealing particularities in the spoken language of racialised difference. Yates and Sclater use rhetorical analysis of 'Enlightenment', progress-directed narratives and the Gothic horror genre to make sense of journalistic representations of GM foods, polarised between trusting optimism and fearful fatalism. The connection with cultural studies also encourages contributors to recognise the historical situatedness of the texts they are working with, as in Ahmed's consideration of generation-specific accounts of racism, and in Apfelbaum's subtle understanding of how the multiple, often partially known histories that follow uprootedness, especially after genocide, provoke conflicting identity effects. It is also partly thanks to work in cultural studies that the chapters in the book are so methodologically bold, focusing as de Certeau urges us on 'stories' and 'practices' rather than methodology (1984: 65). And it is cultural studies, particularly under the influence of feminist and queer theory and theories of cultural difference and hybridity, that enables the writers to consider 'high' and 'low' cultural phenomena alongside each other. Applebaum moves confidently between literature and the everyday autobiographical voice without losing the specificity of either. Contributors treat seriously some banal but powerful elements of culture – the images of men's bodies, specifically 'beefcake' advertisements considered by Gill and her co-authors, the tabloid presentations of expert scientists, Frankensteins and mutant fish in Yates and Day Sclater's chapter, young working-class white boys' unstructured, inconsequential talk about themselves in Frosh and his colleagues' chapter. Marshall and Woollett adopt the video diary method from its familiar television context and pay attention to the musical 'background' of the shots. They, along with Gill and her co-writers, also focus on visual culture, a realm often passed over by psychologists in their search for underlying cognitive significance.

This seriousness about popular culture does not imply uncritical relativism. For Yates and Day Sclater there is 'good' and 'bad' popular culture, depending on whether or not it offers a 'transitional' space for exploring emotional possibilities (p. 143). For Gill and her co-writers, even 'bad' popular culture can have interesting, transformative aspects; for instance, when objectifying visual images fracture masculinity's relationship to femininity and desire. Even Frosh and his co-authors find important diversities within racialised masculinities, which at least offer potential for understanding these negative aspects of everyday lived culture.

It is often through cultural studies that writers in this book take on ideas from psychoanalysis. What results is by no means orthodox psychoanalysis, but rather partial deployments of psychoanalytic concepts like those that have characterised the most creative and influential recent uses of psychoanalysis in literary and cultural theory (Bhabha, 1994; Butler, 1993; Mulvey, 1975). Yates and Day Sclater, in the piece that comes closest to a direct use of psychoanalytic ideas, argue that Winnicottian notions of transitional space, where anxieties and uncertainties are negotiated, help us understand the emotional intensity of late-modern culture – particularly where food, a highly meaningful, 'real and imagined' part of our environment (p. 140), is at stake. Yet they imbue the psycho-analytic concepts with an ambiguity that necessitates a parallel analysis at the level of culture. Ushher and her co-authors, in a less obviously psychoanalytically inflected piece, outline the unconscious ambivalences and fragmentation of subjectivities and the splitting of femininity as they are played out around PMS (premenstrual syndrome) in the spheres of popular culture and everyday life.

Revisiting critical psychology: from method to practice, from language to culture

Contemporary forms of cultural psychology also have important connections with the tradition of critical psychology. That tradition's distinctiveness can be identified with its approaches first to method, second to language. Since the 1960s critical psychologists have argued for the political, human and scientific value of qualitative methods, of listening to people, watching and understanding them, rather than measuring them (Fox and Prilleltensky, 1997). Contemporary cultural psychology, though, is less interested in listening to ignored individual experiences or treating research as a kind of adjunct to identity politics, and more, under the influence of post-structuralist and postmodernist theory, in 'thinking through' the complex dialogues between self and other, and the patterns of truth and fiction involved when 'research' becomes the generation of plausible narrative (de Certeau, 1984; Shweder, 1991: 108–10). Such work does not have to involve qualitative research. As Fine and her colleagues' chapter shows in its use of attitude scales to explore the relationship between feminism and perspectives on difference, quantitative work can also be conducted within the new forms of cultural psychology (see also Unger, 1983). Moreover, qualitative work done within this framework need not be relativist and impossible to evaluate. The chapters in this volume, for instance, make epistemological sense within contemporary social science, for they use a span of evidence, argument and theory that is accepted as adequate. However, unlike in much critical psychology, where particular varieties of method are endlessly debated, methodological diversity is quite compatible with the common project of these writers. In their concerns, practice, performance or pragmatics has displaced method. Psychology has become a matter of achieving effective analyses and understandings, an aspect of the continuous performance of culture. This perspective supports methodological scepticism and creativity, as well as an ability to view research participants as collaborators, even theoreticians.

The second distinctive feature of contemporary critical psychology is what is often referred to as its 'turn to language'. Work on the symbolic elements of cultures has become a much larger part of psychology as the discipline has taken on post-structuralist and postmodernist concerns with the failure of meaning to emerge self-evidently from language, the importance of examining representational structure, and the role of representations in constructing human subjectivities. The resulting field, generally called 'discourse analysis', is broadly divisible, as Griffin discusses in this volume, into more technical, conversation-analytic research on discursive structure, and more sociological or political, Foucauldian research on discursive power. As Edward Said (1984: 3) points out,

the theoretical origins of post-structuralism and postmodernism were 'insurrec-
tionary', but their popularisation, particularly in US literary theory, led to narrow
'textuality' of the kind that is often said to characterise the first tendency in
discourse analysis. Many critical psychologists remain, like other psychologists,
preoccupied with psychology's relation to science. Language, or text, is a
scientifically respectable object of study, which the first tendency retains. This
narrowness of object can be to its detriment, limiting its remit to 'reflexivity, an
idealised notion of conversation . . . and pluralism served up on a linguistic base'
(Parker, 1989: 138). The second tendency, to which the work in this volume is for
the most part closer, runs a different risk: that of overgeneralising about large
ideological and discursive structures from small pieces of text (Malson, 2000).
Language itself, though, often disappears as an object of study in both tendencies,
being viewed as a guide, in the first case to underlying cognitive structures, and in
the second, to broad ideological structures (Squire, 1995).

The 'turn to culture' demonstrated in this volume is in some ways a successor
to the 'turn to language'. The contributors spend little time debating the conceptualisations of language, cognition and power that could define their place in
discourse analysis. In these chapters, language acts as a bridge between popular
culture and subjectivity, rather than as a reified analytic category. Language and
its failures are seen as constituting culture and its lacunae, but this element in the
construction of cultural phenomena need not, as Griffin suggests, be separated out
from others. Malik, for instance, whose work turns on the translatability and the
connotations of the terms 'distress' and 'depression', integrates these concerns into
her consideration of psychiatry, migration, racism and cultural difference. Ahmed
emphasises the importance of the context of discourse production, and of who,
exactly, is producing it. Perhaps it is indicative that many contributors invoke
'narratives', large, historically evolving, and often fairly untidy and incomplete
linguistic structures, with clear cultural variability, to describe both cultural
phenomena and their own work. They themselves produce stories very different
from the rather untypical closed narratives, similar to detective stories, that
characterise mainstream psychological research (Squire, 1990). Their open
narratives are indeed more like hypertext in the alternative interpretive pathways
they allow. And they are committed to researching cultural formations as if they
too are open narratives, with many possible sequences and endings, still in the
process of being told by their makers.

Postscript: Bad science

There is another strand of recent psychological work on culture: that of biological
and evolutionary psychologists, who provide explanations for the cultural similarities and differences they identify in terms of their reproductive benefits,
and who aim to substantiate these explanations with robust evidence of the physiological underpinnings and genetic determination of many aspects of culture. Such
concerns are not new. The 'cross-cultural', etic variety of cultural psychology
often assumes that cultural universals and variations in them are based on

biological underpinnings, and emic research persistently though often implicitly identifies 'culture' with biological 'race', as Malik's review of research of this kind about the emotions points out. Gender too is frequently understood, in psychology and popularly, as biological, as Ussher and colleagues' account on the psychopathologisation of PMS demonstrates. However, evolutionary psychology's stronger claims generate massive interest, in psychology and the media, and it was partly in response to these often overinflated claims that this book was written. Chapter 2, by Lynne Segal, is devoted to demolishing them (an even more extensive critique is to be found in Segal, 1999).

From the perspective of contributors to this volume, evolutionary psychology's problems can be summarised as stereotype, syllogism, biological reductionism and, at the level of rhetoric, an unpersuasive mix of arrogance and defensiveness. First, stereotypes. Evolutionary psychology resorts to these surprisingly often in its descriptions of cultural phenomena. Popular concepts of gender differences in, for instance, aggression, communication and visuospatial intelligence, based on contested and ambiguous research, are treated as empirically proved, and from them the sexes are concluded to have distinct, almost speciated reproductive interests. The role of syllogism also emerges clearly in such arguments. As Segal notes (p. 34), in evolutionary psychology a widely observed behaviour quickly becomes a biologically founded, 'universal' one, whose genetic cause can be assumed. The argument seems to go like this: Differences between women and men in, for instance, communication styles are widely observed. Other differences between women and men in, for instance, muscle mass, or susceptibility to heart attacks, are also widely observed. These differences have been explained biologically. Therefore, communication differences can be explained biologically.

The power of such syllogisms comes from the third problematic factor in evolutionary psychology: its biological reductionism. Segal (p. 36) gives as one example the assertion that widespread findings of preferences for light-skinned reproductive partners suggest that lighter skin indicates greater fertility, rather than that they suggest the powerful effects of western colonial and postcolonial ideologies. Such resorts to biology when social factors provide simpler and more complete explanations seem naive in a social scientist – or, indeed, any scientist. The biology itself is questionable. Genetic explanations tend to be based on single studies of biological relatives or small-scale research on genetic markers, which are rarely replicated, so the explanations are 'disputed or dropped', as a science journalist recently remarked wearily (*Guardian*, 23 April 1999: 11). The alleged genetic mechanisms behind culture are acknowledged to be too complex for current discovery, so much evolutionary psychology, though taken as substantiated, remains at the level of speculation, and often bears little relation to the complexities of contemporary biological knowledge. Examples are ideas of cultural phenomena as gene-analogous 'memes' (Dawkins, 1989); Pinker, 1997), or as 'nested' within evolved biological parameters of human cognition (Plotkin, 1998: 241–2). More specific hypotheses, like the notion of human communication as reducible to the evolutionary advantage it confers on a highly social species with a long childhood, are equally tendentious. Henry Plotkin tries to tie down the theory by referring to the thirty million DNA base pairs by which humans differ from chimpanzees, among which 'must' be those that code for language, though a description of them and their functioning is neither feasible nor likely to account for all human linguistic capabilities (1998: 136).

Plotkin provides examples of the slightly ludicrous rhetoric of much evolutionary psychology when he insists on calling cultural knowledge and exchange 'extra-somatic storage' and 'extragenetic transmission', and meanings 'replicators' (1998: 250, 247, 256). A deeply un-Darwinian biological messianism also appears in evolutionary psychology's frequent populist framings of evolution as design: mind is 'designed by natural selection to solve' our ancestors' problems, for instance (Pinker, 1997: x). In other rhetorical attempts to get culture under control, it is often said to be the result of an evolved complex neural computer, 'hard-wired' in. 'Culture really is big science', Plotkin (1998: 223) boosterishly assures us; unappetisingly, the evolutionary psychology of culture sets itself up as a new frontier where men are fighting each other for genes, machines and research budgets.

The popularity of evolutionary psychology indicates the power of the drive within psychology, and elsewhere, towards the apparent truth and the comforting conservatism of biological explanations. Of course, evolutionary psychologists acknowledge that biology is not a sufficient explanation for the whole of culture. They emphasise that biological determinants can, and often should, be worked against. Pinker (1997), for example, presents himself as a feminist of the emotions, if not the intellect, when he argues that sex differences are not validated by their biological basis; resistance to them may even be morally compulsory. Yet evolutionary psychology preserves, through its far from scientific belief in a biological foundation to such differences, a sense of knowing the truth, and knowing the absolute limits to social change.

As Segal notes, the resurgence of such a 'biology' of culture is probably related, as with sociobiology in the 1970s, to dramatic, ongoing and contested changes in discourses and practices around gender, race and sexuality. Today, however, this 'biology', however specious, has been far less challenged than twenty years ago, perhaps partly because of the shifting and more uncertain nature of social change movements themselves.[5] Yet it seems a mistake to let evolutionary psychology declare itself the undisputed, 'scientific' truth of culture when it is so inadequate as science or indeed as any other kind of explanation of cultural phenomena.

Later in Part I, Segal comprehensively questions evolutionary psychology's imperialism about culture. Arriving at a picture of cultural psychology that does not ignore biological factors but recognises the complexity of their operation within the 'bestiary' that is natural history (Bagemihl, 1999: 265),[6] she argues for 'epistemic diversity' (p. 40). The other chapters in this book set about developing psycho-cultural approaches to psychology that focus on the mutually determining relationships between subjects and culture, and on 'culture' as a matter of symbolic, theoretical and everyday activities carried out by psychologists, as well as by the people they study.

In Chapter 1, Griffin explores cultural psychology's relations to mainstream psychology, and to anthropology, sociology and cultural studies, particularly to studies of youth culture. She argues that this kind of work should focus on observing and understanding practices as much as on eliciting, recording and analysing language.

Part II, 'Culture and social formations', looks at how people create and sustain the meanings of social categories such as gender, 'race' and class, and how in the process they often 'talk back' to dominant understandings of these categories. An interest in culture seems, as in this book, to encourage psychological work that is sensitive to postcolonial, 'hybrid' identities. Such identities are shaped by migration, discrimination, poverty, and minority ethnic, racial and religious statuses. They appropriate elements of dominant western cultures, but they themselves also come to inflect those cultures, and in addition they retain and transform aspects of 'other', marginalised cultural identities. At the same time, the chapters in this section are very aware of the problems and limits of such hybridity in effecting personal and social change.

An address to 'culture' should cause psychologists to pay attention not just to everyday lived culture but also to mass-audience popular culture and its articulation with subjectivity. Part III, 'Culture and representations', examines the interaction between specific written and visual representations and everyday lived culture, looking both at how those representations shape subjectivity and at how people's engagement with them, as active cultural consumers and producers, changes them.

Attention to culture can also help us negotiate between concepts of subjectivity as a social construct and as a powerful personal experience (Bhabha, 1994). Part IV, 'Culture and the emotions', explores this negotiation, looking at the idiosyncratic meanings cultural forms have for individuals, the more general unconscious significances that ideologies and social formations take on – and the possibilities and problems presented by deploying such psychoanalytic concepts in the field of cultural psychology. Finally, the Conclusion assesses common factors in the contributors' disparate research and theorisation, sets them in the context of developments in cultural theory and critical psychology, and evaluates their significance for the psycho-cultural 'third space' it sees opening up in contemporary work on culture and subjectivity.

Notes

1 Unger is referring here to gender, but the argument can be generalised to other aspects of culture.
2 Ussher and her co-writers note this possibility in relation to premenstrual experiences later in the book.
3 Gilroy uses this term to refer specifically to 'Britain's black cultures' (1993: 1), and its significance is somewhat diluted by my extension of its application.
4 Williams uses this phrase to characterise Arnold's deification of culture.
5 Some on the British Left have even adopted the evolutionary-psychological framework (Singer, 1998).
6 Bagemihl uses this term to describe 'sexual and gender variance' in animals, features

that are commonly stereotyped in evolutionary psychology, but it can usefully be extended to cover animal variations more generally (1999: 265).

References

Bagemihl, B. (1999) *Biological Exuberance*, London: Profile Books.

Bhabha, H. (1994) *The Location of Culture*, London: Routledge.

Bhachu, P. (1997) 'Dangerous design: Asian women and the new landscapes of fashion', in A. Oakley and J. Mitchell (eds) *Who's Afraid of Feminism?*, London: Hamish Hamilton.

Brown, P. (1973) *Radical Psychology*, New York: Harper & Row.

Butler, J. (1993) *Body Matters*, London: Routledge.

—— (1997) *The Psychic Life of Power*, Stanford, CA: Stanford University Press.

Certeau, M. de (1984) *The Practice of Everyday Life*, Berkeley: University of California Press.

Clark, K. and Clark, M. (1947) 'Racial identification and preference in Negro children', in E. Maccoby and E. Hartley (eds) *Readings in Social Psychology*, New York: Holt, Rinehart & Winston.

Clifford, J. (1988) *The Predicament of Culture*, Cambridge, MA: Harvard University Press.

Clifford, J. and Marcus, G. (eds) (1986) *Writing Culture*, Berkeley: University of California Press.

Cole, M. (1996) *Cultural Psychology: A Once and Future Discipline*, New York: Belknap Press.

Dawkins, R. (1989) [1976] *The Selfish Gene*, Oxford: Oxford University Press.

Derrida, J. (1995) *On the Name*, Stanford, CA: Stanford University Press.

Fox, D. and Prilleltensky, I. (1997) *Critical Psychology*, New York: Hamish Hamilton.

Gilroy, P. (1993) *Small Acts*, London: Serpent's Tail.

Hall, S., Hobson, D., Lowe, A. and Willis, P. (1980) *Culture, Media, Language*, Birmingham: Hutchinson and the University of Birmingham.

Henriques, J., Hollway, W., Urwin, C., Venn, C. and Walkerdine, V. (1998) *Changing the Subject*, London: Routledge. First published 1984.

Jacobs, R. (2000) 'Narrative, civil society and public culture', in M. Andrews, S. Sclater, C. Squire and A. Treacher (eds) *Lines of Narrative*, London: Routledge.

Kuper, A. (1999) *Culture: An Anthropologist's Account*, London: Harvard University Press.

MacPherson, P. and Fine, M. (1995) 'Hungry for an us: adolescent girls and adult women negotiating territories of race, gender, class and difference', *Feminism and Psychology* 5(2): 181–200.

Malson, H. (2000) 'Fictional(ising): ontological assumptions and methodological productions of ("anorexic") subjectivities', in M. Andrews, S. Sclater, C. Squire and A. Treacher (eds) *Lines of Narrative*, London: Routledge.

Mercer, K. (1994) *Welcome to the Jungle*, London: Routledge.

Mulvey, L. (1975) 'Visual pleasure and narrative cinema', *Screen* 16: 6–18.

Parker, I. (1989) *The Crisis in Modern Social Psychology – And How to End It*, London: Routledge.

—— (1992) *Discourse Dynamics*, London: Sage.

Pinker, S. (1997) *How the Mind Works*, London: Penguin.

Plotkin, H. (1998) *Evolution in Mind*, London: Penguin.

Reicher, S. (1984) 'St. Paul's: a study in the limits of crowd behaviour', in J. Murphy, M. John and H. Brown (eds) *Dialogues and Debates in Social Psychology*, Milton Keynes: Open University Press.

Riley, D. (1988) *'Am I That Name?' Feminism and the Category of 'Women' in History*, Minneapolis: Minnesota University Press.

Rose, N. (1996) *Inventing Our Selves*, Cambridge: Cambridge University Press.

Said, E. (1984) *The World, the Text and the Critic*, London: Faber & Faber.

Sapir, E. (1994) *The Psychology of Culture*, New York: Houton de Gruyter.

Segal, L. (1999) *Why Feminism?*, Cambridge: Polity Press.

Shweder, R. (1991) *Thinking Through Cultures*, Cambridge, MA, and London: Harvard University Press.

Singer, P. (1998) 'Darwin for the left', *Prospect*, June: 26–30.

Spivak, G. (1996) 'Diasporas old and new: women in the transnational world', *Textual Practice* 10(2): 245–69.

Squire, C. (1990) 'Crisis what crisis? Discourses and narratives of the "social" in social psychology', in I. Parker and J. Shotter (eds) *Deconstructing Social Psychology*, London: Routledge.

—— (1995) 'Pragmatism, extravagance and feminist discourse analysis', in S. Wilkinson and C. Kitzinger (eds) *Feminism and Discourse*, London: Sage.

Triandis, H. and Berry, J. (1980) *Handbook of Cross-cultural Psychology*, Boston, MA: Allyn & Bacon.

Unger, R. (1983) 'Through the looking glass: no wonderland yet! The reciprocal relationship between methodology and models of reality', *Psychology of Women Quarterly* 8: 9–32.

—— (1999) 'Some musings on paradigm shifts: feminist psychology and the psychology of women', *Psychology of Women Section Review* 1(2): 58–62.

Unger, R. and Sanchez-Hucles, J. (1993) 'Integrating culture', *Feminism and Psychology* 17(4): 365–72.

Walkerdine, V. (1997) *Daddy's Girl: Young Girls and Popular Culture*, London: Macmillan.

Williams, R. (1958) *Culture and Society*, London: Penguin.

Wollen, P. (1993) *Raiding the Icebox*, Bloomington: Indiana University Press.

Woollett, A., Marshall, H., Nicholson, P. and Dosanjh, N. (1994) 'Asian women's ethnic identity: the impact of gender and context in the accounts of women bringing up children in East London', *Feminism and Psychology* 4(1): 119–32.

1 More than simply talk and text

Psychologists as cultural ethnographers

Christine Griffin

In a variety of ways, all the contributors to this volume are calling for a fuller and more nuanced understanding of culture and the cultural in psychological research and practice. This book is concerned with a perspective that has become known as the 'new cultural psychology' (Shweder, 1990), and sets out to explore this emerging approach in all its diversity. The debates on the 'new cultural psychology' revolve around two related but distinct issues: first, the critiques of mainstream psychology as Anglocentric and the advocacy of a more culturally sensitive psychology which is politically engaged (e.g. Fox and Prilleltensky, 1997); and second, calls for a deeper understanding of the relationship between psychology and the cultural domain. This latter aspect of the 'new cultural psychology' involves a connection with debates in the humanities and cultural studies, as well as in social anthropology and the new cultural geography (e.g. Pile and Thrift, 1995). In particular, a consideration of the relationship between psychology and the cultural domain involves an engagement with post-modernism(s), post-structuralism(s), feminism(s) and more recent approaches to the practice of ethnography. A major implication of such an engagement for contemporary western psychology concerns the 'new' theories of the subject and subjectivity which have emerged from post-structuralism and psychoanalytic perspectives (e.g. Henriques *et al.*, 1984; Walkerdine, 1996), and which are covered in depth elsewhere in this volume. This new approach to subjectivity also involves an engagement with new understandings of 'difference', including cultural difference, informed by postmodernism and post-structuralist ideas (Ferguson *et al.*, 1990).

A further area of debate around the relationship between psychology and the cultural domain relates to methodology, and especially the restricted range of research methods which are deemed acceptable in psychological research, and their limitations for appreciating the complexity (or even the possibility) of cultural forms and practices. My aim in this chapter is to devote some attention to this latter issue, and to consider the theoretical and methodological implications for constructing a critical cultural psychology which could appreciate the diversity of the cultural domain. My intention is to consider the potential value of those aspects of cultural studies (or research which engages with the cultural, to use a broader term) which have their roots in social and cultural anthropology as well as drawing on ethnographic practices and research methods. My argument, then, is for a broadening of the theoretical and methodological arena of contemporary cultural psychology, and I will draw on a number of examples from recent empirical research to illustrate my points. I will begin by considering some of the recent texts on the 'new cultural psychology'.

The 'new cultural psychology' and recent approaches to the relationship between culture and psychology

Interest in the relationship between culture and psychology has been most pervasive among those psychologists who have operated on the margins of the discipline, many of whom would dispute psychology's insistence on its foundation in positivism and the scientific method, and its adherence to an impossible position of political neutrality and scientific objectivity (e.g. Sampson, 1977; Unger and Sanchez-Hucles, 1993). In 1995, US psychologists Nancy Rule Goldberger and Jody Bennet Veroff compiled a reader on culture and psychology which reprinted key texts from anthropology (Geertz, 1975); psychiatry (Kleinman, 1988); clinical psychology (Jones and Thorne, 1987); child development (Ogbu, 1981); feminism (Moraga, 1983); as well as academic social and cognitive psychology (Jahoda (1977) and Helms (1992) respectively). In this text Goldberger and Veroff and several other contributing authors argue for 'a multicultural perspective in studying and understanding human behavior' (1995: 3) in a challenge to the pervasive Anglocentrism of mainstream psychology.

The emergence of what these authors term 'cultural psychology' (Goldberger and Veroff, 1995: 7) involves more than studies of cultures other than the Anglo-European or Anglo-American norm. It involves 'studies of the interactive effects between cultures that coexist in a larger societal context' (Goldberger and Veroff, 1995: 7). It also involves a concern with the potential impact of specific cultural influences on individuals living within those cultures. As Goldberger and Veroff point out, this is an interdisciplinary project, which involves engagement with debates in (at least) anthropology, philosophy, cultural studies, education, sociology, literary studies and linguistics, as well as cultural geography and the perspectives of postmodernism and post-structuralism.

A key figure in the emergence of 'cultural psychology' has been Richard Shweder (1990), who sees the field as the study of 'intentional worlds', or of how meanings and interactions are products of the inevitable interdependence of psyche and culture (see also Sampson, 1993). Shweder's argument has much in common with ideas derived from post-structuralism which challenge the long-held distinction between individual and society so central to mainstream social psychology. As the authors of the influential text *Changing the Subject* recognised in 1984, this challenge presages a profound transformation in psychology's theory of the self, since it is no longer possible to (pretend we can) say where the 'individual self' ends and 'society/culture' begins (Henriques *et al.*, 1984). However, Shweder does not couch his arguments in terms of the transformed theory of the subject informed by psychoanalysis which is characteristic of much post-structuralist work.

Fundamental to what Shweder terms 'cultural psychology' is its challenge to the assumption of mainstream psychology that humans have an inherent central processing mechanism which is outside of and distinct from the sociocultural environment, although the two may influence each other. The goal of this central processing mechanism is assumed to be psychological unification. For Shweder and many others, such an assumption is profoundly flawed, and the preferred concept of the self is as a socially constructed entity in which psychological unification is treated as a narrative project rather than as an idealised and attainable goal (see also Moghaddam and Studer, 1997). Many critics of mainstream psychology prefer this social constructionist or narrative theory of the self, in which we are assumed to make ourselves up as we go along, and language is seen to play a key role in this process (e.g. Harre, 1989; Malik, Chapter 10, this volume). Language, however, is not treated as simply a tool for reflecting 'how things are in the world', but as a profoundly social form which is always located and (re)produced in specific cultural, historical and political contexts (see Ahmed, Chapter 5, and Ussher *et al.*, Chapter 6, this volume). Debates about language and meaning are therefore central to the work of cultural psychologists and other critical and discursive psychologists who have followed what Ian Parker and Erica Burman have termed 'the turn to text' (Burman and Parker, 1994).

However, the various readings included in the Goldberger and Veroff text *Culture and Psychology* still have more to say about the Anglocentrism of psychology and the need for a more culturally sensitive set of psychological theories and practices than about the links between psychology and the cultural domain – or how a psychologist might theorise and research the cultural.

The domain of the cultural: enter the study of contemporary culture

So what is generally meant by the term 'culture'? In their classic content analysis, carried out during the early 1950s, Kroeber and Kluckhohn defined culture as follows:

> Culture consists of patterns, explicit and implicit, of and for behavior acquired and transmitted by symbols, constituting the distinctive achievement of human groups, including their embodiments of artifacts; the essential core of culture consists of traditional (i.e. historically derived and selected) ideas and especially their attached values; culture systems may, on the one hand, be considered as products of actions, on the other as conditioning elements of further action.
>
> (1963: 357)

This lengthy definition owes much to anthropological approaches to the study of culture, with its emphasis on tradition and artefacts, and its relative lack of attention to the construction of the self within and through the cultural domain. Goldberger and Veroff, who quote the above extract, put the self back in when they point out that more recent understandings of culture have tended to view it as 'a system of shared meanings that grow out of cultural qualities [e.g. common rituals, beliefs, values, rules and laws] and provide a common lens for perceiving and structuring reality for its members' (1995: 10–11). Goldberger and Veroff also point to the extension of this definition to include the notion of culture as tied to a sense of group membership and identity that may be focused around gender, class, ethnicity, sexuality and/or age. They prefer the term 'intercultural psychology' over 'cultural psychology', since their primary interest is in 'studies of the interactive effects between cultures that co-exist in a larger societal context' (1995: 7). However, many of the psychological contributors to *Culture and Psychology* concentrate on challenges to the Anglocentrism of mainstream psychology rather than examining the interface between a 'new cultural psychology' and the study of culture in the broadest sense, which has been the domain of cultural studies. As a consequence, what is missing from Goldberger and Veroff's reader is issues such as the diverse ways in which subjectivities are constituted in the cultural domain; and in which cultural practices operate to (re)produce social relations around gender, class, 'race', age and sexuality in specific contexts. In other words, Goldberger and Veroff's landmark collection on culture and psychology still pays minimal attention to key debates within one of the main approaches to have engaged with the cultural domain: cultural studies.

Cultural studies is an interdisciplinary approach to the study of social and political life which has become something of a discipline in its own right (Shiach, 1999). It has transformed contemporary understandings of culture and the cultural, and has had some profound impacts on debates within anthropology (Clifford and Marcus, 1986). For Raymond Williams, a major influence on the study of contemporary culture in Britain, the term *culture* refers to 'a whole way of life', and culture is seen to act as a conduit for identity, style, ideology and politics (Williams, 1976). In cultural studies, culture is viewed less as a system of *shared* meanings than as a system of *continually contested meanings* in which 'societies' and 'individuals' are (re)produced and transformed, but within a nexus of social relations around domination and subordination.

So, for example, the cultural studies text *Out There: Marginalization and Contemporary Cultures* (Ferguson *et al.*, 1990) addresses various aspects of 'the invisibility of the centre' in contemporary US society, in which 'dominant discourse tries never to speak its name. Its authority is based on absence' (Ferguson *et al.*, 1990: 11). The dominant group seldom needs to speak its name: it is defined in contrast to the more explicit naming of marginal and subordinated subjects. The processes through which such groups are constructed as Other along dimensions of gender, 'race', class, sexuality and so on is profoundly cultural, and involves the use of language as an instrument of power (Ferguson *et al.*, 1990). These processes are reflected in such mundane and pervasive practices as the television or radio news-reader identifying those who have died in accidents or 'natural' disasters as follows: 'ten people were killed, including two women and three children'. We do not need to be informed that the remaining five victims are adult males, and it is through such apparently trivial practices that the cultural norm of (in this case) adult male-ness is reproduced. Cultural studies has been concerned with these and many other everyday practices through which the cultural domain operates, but this approach owes little to social-psychological theories or to mainstream anthropology, relying more on post-structuralist theory, postmodernism and feminist, Marxist and postcolonial analyses.

As Morag Shiach points out in her recent reader *Feminism and Cultural Studies*, 'there is no single story of cultural studies' (1999: 1). The field, she argues, is an 'interdisciplinary space' marked by a common project: an attempt to take culture seriously as a focus for systematic analysis and political engagement, and to address 'popular culture' as well as so-called 'high culture' (Williams, 1961). In Britain cultural studies emerged at a particular historical and political period in postwar Europe and a heightened moment of radical political engagement around 1968 (Hall *et al.*, 1980). One important facet of this project was to challenge the representation of contemporary working-class culture(s) as inferior or barbaric compared to traditional forms of 'high' culture. This involved the (re)formulation of Marxist, feminist and/or psychoanalytic perspectives to question dominant constructions of marginalised and subordinated cultures and peoples (e.g. Bhabha, 1994; Ferguson *et al.*, 1990; Hall and Jefferson, 1975).

The project also meant transforming notions of the cultural, and what could be counted as part of 'culture'. Morag Shiach (1999) argues that cultural studies has understood 'culture' in a number of different ways: 'as specific texts; as the practices which construct national, class or gender identities; or as the inter-connection of different modes and systems of communication' (1999: 3). Her eventual definition runs as follows: 'overall . . . cultural studies is interested in the *practices and texts* through which individuals and groups come to understand or to imagine themselves as social beings' (1999: 3; emphasis added). Some of those taking a post-structuralist perspective within psychology might well question Shiach's distinction between 'individuals' and 'groups', preferring to speak of 'individual subjectivities' as being constituted through discourse as specific kinds of social being (Hollway, 1989; Walkerdine, 1996).

Cultural studies has obvious areas of overlap with what has been termed the 'new social psychology' in its critical and discursive forms. The overlap is especially clear in relation to recent work on identity (e.g. Shotter and Gergen, 1989). However, I am particularly interested in Shiach's juxtaposition of the terms 'practices' and 'texts'. It seems to me that while much of recent critical and discursive psychology has been extremely interested in the *texts* through which individuals and groups are constituted or constitute themselves, far less attention has been devoted to the role of cultural *practices*. This is partly a consequence of the theoretical and conceptual priorities of the 'new social psychology', but also a result of the latter's research methods. Critical and discursive psychology tend to employ informal interviews and related techniques for the qualitative analysis of spoken and written texts, devoting relatively less attention to the use of observational methods, especially ethnography, and to the operation of specific cultural *practices*.

The 'new social psychology' and the cultural domain

The 'new social psychology' is a diverse and constantly changing set of approaches to the study of human life which share a critical perspective on positivist psychology, especially in its more rigidly experimental forms (e.g. Edwards, 1997; Fox and Prilleltensky, 1997). One of the approaches within this 'new social psychology' is generally referred to as 'discursive psychology' (Edwards, 1997; Potter and Edwards, 1992). Discursive psychology uses research methods derived from a combination of conversation analysis and ethnomethodology, and tends to offer a fine-grain analysis of the action orientation of talk (see Wetherell (1998) and Widdicombe and Wooffitt (1995) for discussions). This perspective is often contrasted with that of so-called 'critical discourse analysis' (e.g. Hollway, 1989; see Burman and Parker (1994) for review). The latter draws on post-structuralism and/or Foucauldian theories to present analyses which are concerned with the interrelation of discourse, power and subjectification. The distinction between these two approaches to 'discourse analysis' is sometimes likened to a distinction between 'micro' and 'macro' levels of analysis (Willott and Griffin, 1997). In addition, the two approaches tend to use the term 'discourse' in rather different ways. For those involved in 'discursive psychology', the term 'discourse' is often (but not always) used to refer to 'spoken or written text' (e.g. Potter and Wetherell, 1987), while for the post-structuralist/Foucauldian approach to critical discourse analysis, 'discourse' usually refers to 'patterns of meaning which organise the various symbolic systems human beings inhabit, and which are necessary for us to make sense to each other' (Parker *et al.*, 1999: 3; see also Burman and Parker, 1994).

To some extent, this crude bifurcation between 'discursive psychology' and 'critical discourse analysis' oversimplifies a varied set of approaches to the qualitative analysis of talk and text in psychology. Some approaches are not so easily incorporated within this bipolar distinction, such as the psychological study of argumentation and rhetoric (e.g. Billig, 1987) and some feminist psychology (e.g. Burman *et al.*, 1996; Gergen and Davis, 1998; Unger, 1999). There is also what is termed 'critical psychology', which cuts across most areas of psychology and adopts an approach which is closer to action research or a form of politically engaged community psychology (e.g. Fox and Prilleltensky, 1997). 'Critical psychology' has some areas of overlap with critical discourse analysis and with discursive psychology, but also some profound differences, especially with regard to post-structuralist theories of the subject and notions of the relation between the self and society. There is a complication to this story, however, since at the grandly named 'Millennium World Conference on Critical Psychology' at the University of Western Sydney in April 1999, 'critical psychology' was constructed by the conference organisers as closely allied to the combination of post-structuralism, feminism and psychoanalytic theory exemplified in the influential text *Changing the Subject* (Henriques *et al.*, 1984). All the above approaches, however, share an interest in qualitative analyses of talk and text; and in meaning and the use of language. All have emerged over the past twenty years (or more) in opposition to the narrowly positivist approach of mainstream psychology and its reliance on quantitative methods. To different degrees all the above approaches share an interest in the importance of 'social context', and have devoted considerable attention to the issues raised by the intersection of culture and psychology. However, if we look at the 'new social psychology' as a whole, we find that cultural studies approaches still have relatively little impact at theoretical or methodological levels, with the possible exception of critical discourse analysis (see Parker *et al.*, 1999), and the work of others who draw on a combination of post-structuralist, feminist and psychoanalytic theories (e.g. Hollway, 1989; Walkerdine, 1996).

In this chapter I have argued that the 'new cultural psychology', and indeed the 'new social psychology', could benefit from a more extensive appreciation of the role of cultural practices. Discursive psychology clearly treats spoken and written texts *as* practices, viewing talk as a form of action in itself. Potter and Edwards present their Discourse Action Model (DAM) as follows: 'for both participants and analysts, the primary issue is the social actions, or interactional work, being done in the discourse' (1992: 2). Potter and Edwards differentiate discursive psychology from mainstream cognitive psychology, which views individuals' talk and interpersonal interactions as expressions of speakers' underlying cognitive states. Potter and Edwards are concerned instead with 'the nature of knowledge, cognition and reality: with how events are described and explained, how factual reports are constructed, how cognitive states are attributed' (1992: 2). Such 'discursive topics' are then 'examined in the context of their occurrence as situated and occasioned constructions whose precise nature makes sense, to participants and analysts alike, in terms of the social actions those descriptions accomplish' (1992: 2–3). Potter and Edwards are interested in the role of talk and text as *occasioned* constructions and as situated actions/practices.

This conceptual move enables Potter and Edwards to develop a powerful critique of what they term *perceptual-cognitivism*. It is not equivalent, however, to the analyses of texts *and practices* that might emerge from the use of sustained ethnographic observation as well as interview methods, in those studies which take a broader interest in the cultural domain. There are examples of such analyses throughout this volume, for instance in Fine *et al.*'s classroom ethnography and textual analysis, and in Frosh *et al.*'s and Marshall and Woollett's emphasis on text as practice. An additional example is Billig's text *Banal Nationalism* (1995), which examines the psychological and political implications of the pervasive cultural practices associated with the iconic national flags of Britain and the USA. *Banal Nationalism* is not based on an ethnographic study in the traditional sense, but Billig looks beyond spoken and written texts to incorporate specific cultural practices (in this case flag-waving in particular contexts) in his analysis of how nationalism and the very idea of the (British and American) nation come to permeate the mundane and taken-for-granted aspects of everyday life.

The emergence of the 'new social psychology' has encouraged an increasing interest in the use of qualitative research methods in psychology, which has eventually resulted in the publication of a number of textbooks in this area aimed at undergraduate and postgraduate readers in psychology. A number of these texts include minimal coverage of observational or ethnographic methods, and some attention is given to visual media, but cultural forms or practices are still largely neglected (e.g. Hayes, 1997; Smith *et al.*, 1995). Other texts covering the use of qualitative methods in psychology do mention observational and/or ethnographic methods in greater depth, but still pay relatively little attention to the potential role of ethnographic methods in researching cultural practices in the broadest sense (e.g. Banister *et al.*, 1994). As a consequence, most psychologists still lack the methodological as well as the theoretical tools to engage with the cultural domain.

The role of ethnography in the study of cultural practices

I will now consider some examples of research about young people that have used ethnographic methods to identify key cultural practices, which would in all likelihood have been overlooked if the researchers had relied on interview methods alone. First, however, I want to consider what is meant by the term 'ethnographic methods'. In western social scientific research, ethnographic methods are associated with critiques of traditional positivist social science and its reliance on 'quantitative' methods. Such methods, which still dominate main-stream psychology, aim to record and analyse information or research material (aka 'data') in primarily numerical terms, using statistical tests and/or computer modelling to link empirical findings to theories. Ethnography, like other 'quali-tative' research techniques, usually sets out to record research material in non-numerical forms, such as via audio- or video-tape-recordings and/or research field-notes, and draws on a wide range of analytic perspectives. Ethnography has not always been used by researchers who are critical of positivism (Hammersley and Atkinson, 1983), but the relationship between ethnography and non-positivist epistemologies is a close one.

Hammersley and Atkinson refer to ethnography as 'participant observation', in that 'the ethnographer participates, overtly or covertly, in people's daily lives for an extended period of time, watching what happens, listening to what is said, asking questions: in fact collecting whatever data are available to shed light on the issues with which he or she is concerned' (1983: 2). Clearly, ethnography has close links with social anthropology, and it has a long history in this and related disciplines. There are many examples of more limited forms of ethnography, involving non-participant observation (for instance, 'fly-on-the-wall' observation), for shorter periods than the one full year of research fieldwork which is required of many Ph.D. students in anthropology. Such 'partial' forms of ethnography as systematic non-participant observation have been employed widely in cultural studies research, as well as in sociology and education (e.g. Griffin, 1985; Walkerdine, 1996; Willis, 1977). The most recent addition to this list is the 'new cultural geography', which draws on arguments from post-structuralism, postmodernism and cultural studies, and employs ethnographic methods to consider the spatial component of cultural practices (e.g. Skelton and Valentine, 1997).

I have chosen youth research as an example of the particular value of observational ethnographic methods for the study of cultural practices for several reasons. Youth research has a strong tradition of interdisciplinary collaboration, and since the mid-1970s the study of youth cultures and subcultures has played a key role in the investigation of cultural practices in specific social and political contexts (e.g. Hall and Jefferson, 1975; Willis, 1977; see Griffin (1993) for review). In addition, feminist work has made a distinctive contribution to this research, as it has to the 'new social psychology' and to recent approaches to cultural psychology (e.g. Hollway, 1989; McRobbie and Garber, 1975; Moraga, 1983).

I want to illustrate some of the advantages of ethnographic methods for a critical cultural psychology using the example of Valerie Hey's (1997) feminist ethnographic study of girls' friendship groups in two urban secondary schools during the mid to late 1980s. In *The Company She Keeps*, Hey describes the various stages of the research process: beginning with short visits to a number of different classes in one of the schools; deciding to carry out participant observation in one class for three terms; conducting informal interviews with individual teachers, girls and with girls' friendship groups from a range of social classes and ethnicities; and a period spent 'shadowing' a friendship group and some individual girls. Hey's work, like other research by feminists, indicates the extent to which reactions to the researcher and/or the research topic can make important contributions to the analysis (see Griffin, 1987). Such insights are generally absent from reports of psychological studies, while research involving ethnographic methods would seldom ignore such events.

Part-way through the project, Hey began to take notice of the notes that girls passed between themselves while in school, and collected over seventy notes as a form of cultural artefact. She discusses the difficulties and dilemmas she experienced in making such private and secret texts publicly available as part of her research data: 'everything about this material conspired to render it unavailable as data' (1997: 51). Hey comments that 'if I had not also been attending to the flux of girls' friendships through observations and interviews I would have had little purchase upon the [notes'] actual sequence, let alone their importance [as] fragmentary moments in the making of schoolgirl selves' (1997: 51). That is, if Hey had only conducted an analysis of the notes as written texts, she would have had a more limited appreciation of their role as *material* manifestations of girls' complex and intense interpersonal relationships. If she had only carried out interviews with girls, even in a longitudinal study, she would not have been able to appreciate the hidden and secretive nature of the girls' friendship groups, which were designed to keep all adults and young males on the outside (Hey, 1997). The combination of individual and group interviews and the analysis of written texts with systematic observation enabled Hey to examine the passing of notes as a specific *cultural practice* through which these girls came to construct and imagine themselves as social beings (see Shiach, 1999). For me, this study falls well within the remit of 'cultural psychology', even though Valerie Hey's work is more widely known in feminist youth research and the sociology of education. Yet the analysis presented in *The Company She Keeps* exemplifies those elements which are generally missing from most research in mainstream psychology, and from much of the 'new social and cultural psychology' as well.

One recent textbook on 'varieties of discourse analysis' in psychology and other areas of social research does take a broader view of what constitutes the text, and of the range of research methods available to social researchers. *Critical Textwork* by Ian Parker and the Bolton Discourse Network (1999) includes chapters on qualitative (discourse) analysis of spoken and written texts, from interviews and letters to fiction and classroom talk; visual texts such as comics, adverts, television and film; and physical texts such as cities, organisations, gardens, sign language and bodies. The book ends with chapters on ethnography, the language of silence in research, and action research around self-advocacy and change. The contributors are postgraduates, lecturers, professors and other researchers and practitioners from a range of social science disciplines, which might account for the book's breadth of focus.

Critical Textwork is a timely example of my argument that the 'new social psychology' needs to adopt a far broader repertoire of research methods and analytic perspectives for understanding social life; to embrace a broader notion of what can constitute the text for research purposes; and to develop a more sophisticated theoretical framework which will enable researchers to appreciate the relevance and importance of the cultural domain, not as background context but as a central player in human social life. *Critical Textwork* enables researchers to use a range of qualitative methods including ethnography to appreciate the cultural domain in all its complexity. Unlike most other texts on methodology from the 'new' social psychology, the book has a range of references to 'culture' in the index, although it still has relatively little to say about the kind of specific cultural practices illustrated by Valerie Hey's research (see Humphreys (1999) as one exception).

One of the reasons for the continuing neglect of the study of cultural practices in much of the new social psychology is the context in which this perspective emerged. Severe funding cuts in the social sciences, especially in radical research, meant that ethnographic research was in decline during the mid-1980s, just as the 'new' critical and discursive psychologies were emerging in Britain and elsewhere. Moreover, the arguments of postmodernism and post-structuralism which combined with feminism to mobilise these 'new' critical voices in and about psychology (e.g. Henriques *et al.*, 1984) also presented a profound criticism of the key assumptions and practices of ethnographic research. These criticisms precipitated something of a crisis within anthropology (see Clifford and Marcus, 1986). They challenged the tendency towards naive realism in ethnographic research, the uncritical imposition of the researchers' authorial analyses over the voices of its subject/respondents, and the relatively simplistic opposition between self and society on which most ethnographic research relied at that time (see Griffin (1993) for a review of this process in British and US youth research). Ironically, many of these difficulties led cultural studies to shift away from ethnographies and the view of the subject as an actor constrained by circumstances, towards a view of the subject as text, as cultural studies drew increasingly on theories of semiotics and then post-structuralism (see Cohen and Ainley (1999) for a critique). In recent cultural studies, subjects are frequently represented as narrators of the self and the world, in a move which has many parallels with recent developments in critical social psychological approaches to identity (e.g. Shotter and Gergen, 1989). A literal application of this perspective has led to a relative neglect of those cultural practices which do not fit easily within analytic frameworks designed around notions of 'stories' and 'texts'.

So if recent forms of 'discursive psychology', 'critical psychology' and even cultural psychology have not addressed the domain of the cultural fully, what might a psychology which was more fully equipped, both theoretically and methodologically, to appreciate and examine the domain of the cultural, look like? If psychology is to take 'culture' and the study of culture seriously, then it must develop a far broader notion of what constitutes the domain of psychological knowledge. Ethnographic methods are not necessary for an analysis of the cultural domain, but they can make a distinctive contribution to research, and should not be overlooked as an important form of qualitative research for psychologists with an interest in cultural practices. I am not advocating the more extensive use of ethnography by psychologists simply as a means of providing a fuller appreciation of the social context in which particular spoken or written texts are produced, but as a fundamental part of the analysis itself.

One of my main arguments in this chapter is that in order to understand the relationship between psychology and the cultural domain, most researchers in the 'new cultural psychology' need (1) a more sophisticated and complex notion of culture, and (2) a broader range of research methods than simply interviews and questionnaires. By 'culture', I prefer the sort of concept used in cultural studies, as in Shiach's definition, to the view of culture as social context which is favoured by more mainstream cross-cultural psychologists. The view of culture as context represents the cultural domain as a form of backdrop to specific practices, whereas the cultural studies perspective tends to treat those practices as a central part of culture itself, and of the ways in which we all construct ourselves as social beings (Shiach, 1999). If critical cultural and social psychologists are to employ this latter view of culture, then it is important to have the appropriate research tools with which to reflect a range of cultural practices in all their complexity, and the conceptual framework to appreciate the role such practices might play in the construction of subjectivities.

References

Banister, P., Burman, E., Parker, I., Taylor, M. and Tindall, C. (1994) *Qualitative Methods in Psychology: A Research Guide*, Buckingham: Open University Press.

Bhabha, H. (1994) *The Location of Culture*, London: Routledge.

Billig, M. (1987) *Arguing and Thinking: A Rhetorical Approach to Social Psychology*, Cambridge: Cambridge University Press.

—— (1995) *Banal Nationalism*, London: Sage.

Burman, E. and Parker, I. (eds) (1994) *Discourse Analytic Research: Repertoires and Readings of Texts in Action*, London: Routledge.

Burman, E., Alldred, P., Bewley, C., Goldberg, B., Heenan, C., Marks, D., Marshall, J., Taylor, J., Ullah, R. and Warner, S. (1996) *Challenging Women: Psychology's Exclusions, Feminist Possibilities*, Buckingham: Open University Press.

Clifford, J. and Marcus, G. (eds) (1986) *Writing Culture*, Berkeley: University of California Press.

Cohen, P. and Ainley, P. (1999) 'In the country of the blind: youth studies and cultural studies in Britain'. Unpublished paper, Centre for New Ethnicities Research, University of East London.

Edwards, D. (1997) *Discourse and Cognition*, London: Sage.

Ferguson, R., Gever, M., Min-ha, T. and West, C. (eds) (1990) *Out There: Marginalization and Contemporary Culture*, New York: New Museum of Contemporary Art.

Fox, D. and Prilleltensky, I. (eds) (1997) *Critical Psychology: An Introduction*, Thousand Oaks, CA: Sage.

Geertz, C. (1975) '"From the native's point of view": on the nature of anthropological understanding', *American Scientist* 63: 47–53.

Gergen, M. and Davis, S. (eds) (1998) *Toward a New Psychology of Gender: A Reader*, New York: Routledge.

Goldberger, N.R. and Veroff, J.B. (eds) (1995) *The Culture and Psychology Reader*, New York: New York University Press.

Griffin, C. (1985) *Typical Girls? Young Women from School to the Job Market*, London: Routledge & Kegan Paul.

—— (1987) 'Young women and the transition from school to un/employment: a cultural analysis', in G. Weiner and M. Arnot (eds) *Gender under Scrutiny: New Inquiries in Education*, Milton Keynes: Open University Press.

—— (1993) *Representations of Youth: The Study of Youth and Adolescence in Britain and America*, Oxford: Polity Press.

Hall, S. and Jefferson, T. (eds) (1975) *Resistance through Rituals: Youth Cultures and Subcultures in Post-war Britain*, London: Hutchinson.

Hall, S., Hobson, D., Lowe, A. and Willis, P. (1980) *Culture, Media, Language*, London: Hutchinson.

Hammersley, M. and Atkinson, P. (1983) *Ethnography: Principles in Practice*, London: Tavistock.

Harre, R. (1989) 'Language games and the texts of identity', in J. Shotter and K. Gergen (eds) *Texts of Identity*, London: Sage.

Hayes, N. (ed.) (1997) *Doing Qualitative Analysis*, Hove, Sussex: Psychology Press.

Helms, J. (1992) 'Why is there no study of cultural equivalence in standardized cognitive ability testing?', *American Psychologist* 47: 1083–1101.

Henriques, J., Hollway, W., Urwin, C., Venn, C. and Walkerdine, V. (1984) *Changing the Subject: Psychology, Social Regulation and Subjectivity*, London: Methuen.

Hey, V. (1997) *The Company She Keeps: An Ethnography of Girls' Friendships*, Buckingham: Open University Press.

Hollway, W. (1989) *Subjectivity and Method in Psychology*, London: Sage.

Humphreys, M. (1999) 'Ethnography: reading across culture', in I. Parker and Bolton Discourse Network (eds) *Critical Textwork*, Buckingham: Open University Press.

Jahoda, G. (1977) 'In pursuit of the emic–etic distinction: can we ever capture it?', in Y.H. Portinga (ed.) *Basic Problems in Cross-Cultural Psychology*, London: Academic Press.

Jones, E.E. and Thorne, A. (1987) 'Rediscovery of the subject: intercultural approaches to clinical assessment', *Journal of Consulting and Clinical Psychology* 55: 488–95.

Kleinman, A. (1988) *Rethinking Psychology: From Cultural Category to Personal Experience*, New York: Macmillan (The Free Press).

Kroeber, A.L. and Kluckhohn, C. (1963) *Culture: A Critical Review of Concepts and Definitions*, Cambridge, MA: Harvard University Press.

McRobbie, A. and Garber, J. (1975) 'Girls and subcultures: an exploration', in S. Hall and T. Jefferson (eds) *Resistance through Rituals*, London: Hutchinson.

Moghaddam, F.M. and Studer, C. (1997) 'Cross-cultural psychology: the frustrated gadfly's promises, potentialities and failures', in D. Fox and I. Prilleltensky (eds) *Critical Psychology: An Introduction*, Thousand Oaks, CA: Sage.

Moraga, C. (1983) 'La Guerra', in C. Moraga and G. Anzaldua (eds) *This Bridge Called My Back: Radical Writings by Women of Color*, New York: Kitchen Table Women of Color Press.

Ogbu, J. (1981) 'Origins of human competence: a cultural-ecological perspective', *Child Development* 52: 413–29.

Parker, I. and Bolton Discourse Network (eds) (1999) *Critical Textwork: An Introduction to Varieties of Discourse and Analysis*, Buckingham: Open University Press.

Pile, S. and Thrift, N. (eds) (1995) *Mapping the Subject: Geographies of Cultural Transformation*, London: Routledge.

Potter, J. and Edwards, D. (1992) *Discursive Psychology*, London: Sage.

Potter, J. and Wetherell, M. (1987) *Discourse and Social Psychology: Beyond Attitudes and Behaviour*, London: Sage.

Sampson, E.E. (1977) 'Psychology and the American ideal', *Journal of Personality and Social Psychology* 35: 767–82.

—— (1993) *Celebrating the Other: A Dialogic Account of Human Nature*, Hemel Hempstead: Harvester Wheatsheaf.

Shiach, M. (ed.) (1999) *Feminism and Cultural Studies*, Oxford: Oxford University Press.

Shotter, J. and Gergen, K. (eds) (1989) *Texts of Identity*, London: Sage.

Shweder, R. (1990) 'Cultural psychology: what is it?', in R. Shweder (ed.) *Cultural Psychology: Essays on Comparative Human Development*, Cambridge: Cambridge University Press.

Skelton, T. and Valentine, G. (eds) (1997) *Cool Places: Geographies of Youth Cultures*, London: Routledge.

Smith, J., Harre, R. and Van Langenhove, L. (eds) (1995) *Rethinking Method in Psychology*, London: Sage.

Unger, R. (1999) *Twenty-Five Years of Feminist Psychology*, Thousand Oaks, CA: Sage.

Unger, R. and Sanchez-Hucles, J. (1993) 'Gender and culture: Special Issue', *Psychology of Women Quarterly* 17(4).

Walkerdine, V. (1996) *Daddy's Girl: Young Girls and Popular Culture*, London: Macmillan.

Wetherell, M. (1998) 'Positioning and interpretative repertoires: conversation analysis and post-structuralism in dialogue', *Discourse and Society* 9(3): 387–412.

Widdicombe, S. and Wooffitt, R. (1995) *The Language of Youth Subcultures*, London: Harvester Wheatsheaf.

Williams, R. (1961) *The Long Revolution*, Harmondsworth: Penguin.

—— (1976) *Keywords: A Vocabulary of Culture and Society*, Oxford: Oxford University Press.

Willis, P. (1977) *Learning to Labour: How Working Class Kids get Working Class Jobs*, Farnborough: Saxon House.

Willott, S. and Griffin, C. (1997) '"Wham bam, am I a man?" Unemployed men talk about masculinities', *Feminism and Psychology* 7(1): 107–28.

2 Gender, genes and genetics

From Darwin to the human genome[1]

Lynne Segal

For several years now we have seen the heightening of old battles between 'Science' and 'Culture', with Darwin reinstated as the figurehead of Science. Today, it is no longer physics, with its military utility, but molecular biology, with its commercial stakes, which has become the new King of Science. Not atomic energy, but recombinant DNA, is the object of the latest form of veneration – now the final arbiter of human circumstance and potential. The loss of belief in the legacies of both Marx and Keynes as guides for social change, and the intensified attacks on Freud as a diviner of self-knowledge, have something to do with the current return to Darwin. So too does another feature of our times: the continuing shifts and disruptions in gender relations, gender practices and identities, alongside persistent feminist questionings, have encouraged an enthusiastic 'backlash' reception for new theories endorsing genetic origins for normative investments in sexual difference.

'Feminists, meet Mr. Darwin!', science columnist Robert Wright announces from the USA (1994: 34). Feminist theorists have for decades been questioning the inevitability of the old gender order, emphasising its specifically social origins. More recently, they have incorporated post-structuralist analysis and deconstruction to describe what they see as the coercively reiterated, and thereby discursively constructed, constraints of gender (Butler, 1990; Gergen and Davis, 1997). A provocative flaunting and celebration of the instabilities and fluidities of gender identities has developed to mock biological presumptions, highlighting their cultural or semiotic formation – apparently all ready for subversion and change! More generally, gender anxieties and disruptions are a constant source of debate, from media apprehension over the boys thought to be 'losing out' when compared with girls in school to the emergence of women bosses or the visibility of transsexual identities. In this context it is hard not to suspect that some part of the current return to Darwin, genes and genetics is a reactive response to the well-documented anxieties generated by uncertainties around gender issues (Dunant and Porter, 1996: 2; Samuels, 1993: 222). Certainly, those who think they have found the fundamental constraints on gender and sexuality seem to offer some consolation for such anxieties. For here we can learn that sexual polarity is encoded in our 'selfish' genes; has been there for millennia; is always likely to be with us, at least to some extent. Within the discipline of psychology, the growing appeal of evolutionary explanations of human behaviour has been used to undermine the efforts of those, like the other contributors to this collection, who have been seeking a richer understanding of the place of culture in human conduct, and calling, in the words of Christine Griffin (Chapter 1), for psychologists to become 'cultural ethnographers'.

It may seem an odd time for the return of any form of fundamentalism, biological or otherwise, with universal truths now derided as fraudulent 'grand narratives' by the post-structuralist critics favoured in literary and cultural studies (Lyotard, 1984). But that, as we shall see, only heightens the battle. The stakes are high. The goal is not just conceptual containment of potentially unlimited shifts in gender beliefs and practices, though without doubt the media is most attentive to reports of their immunity to cultural flexibility (Martin, 1992). It is also a return to the allegedly more rigorous authority of the biological sciences to explain much that has recently been studied through a cross-disciplinary cultural lens. The hope is to defeat, once and for all, those cultural theorists who assume that 'ideas that draw upon the authority of nature nearly always have their origin in ideas about society' (Ross, 1994: 15).

From Richard Dawkins, the authorised populariser of science in Britain, occupying the Chair for the Public Understanding of Science specifically created for him at Oxford University by Microsoft millionaire Charles Simonyi, we can learn 'the first axiom of science': 'Plants and animals alike all – in their immensely complicated, enmeshed ways – are doing the same fundamental thing, which is propagating genes' (cited in Hughes, 1998). The eternal truths of Darwin's grand narrative, reinterpreted anew, have returned with a vengeance to reshape intel-lectual agendas at the close of the twentieth century, just as strongly as they did in the nineteenth century. And yet, only a generation ago, appeals to evolutionary biology to explain cultural practices or social hierarchy were fiercely denounced as justifications for conservative prejudices. Then, these accounts still triggered the memory of the appropriation of Darwin's ideas earlier in the twentieth century, when they were used to justify all manner of eugenic campaigns exemplify-ing the most noxious class, 'race' and anti-immigrant prejudices, well before Hitler's genocidal practices began to make such prejudices widely unacceptable (Kevles, 1985). Today, mirroring that earlier time, the most reductive forms of evolutionary theory are advanced by actively committed social reformers. For example, Tony Blair's favourite think-tank, Demos, has explored the supposed implications of evolutionary psychology for the shaping of social policy in Britain, in 'Matters of life and death: the world view from evolutionary psychology' (1996).

Darwinian predictions

Darwin argued that all living things are related, having descended from a common origin. Species have appeared and disappeared over time, through a mechanism of natural selection or 'Survival of the Fittest', ensuring that only those life forms best suited to survive and reproduce themselves in any specific habitat continue to exist (Darwin, 1968). Alongside the random mutations generating 'natural selection' for survival, Darwin also wrote of 'sexual selection' for effective procreation in sexually reproducing species, producing 'a struggle between the males for possession of the females', as well as choice and selection of males by females (1968: 136). Reflecting the creed of imperial England, Darwin saw sexual hierarchy conjoined with racial hierarchy, producing white males at the pinnacle of evolution. However, today's Darwinians generally distance themselves formally, though not always effectively, from the Victorian racist dynamics of 'sexual selection', even as they militantly affirm its sexist dynamics: males have an inherent advantage in the evolutionary '*arms race*' (Dawkins and Krebs, 1979: 489).

Patriarchal precedent and capitalist market values seemed embarrassingly prominent in the first blast of neo-Darwinism two decades ago, with the publication of E.O. Wilson's *Sociobiology* in 1975 and Richard Dawkins' *The Selfish Gene* the following year (Wilson, 1975; Dawkins, 1976). In a decade of resurgent feminism, these books promised a genetic underpinning for male dominance and aggression, female passivity and domestication, in terms of 'the optimizing of reproductive fitness' – albeit without any knowledge of actual genetic determinants. Sexual selection for competitive reproductive advantage was the aspect of Darwin's work that emerged as *the* fundamental postulate of sociobiology. Sociobiology was an elaboration not so much of Darwin's own writing as of its extension to accounts of differential 'parental investment' in offspring (in sperm, egg, and the raising of progeny to reproductive age), first proposed by the US biologist, Robert Trivers, in 1974.

Trivers' (1974) conjecture is that promiscuous male behaviour evolved to promote the maximum spread of 'low-cost' copious sperm; prudent and passive female behaviour to accommodate the 'high-cost' requirements of the far fewer female eggs. Dawkins reiterates this argument, concluding: 'it is possible to interpret *all* other differences between the sexes as stemming from this *one* basic difference. . . . Female exploitation begins here' (1976: 153; emphasis added). The search for single overarching principles unifying all forms of knowledge drives this return to Darwin. All human behaviour, E.O. Wilson echoes, faithfully obeys this one biological principle (1978: 552).

Inside the academy, such genetic reductionism was briefly held at bay by vigorous rebuttal from biological and social scientists (Hubbard, 1982; Montague, 1980; Rose, 1982; Sahlins, 1977). Given that at this time sociobiologists could not even pretend to have direct knowledge of their ontologically founding category – human genes, the designated units for natural selection – there could be no convincing verification, or falsification. It would seem an awkward failing for theorists whose mantra was scientific rigour; whose goal was the defeat of loose or sentimental thought and language. The situation is little different today, genetic boosterism notwithstanding.

However, the capital investment pouring into 'biotechnology' since the 1980s, bringing together new microelectronic technology and procedures for gene splicing, generated vast hopes of commodifying and patenting new procedures for the production of plant, animal and even human life. The 'genetic revolution' had arrived, and ushered in the multi-billion-dollar Human Genome Project, attempting to map all the genes of human DNA – with massive government support, first in the USA, since accelerating elsewhere (Kevles, 1992). Old visions of a brave new world have been re-awakened, with scientists in control of genetic modification. The spread of neo-Darwinian ideas continues to accelerate; yet what we find today is a muddled mix of genetic determinisms. One minute they are used to set limits on the potential for possible change in human society and culture; the next minute to promise the removal all human 'deficiencies', in a future where nothing is impossible.

The rise of evolutionary psychology

The ambivalent pull of new Darwinian thinking is nowhere stronger than in mainstream psychology, some of whose scholars have moved effortlessly from an earlier emphasis on 'learning' in the explanation for human 'social behaviour' to promoting the greater utility of modern Darwinism, or new evolutionary psychology, for the same purpose. In Britain John Archer, in the forefront of analysing the acquisition of sex differences primarily in terms of social learning theory in the heyday of environmentalism in the 1970s, has now switched his emphasis to argue that 'evolutionary theory accounts much better for the overall patterns of sex differences and for their origins' (Archer, 1996: 914). Anne Campbell, formerly studying the cultural dynamics of working-class 'girl gangs', now highlights evolutionary arguments to explain the nature of female aggression (Campbell, 1999).

Evolutionary psychology has become the most conspicuous 'new' theoretical perspective within psychology during the past decade, its exponents certain it will consummate their dream of unifying psychology with hard science, within the conceptual framework of natural selection (Tooby and Cosmides, 1992: 49; Buss, 1995). Nowadays, evolutionary psychologists rely less on animal studies than did their sociobiological predecessors. Instead they are on the lookout for universals of human behaviour. On finding any hint of them, they immediately assume some genetic explanation: any putatively universal behaviour, it is argued, must be adaptive, and must have been 'selected' for. If the universality relates to gender, it has been selected in order to encourage 'the reproductive strategies appropriate for their own sex' (Archer, 1996: 916). As we saw with sociobiology, it is just such presumed sex-differentiated reproductive strategies which take us back to the issues most strongly disputed by those who have recently been contesting men's institutionalised dominance over women: the inevitability of men's sexual promiscuity, harassment or violence; the inequality of women's domestic burdens and parenting responsibilities.

In a recent overview, four leading evolutionary psychologists summarise achievements to date. They list thirty empirical 'discoveries' about human behaviour generated by evolutionary theory, many of them explaining gender contrasts such as sexually dimorphic mating strategies, male risk-taking and patterns of male homicide (Buss *et al.*, 1998: 544). Yet one does not have to believe that evolution and genetics play no role in human affairs (indeed, it would be hard to make much sense of such a claim) to point out that the apparent universality of certain practices does not entail a genetic origin. The weight of historical, anthropological and sociological evidence suggests enormous variability in the areas of human sexual conduct that evolutionary psychology assumes are universally dimorphic. Even if we choose to overlook this evidence, it would still be the case that the claimed universality of behaviour patterns could as easily be seen as a cultural effect as it could be seen as an evolved adaptation operating as a *cause* of men's relatively greater access to economic resources and social power and privilege.

David Buss is best known for his body of research on what he calls 'mating strategies' across thirty-five cultures, showing that men *claim* to be far more promiscuous than women, and readier to have sex with any female strangers so long as they are young and attractive. Women, in contrast, are said universally to report desiring (or having 'mating preferences' for) ambitious, industrious men with good financial resources (Buss, 1994). But this pattern is precisely what those who stress the *cultural* rather than the biological basis of contrasting sexual conduct would themselves predict, whether via individually based 'learning theory' or discursively mediated 'social construction' perspectives. In male-dominated societies boys learn to see heterosexual activity as a confirmation of masculinity and know that boasting about their desire to perform it is the single easiest way of proclaiming their 'virility'. Girls learn to value committed relationships over casual sex, or discover that they ought to suggest such values if they are not to suffer the consequences of being labelled whatever is the local vernacular for 'slag'.

The shallowness of the biological explanation of men's sexual braggadocio and women's circumspection is revealed in other studies. As Dorothy Einon suggests from her research, in which heterosexual men reported having three or four times the number of sexual partners that women reported having, the figures just don't compute: a tiny minority of enormously sexually active 'young and attractive' women would, despite all their protestations, have to be obliging an army of dedicatedly randy men (Einon, 1998). In contrast to the findings of evolutionary psychologists, the one constant of historical and sexological research on the pursuit of human sexual pleasure is, in fact, its frequent *negative* correspondence with reproductive ends (Bagemihl, 1999; Lauman *et al.*, 1994; Wellings *et al.*, 1994).

Martin Daly and Margo Wilson's popular evolutionary theory of male violence and homicide is even less persuasive, relying on the notion of 'kin selection' in which our genes are selected for co-operative or helping behaviour towards those with shared genes. The theory claims to explain why husbands are far more likely to murder their wives (genetically unrelated) than their biological children, and why a child is much more likely to be murdered, or physically abused, by a step-parent than a child with two biological parents (Daly and Wilson, 1988). It would not explain why an overwhelmingly greater number of human parents willingly adopt children, and most typically display remarkable love and concern for them.

It would not explain why midwives in both the USA and Britain have been reporting for several years now that violence against women often begins when that woman is pregnant with a man's baby. The latest figures reported in the UK estimate this to be true for one-third of women who are attacked (HMSO, 1998). It is, of course, precisely when they are made pregnant by their live-in partners that 'females' cannot be impregnated by rival males: the time when they most fully 'obey' the so-called 'Darwinian' rules for 'kin-selection', carrying 50 per cent of the aggressor's genes.

A total absence of 'scientific rigour' often accompanies the postulated 'paradigm shift' to an evolutionary psychology designed to secure that rigour. The ability to imagine an evolutionary scenario for supposed universal behaviours does nothing at all to establish the explanation's validity. As Looren de Jong and Van Der Steen observe of the controversies generated by Cosmides and Tooby's work on supposed universal cognitive adaptations (like that for 'cheater detection'), talk of 'natural selection' is merely an empty generalisation unless it can delineate something about the evolutionary history of a trait (Looren de Jong and Van Der Steen, 1998: 196). To the chagrin of psychologists like Steven Pinker, this is also the view of the famous language theorist, Noam Chomsky, who, despite stressing the innateness of 'the language faculty', rejects the adaptationist account of language development as a mere 'fairy tale' (Chomsky, 1996: 15). Indeed, one might be tempted to dismiss evolutionary psychology's speculations altogether, were it not for the media fascination with them.

Against the grain of the trend to focus on gender rather than race, some evolutionary psychologists have even managed to restore a classically ethnocentric way of applying evolutionary theory. Leslie Zebrowitz, for instance, suggests it is adaptive for men to prefer 'lighter-skinned women'. The explanation on offer is that light skin is a sign of fertility: women's skin is said to darken during periods of infertility, such as pregnancy, ingestion of contraceptives, and throughout infertile phases of the menstrual cycle. Light-skin preference cannot be attributed to western standards of beauty, we are assured, as it is documented cross-culturally (Zebrowitz, 1997). Yet given the higher status accorded to lighter-skinned people in most cultures over the past four hundred years, after certain global episodes like slavery and colonialisms, old and new, it is not too taxing to offer a few abiding cultural explanations for empirical findings such as these.

'New' evolutionary theorists claim that they now eschew rigid biological determinism with their suggestion that genetic and environmental forces always interact. Yet, as Tooby and Cosmides clarify in *The Adapted Mind*, when they outline what they call the 'psychological foundations of culture', this inter-actionism still means that 'content-specific evolved psychologies constitute the building blocks out of which *cultures themselves* are manufactured' (Tooby and Cosmides, 1992: 207). This account is presented as less biologically reductionist than previous sociobiological explanations, but it can be seen as exactly the opposite: culture never exists autonomously from genetic selection. As we shall see, what its chief critics argue from their actual, rather than speculative, biological and palaeontological work is that we would understand the relation between genes and culture much better if we assumed the reverse. For there is no unitary or general standard of fitness in biology. What fitness entails is context specific.

The case for theoretical pluralism

Some biologists have watched in bewilderment as psychologists resort to notions of gene selection to explain human behaviour, while 'the technical literature of evolutionary genetics has emphasized more and more the random and historically *contingent* nature of genetic change over time' (Lewontin, 1998: 60). Their conflict, they say, is not with Darwin but with the misuse of Darwin, whom they hope to rescue from his new friends (Eldredge, 1995; Rose, 1997: 176). As many molecular biologists have noted, genes (and the gradual, small changes which constitute mutation) are not the *only*, and far from the *necessary*, driving forces of evolution. In Steven Rose's recent critique of those he calls the 'ultra-Darwinians', 'the individual gene is not the only level at which selection occurs'; 'natural selection is not the only force driving evolutionary change'; 'organisms are not indefinitely flexible to change'; 'organisms are not mere passive responders to selective forces but active players in their own destiny' (Rose, 1997: 246).

No unifying principle drives either genetic or social change. On the one hand, simply tweaking a rat's whiskers causes changes in gene expression in the sensory cortex (Plomin, 1994: 14). On the other hand, quite staggering changes in the nature of the world have occurred with very few, if any, ties to genetic change. What we find is precisely an *incommensurability* between world history and human evolution, not a reflection of the limitations of human biology, but rather the negation of such limitation (Gould, 1996: 220).

The current enthusiasm for the idea that our gene histories determine our cultural futures thus occurs despite, not because of, new genetic knowledge. Human culture can always be passed on immediately to one's heirs (biological or otherwise) in speedy and direct Lamarckian fashion; while genetic evolution must move along the inordinately slower, indirect pathways of random mutation, natural selection and contingency. The central point, made repeatedly by the critics of those evolutionary psychologists busy reversing the reel to explain why we are the way we are, is that changes in genetic structure, which may survive as adaptations to particular environments, are precisely what Darwin saw them to be: '*local adaptations*'. The adaptations that may enable an organism to survive in one situation are not optimal in any general way; they will differ from changes which promote survival in another situation. Genes which were not selected for may also survive (as 'exaptations' or 'spandrels') because they just happen to reside alongside genes which were optimal for adaptation, or simply as by-products or co-options of features which survived as contributing to reproductive fitness.

Illustrating the non-adaptationist account of human mental functioning, Gould (1996), Lewontin (1993), Robert Brandon (1990) and many other researchers have often commented that the complexity of the human brain and its extraordinary endowment, for example, was *not* selected for in order to enable humans to read and write – skills which emerged many centuries after the appearance of those bigger brains. Rather, these skills emerged as by-products of the potential of the already evolved brains. Indeed, historical evidence supporting adaptive explanations is lacking for all higher mental processes, which is what makes their postulation by evolutionary psychologists so facile (Richardson, 1996). Against the fundamentalist or ultra-Darwinians, Darwinian pluralists like Gould, Lewontin or Rose argue that what millions of years of genetic change has selected for in human species is not any single set of 'natural' rules for development, 'sexual' or otherwise; rather, it has brought about the far more impressive open trend towards ever greater complexity, ever greater adaptability. 'If biology is indeed destiny', Rose concludes, 'then that destiny is constrained freedom' (1997: 245). Inside biology there is a multiplicity of explanatory levels, although many within the field constantly have to battle against media promotion of genetic foundationalism in order to point this out.

Gene talk versus social change

Inside psychology the same battle rages. Gene talk is becoming ubiquitous. Every area of human behaviour, no matter how clearly culturally diverse and complex – from good mothering to divorce and moral turpitude – is abruptly thrust back on to genetic foundations. Such is the force of the current hegemony of genetic anti-culturalism that few people even bother to look at the lamentably inconclusive nature of the research which galvanises media attention (Fausto-Sterling, 1992; Hubbard and Wald, 1993). Yet such claims only sound intelligible to those who have already closed their eyes to the complexities of the behaviour of living things, not to mention the mobilities of language and representation.

Even if we could trace a complex human behaviour to a particular 'gene' sequence, this correspondence would not tell us as much as we might hope. Genetic activity is not constant, but modified by the presence or absence of other genes in the genome, by the cellular environment, and by a multitude of external circumstances, from temperature or exposure to different metals to viral infection and the presence or absence of other social and physical environmental features. Thus the same behavioural outcome can result from quite different gene sequences. *If* we could agree on how to identify behaviour phenotypically (itself profoundly contentious) and *if* we had some idea how to connect it with a particular gene sequence, the molecular underpinnings would still remain forbiddingly convoluted. This is why trying to understand even genetically 'simple' diseases, like haemophilia, proves hugely complicated, as Lewontin explains: 'hemophiliacs differ from people whose blood clots normally by one of 208 different DNA variations, all in the same gene' (1993: 69). Many scientists now point to the dangers arising from the increasing array of diagnostic DNA tests, and the inevitability of their misuse. Like the biologist Ruth Hubbard, they fear that 'gene hunters' are securing an ideological climate which diverts attention away from the analysis of environmental and social problems, in a deplorable repetition of the thinking and rhetoric of eugenicists in the early decades of the twentieth century (Hubbard and Wald, 1993).

It is here that the predilections of evolutionary psychologists for stressing the genetic constraints on human social relations, especially in patterns of sexual and gender interactions, give way to the reckless illusions of some molecular biologists and their political and commercial sponsors, imagining utopian futures where individuals are able to breed flawless offspring, 'perfect babies'. Such presumptions do not just deny the intrinsic uncertainties and complexities in human genetics. They also encourage the reduction of social problems to flimsy biological speculations, and elevate dreams of genetic omnipotence and normalisation. In an inversion of earlier beliefs, it is now 'nature', rather than 'nurture', which is presumed infinitely malleable, at least potentially. This is despite the billions invested in human biotechnology over the past forty years, so far producing so little in useful treatments – with the notable exceptions of the synthesis of a bacterial protein for use in haemophilia, and the engendering of the secretion of human growth hormones in sheep (Jones, 1997: 63). The British geneticist Steve Jones has been among the most anxious to acknowledge that the idea of curing known inherited disease by replacing DNA is a 'piece of biological hubris': 'How the DNA in a virtually formless egg is translated into an adult body remains almost a mystery' (1997: 62). However, the move to aggrandise the notion of 'genetic disease' and its biological elimination continues apace. It includes psychological states – such as homosexual desire – which may well be neither genetic nor diseases, and has been extended to explain the social 'impairments' of homelessness and poverty, as in the writing and speeches of molecular biologist David Koshland when editor of *Science* magazine in the 1980s (Koshland, 1989: 189; see also Yoxen, 1984).

Two contradictory trends have intensified rather than resolved old clashes between culture and science, to the detriment of useful collaboration. On the one hand, the rise of cultural studies encouraged interdisciplinary efforts to blur the demarcations between distinct disciplinary sources of knowledge, strongly supported by most (but not all) feminist scholarship. This work emphasised the constitutive role of language and cultural context in different areas of scientific thought and practices. On the other hand, such understandings exacerbated a counter-trend, sometimes taking the form of a direct backlash against cultural studies and feminist critique, in which the very notion of 'culture' is vanishing from the favoured conceptual framework of the social and biological sciences, connected with the trend to replace 'social' with 'life' or 'human' sciences. As Evelyn Fox Keller notes, 'in terms that increasingly dominate contemporary discourse, "culture" has become subsumed under biology' (1992: 297). Evolutionary psychologists have helped to promote this particular disappearing act. Declaring their interest in culture or the effects of nurture on individual development, they nevertheless assume that 'culture is part of our biology' because, as Henry Plotkin suggests, 'the traits that cause culture have been selected for' (1997: 111, 231). More elaborately, Richard Dawkins, Daniel Dennett and Susan Blakemore refer to cultural inheritance as 'memes'. As Dawkins outlines, in strict analogy with the gene, a 'meme' is 'anything that replicates itself from brain to brain, via an available means of copying. . . . The genes build the hardware. The memes are the software' (1998: 302, 308). Responding in dismay to such reductionist axioms, Steve Jones protests: 'Just as geneticists begin to realize how far it is between DNA and organism, their subject is being hijacked. Society is, it seems, little more than the product of genes' (1997: 63). The insistence on a genetic subtext draws attention away from the differing levels of the cultural domain: its diverse institutional and social practices; its complex representations and interpretive strategies.

For epistemic diversity

As I see it, the attempt to abridge culture into biology, or biology into culture, can only impoverish us all. There never can be any single, unified project with the capacity to encompass the different levels of explanation necessary for understanding the complexity of human affairs. Some who have turned to totalising Darwinian or genetic visions have done so in criticism of recent cultural theorists' dismissal of the relevance of the body's evolutionary history and its changing biological potential (McIntosh and Ehrenreich, 1997). They rightly reject the idea that exploring the meanings we attach to bodily states, and their accompanying performative enactments or psychic investments, encompasses all we can achieve in relation to corporeal reality. Such absolute cultural appropriation of the life spans of any living creature is about as foolish as imagining that they are merely machines for the replication of DNA.

One obvious illustration is the issue of human reproduction, so central for ultra-Darwinians, feminists and cultural theorists alike. The ultra-Darwinians see only sexually dimorphic adaptations for the most efficient gene dispersal. The cultural theorists, looking through the lens of culture, know that bodies are produced in particular discourses with strong normative and symbolic meanings. Women's bodies are always defined by their capacity for pregnancy, even though they are reproductively infertile for significant portions of their lives, and their potential for child bearing is something women in the industrialised world choose not to exercise throughout most of their lives. The gene's-eye view of maximum reproductive advantage explains next to nothing about the complexity and variation in women's lives and experiences: why women today have fewer children, why they have them later in life, why in growing numbers they raise them independently of the biological father, why a significant minority choose not to have children at all.

However, this complexity does not mean that we can ignore women's reproductive biology. The female body's biological potential for impregnation can play a crucial role in the desires and fears which govern women's lives, at least some of the time. Moreover, not just cultural meanings but also physiological events are affected by cultural patterns, making reproductive cycles themselves culturally contingent. Thus medical anthropologists Susan Sperling and Yewoubdar Beyene point out that there is no universal biological pattern for the female reproductive cycle. While western women now experience approximately thirty-five years of ovulatory cycles, later menarche, early menopause and prolonged breast-feeding, in non-industrial societies the menstrual cycles experienced by women are approximately four years (Sperling and Beyene, 1997: 145). Sperling and Beyene emphasise the necessity of analysing the autonomous complexity of both biology and culture in reproductive studies, if we are to gain any clear understanding of how either biological plasticity, or cultural diversity, interact to produce reproductive experience. Rather than reinventing overarching laws to account for human behaviour, psychologists have everything to gain from attending to the critical conversations occurring both *among* and *between* cultural and biological theorists and researchers if they are ever to grapple with the constitutive roles of both culture and biology in the even greater complexities of the psychological domain.

Acknowledgement

I am grateful to Corinne Squire for helpful suggestions and clarifications.

Note

1 These arguments are developed more fully within the larger project of assessing the place of feminism at the close of the twentieth century in *Why Feminism? Gender, Psychology, Politics* (Segal, 1999).

References

Archer, A. (1996) 'Sex differences in social behavior: are the social role and evolutionary explanations compatible?', *American Psychologist* 51(9): 909–17.

Bagemihl, B. (1999) *Biological Exuberance: Animal Homosexuality and Natural Diversity*, New York: St Martin's Press.

Birke, L. and Silverton, J. (eds) (1984) *More Than the Parts: Biology and Politics*, London: Pluto Press.

Bleier, R. (1984) *Science and Gender: A Critique of Biology and its Views of Women*, Oxford: Pergamon Press.

Brandon, R. (1990) *Adaptation and Environment*, Princeton, NJ: Princeton University Press.

Buss, D. (1994) *The Evolution of Desire: Strategies of Human Mating*, London: HarperCollins.

—— (1995) 'Evolutionary psychology: a new paradigm for social science', *Psychological Inquiry* 6: 1–30.

Buss, D., Haselton, M., Shackelford, T., Bleske, A. and Wakefield, J. (1998) 'Apatations, exaptions, and spandrels', *American Psychologist* 53(5): 533–48.

Butler, J. (1990) *Gender Trouble: Feminism and the Subversion of Identity*, London: Routledge.

Campbell, A. (1999) 'Staying alive: evolution, culture, and women's intrasexual aggression', *Behavioural and Brain Sciences* 22: 203–52.

Chomsky, N. (1996) *Powers and Prospects: Reflections on Human Nature and the Social Order*, London: Pluto Press.

Daly, M. and Wilson, M. (1988) *Homicide*, New York: Aldine de Gruyter.

Darwin, C. (1968) [1859] *The Origin of Species by Means of Natural Selection*, Harmondsworth: Penguin.

Dawkins, R. (1976) *The Selfish Gene*, Oxford: Oxford University Press.
—— (1998) *Unweaving the Rainbow*, London: Penguin.
Dawkins, R. and Krebs, J.R. (1979) 'Arms races between and within species', *Proceedings of the Royal Society of London Bulletin* 295: 489–511.
Demos (1996) 'Matters of life and death: the world view from evolutionary psychology', *Demos Quarterly* 10.
Dunant, S. and Porter, R. (eds) (1996) *The Age of Anxiety*, London: Virago.
Einon, D. (1998) 'How many children can one man have?', *Evolution and Human Behavior* 19: 413–26.
Eldredge, N. (1995) *Reinventing Darwin: The Great Debate at the High Table of Evolutionary Theory*, New York: Wiley.
Fausto-Sterling, A. (1992) 'Sex and the single brain', in *Myths of Gender: Biological Theories about Women and Men*, New York: Basic Books.
Gergen, M. and Davis, S. (eds) (1997) *Towards a New Psychology of Gender*, London: Routledge.
Gould, S.J. (1996) *Life's Grandeur: The Spread of Excellence from Plato to Darwin*, London: Jonathan Cape.
HMSO (1998) *Why Mothers Die: The Confidential Enquiry into Maternal Deaths*, London: HMSO.
Hubbard, R. (ed.) (1982) *Biological Woman: The Convenient Myth*, Boston, MA: Shenkman.
Hubbard, R. and Wald, E. (1993) *Exploding the Gene Myth*, Boston, MA: Beacon Press.
Hughes, C. (1998) 'The *Guardian* profile, Richard Dawkins: the man who knows the meaning of life', *The Guardian Saturday Review*, 3 October: 7.
Jones, S. (1997) 'Biology and bile', *Prospect*, March: 63.
Keller, E.F. (1992) 'Nature, nurture and the Human Genome Project', in D.J. Kevles and L. Hood (eds) *The Code of Codes: Scientific and Social Issues in the Human Genome Project*, Cambridge, MA: Harvard University Press.
Kevles, D. (1985) *In the Name of Eugenics: Genetics and the Uses of Human Heredity*, New York: Alfred Knopf.
—— (1992) 'Out of eugenics: the historical politics of the Human Genome', in D.J. Kevles and L. Hood (eds) *The Code of Codes: Scientific and Social Issues in the Human Genome Project*, Cambridge, MA: Harvard University Press.
Kevles, D.J. and Hood, L. (eds) (1992) *The Code of Codes: Scientific and Social Issues in the Human Genome Project*, Cambridge, MA: Harvard University Press.
Koshland, D. (1989) 'Sequences and consequences of the Human Genome', *Science* 146: 187–90.
Lauman, E.O., Gagnon, J.H., Michael, R.T. and Michaels, S. (1994) *The Social Organization of Sexuality: Sexual Practices in the United States*, Chicago, IL: University of Chicago Press.
Lewontin, R. (1993) *The Doctrine of DNA: Biology as Ideology*, London: Penguin.
—— (1998) 'Survival of the nicest?', *New York Review of Books*, 22 October: 60–1.
Looren de Jong, H. and Van Der Steen, W.J. (1998) 'Biological thinking in evolutionary psychology: rockbottom or quicksand?', *Philosophical Psychology* 11(2): 196.
Lyotard, J.-F. (1984) *The Postmodern Condition: A Report on Knowledge*, Manchester: Manchester University Press.
McIntosh, S. and Ehrenreich, B. (1997) 'The new creationism', *The Nation*, 9 June: 11–16.
Martin, E. (1992) 'Body narratives, body boundaries', in L. Grossberg, C. Nelson and P. Treichler (eds) *Cultural Studies*, London: Routledge.

Montague, A. (ed.) (1980) *Sociobiology Examined*, Oxford: Oxford University Press.

Plomin, R. (1994) *Genetics and Experience: The Interplay between Nature and Nurture: Individual Differences and Development Series*, Volume 6, London: Sage.

Plotkin, H. (1997) *Evolution in Mind: An Introduction to Evolutionary Psychology*, London: Penguin.

Richardson, R.C. (1996) 'The prospects for an evolutionary psychology: human language and human reasoning', *Minds and Machines* 6: 541–77.

Rose, S. (ed.) (1982) *Against Biological Determinism*, London: Allison & Busby.

—— (1997) *Lifelines*, London: Penguin.

Ross, A. (1994) *The Chicago Gangster Theory of Life: Nature's Debt to Society*, London: Verso.

Sahlins, M. (1977) *The Use and Abuse of Biology*, London: Tavistock.

Samuels, A. (1993) *The Political Psyche*, London: Routledge.

Segal, L. (1999) *Why Feminism? Gender, Psychology, Politics*, Cambridge: Polity Press.

Sperling, S. and Beyene, Y. (1997) 'A pound of biology and a pinch of culture or a pinch of biology and a pound of culture?', in L. Hager (ed.) *Women in Human Evolution*, London: Routledge.

Tooby, J. and Cosmides, L. (1992) 'The psychological foundations of culture', in J. Barkow, L. Cosmides and J. Tooby (eds) *The Adapted Mind: Evolutionary Psychology and the Generation of Culture*, New York: Oxford University Press.

Trivers, R. (1974) 'Parent–offspring conflict', *American Zoologist* 14.

Wellings, K., Field, J., Johnson, A. and Wadsworth, J. (1994) *Sexual Behaviour in Britain: The National Survey of Attitudes and Lifestyles*, London: Penguin.

Wilson, E.O. (1975) *Sociobiology: The New Synthesis*, Cambridge, MA: Harvard University Press.

—— (1978) *On Human Nature*, Cambridge, MA: Harvard University Press.

Wright, R. (1994) 'Feminists meet Mr. Darwin', *The New Republic*, 28 November: 34–6.

Yoxen, E. (1984) 'Constructing genetic disease', in T. Duster and K. Garett (eds) *Cultural Perspectives in Biological Knowledge*, Norwood, NJ: Ablex.

Zebrowitz, L. (1997) *Reading Faces: Window to the Soul*, Boulder, CO: Westview Press.

Part II
Culture and social formations

Introduction

Cultural phenomena are not direct reflections of social circumstances, nor do they always have direct effects on those circumstances. The relationship is often much subtler and harder to trace. Sometimes, too, cultural phenomena outlast the social conditions in which they arose; sometimes they are much more evanescent. The cultural discourses and practices considered in Part II display these complex relations to social formations, particularly social formations of gender and 'race'. Culture is the way we live with such formations, and it enables our actions in and against them.

The first chapter (Chapter 3), 'Cultural contestations in practice: white boys and the racialisation of masculinities' by Stephen Frosh, Ann Phoenix and Rob Pattman, explores what has come to be called the 'crisis of masculinity' through the narratives given by teenage boys of their emergence into masculine identities. Drawing on discourse theory and psychoanalysis, the chapter argues that masculinities arise from a complex process of cultural and personal 'accounting', in which boys take up positions with regard to a variety of dominant and submissive masculine forms. These gendered identities are cross-cut by 'race', ethnicity, class and sexuality. Using illustrations from an interview-based study of London boys, the chapter demonstrates that historically and socially specific discourses of African Caribbean and Asian masculinities are often the cultural resources available to channel the anxieties immanent in the emergence of white masculine identities.

In Chapter 4, 'White girls and women in the contemporary United States: supporting or subverting race and gender domination?', Michelle Fine, Abigail Stewart and Alyssa Zucker deploy feminist theory, cultural analyses of whiteness and social history, while also drawing on two psychological studies of the contemporary roles of white girls and women as critics and facilitators of social inequity. The contributors are interested in the conditions that lead us to see and speak about social justice, or to 'pretend not to see' and paper over striking inequities. Fine uses ethnographic data to document the discursive strategies by which (vocal) white girls frame social inequities (psychologically), deflect conflict as unintentional misunderstanding (not power), represent individualism as normative and valued, and insist that unlimited social choices are universally available. There are nevertheless moments when African American girls pose more radical discursive challenges, and when white girls recognise possibilities of alliance around the politics of gender and racialised difference. Stewart and Zucker use quantitative data from a study of three generations of white, college-educated women in the USA to show that egalitarianism (in contrast with feminism) is associated with the rejection of collective action by women, and less critical views of racism and the power of white men. They suggest that a widely held egalitarian but explicitly non-feminist ideology may lead some white women to protect a system of constraints they believe they can escape. Identification with feminism seems more likely to produce an understanding of other forms of social differentiation; feminism acts to 'culture' social awareness.

In the third chapter in the section (Chapter 5), 'Constructing racism: discourse, culture and subjectivity', Bipasha Ahmed examines the ways in which a group of second-generation middle-class young Bangladeshi adults construct and account for their experiences of racism. Ahmed's study shows how various discursive practices construct racism in descriptions of participants' experiences of racism and their strategies for dealing with it, and how these cultural constructions serve particular functions. In these discourses, racism is constructed as a problem of the past, and therefore only a minor problem now; or as present, but manifesting itself in subtle, covert forms. These discourses place the onus for dealing with racism on the potential victims, thus reinforcing the power relations of racism; but at the same time the discourses offer the interviewees control over racism and their futures. In addition, the discourses mark important differences in generational and class experiences of racism, differences that these interviewees are some of the first to articulate. Finally, the chapter examines how some social psychological theorising may also be perpetuating the power relations of racism by abstracting 'discourse' from the cultural practices of producing discourse.

3 Cultural contestations in practice

White boys and the racialisation of masculinities

Stephen Frosh, Ann Phoenix and Rob Pattman

Theorising culture in practice

The construction of masculine identities has become a major research and media focus in recent years. While some publications on boys and masculinities centre on the 'crisis of masculinity' with its manifestations in relatively low levels of achievement in school and relatively high rates of suicide, violence, and alcohol and drug abuse among teenage boys (Farrington, 1995; Vizard *et al.*, 1995), there have also been some ethnographic and discursive studies which address boys' cultural practices (see Pattman *et al.* (1998) for a review). These studies converge on the idea (first developed by Connell, 1987, 1995) that it is possible to view constructions of masculinity as the products of interpersonal work, accomplished through the exploitation of available cultural resources such as the ideologies prevalent in particular societies.

'Culture' enters the frame here in two main ways. First, as we shall attempt to show in the material presented later in this chapter, the 'cultural resources' upon which boys draw in positioning themselves with regard to masculinities are strongly imbued with features of the social structure out of which they emerge. What we are suggesting here is that relatively 'deep' structural factors, notably social class, 'race' and gender, become worked on in culture to make available subject 'positions' out of which specific subjectivities are constructed. In the research we have been carrying out with teenage boys, this process can clearly be seen in the impact of ethnicity and 'race' on the masculine identities constructed by young men. Thus images of 'whiteness', 'Asianness' and 'blackness' are central to the ways in which masculinities are experienced in Britain today. This, at first sight, appears to be the view of 'culture' often imported into developmental and social psychological studies to explain differences between different 'cultural' groups by racialising, ethnicising and fixing them. This treatment of culture serves, implicitly, to reproduce racism and ethnicism by normalising white English ethnics and treating everybody else as Other in comparison. Our version of culture, however, draws on recent work in anthropology, cultural studies and sociology that sees culture as dynamic and actively constructed (although both historically located and deploying 'tradition'), relational, imbued with power relations and, hence, a site of contestation as well as of commonality (Brah, 1996; Clifford and

Marcus, 1986; Hall and du Gay, 1996). 'Culture' and 'difference' are powerfully intertwined not because of pre-existing and immutable differences between cultures, but because constructions of cultural diversity are frequently used to serve the interests of difference. This understanding makes readings of 'race' and ethnicity central to the constructive process of generating masculinities, rather than suggesting that there is something integrally different about (say) 'white masculinity' in contrast to 'Asian masculinity' or 'black masculinity'. It is, therefore, only possible to analyse culture by examining people's complex, contradictory, socially situated and dynamic everyday practices (see Griffin, Chapter 1, this volume). Since culture is multi-layered, young men in British multi-ethnic schools come into contact with a range of cultures – those seen as national and religious as well as gender and 'youth cultures'. It thus becomes hard to sustain a view of ethnicity or 'race' as fixed identities; rather, the diversity of cultural experiences to which people are exposed makes it clear that ethnicity and 'race' are plural, dynamic and socially constructed concepts – an idea conveyed in the terms 'racialisation' and 'ethnicisation' (Anthias and Yuval-Davis, 1992; Omi and Winant, 1986; see also Fine *et al.* (Chapter 4) and Marshall and Woollett (Chapter 8), this volume).

The second manifestation of 'culture' in the production of masculinities is a more general version of the first. Taking as a starting point the idea that identities are made rather than given, 'culture' becomes not just something distinguishing one set of practices from another, but refers to the general complex of materials out of which, and in interaction with which, subject positions are created. Culture provides the conditions of emergence for identities and the desires and anxieties which underpin them. This means that masculinities are always already imbued with culture; indeed, they are 'cultural' by virtue of being produced from social engagements, understood broadly as patterns of ideological and material encounter between any person and other people, and between people and social institutions (Connell, 1995, 1996; Wetherell, 1996). Methodologically, therefore, studies of 'culture in psychology' need to explore the ways in which identities are socially structured and inhabited and also to recognise the very fluid manner in which these identities can form and change – sometimes in the course of a research interview. Consequently, our own research into 'emergent masculinities' in boys has taken for granted the fluidity of masculine identity construction, assuming, for example, not only that masculinities enacted in the one-to-one interview with our interviewer might differ from those enacted in group discussions, but also that the process of researching this topic will itself contribute to the consolidation and diminishing of particular masculinities among participants. A similar process is perhaps occurring in the study reported by Gill *et al.* (Chapter 7), this volume. Research is thus reactive not just as an unwanted or uncontrollable side-effect, but simply because it is part of 'culture', the process of production out of which identities emerge.

In this chapter we explore issues around the 'culture' of masculine identity construction through one pervasive feature of boys' accounts of masculinities: racialisation. The chapter focuses on the two aspects of culture described above as demonstrated in white boys' narratives. First, we examine how the cultural resources available to boys for constructing masculinities are racialised in everyday practices. Second, we deal with the ways in which white boys' use of racist discourses demonstrates the intersections of gender and 'race' in the construction of their identities.

The chapter draws on some research we have been carrying out with seventy-eight 11 to 14-year-old boys from a variety of London schools, who have been interviewed individually and in groups about various aspects of their lives, the main focus being the ways in which they experience themselves as young men.[1] The interviews follow a semi-structured format, but encourage the boys to express themselves in 'narrative' terms. In line with our aspiration to create a collaborative context for boys to talk about themselves, our interviewer, Rob Pattman (a white man), adopted an informal style with an emphasis on trying to understand the boys' lives and generally being sympathetic to them. He saw his task as encouraging the boys to talk about themselves, and he worked hard to create a non-judgemental and affirming atmosphere. More generally, we see the interview as 'co-constructed'; out of it emerge narratives of identity which might be quite new and unstable, but are nevertheless part of the complex work of producing masculinities. We are not suggesting, therefore, that the interviews index pre-existing masculine identities, but rather that the challenging conversational/discursive process taking place between the interviewer and those he interviews is itself part of the cultural construction of masculine forms.

Claiming/contesting 'authentic' cultural practices: racialisation of masculinities in process

British and US research with young people suggests that young black men of African Caribbean descent are viewed in some ways as 'super-masculine'. They are constructed as possessing the attributes that are seen by young men as indicative of the most popular forms of masculinity: toughness and authentically male style in talk and dress. Paradoxically, while they are feared and discriminated against because of those features, they are also respected, admired, and gain power through taking on characteristics which militate against good classroom performance (Back, 1996; Mac an Ghaill, 1988). Sewell (1997) found that many of the 15-year-old black boys he studied both were positioned by others, and positioned themselves, as superior to white and Asian students in terms of their sexual attractiveness, style, creativity and 'hardness'. They are 'Angels and Devils in British (and American) schools. They are heroes of a street fashion culture that dominates most of our inner cities' (Sewell, 1997: ix). At the same time, they are the group of pupils most likely to be excluded from schools.

From their research in the US context, Majors and Billson (1992) refer to this subject position as 'cool pose' – an aggressive assertion of masculinity that allows control, inner strength, stability and confidence in the face of the adverse social, political and economic conditions which many African American men face. 'Cool pose' fits many of the characteristics associated with popular masculinity.

However, it also imposes costs on those black boys and men who cannot deal with it as one among many masculine identities, but who want others to believe that they 'really' possess it, that this is the 'truth' of them. What this means is that rather than developing a set of identities which might be adaptable to different contexts, many black males find themselves trapped within this particular discursive construction of masculinity, experiencing it as 'true' or 'ideal' masculinity which, because they are African American, they should possess. At the same time it closes down other ways of doing masculinity. The costs involved here can include, for example, the suppression of motivation to learn and emotional expressiveness. Moreover, those boys who attempt to inhabit this prescriptive cultural construction of masculine positions but who experience themselves or are judged by others as 'unsuccessful' in doing so, have to deal with failing cultural practices which many have essentialised as natural to black men.

Research of this kind exemplifies the way that, in Britain and the USA, masculinity as a 'practical accomplishment' (Connell, 1995) involves the construction of masculinities as culturally differentiated along racialised lines. This racialisation contradicts, but coexists with, the common, difference-denying 'equality' discourse that dominates the talk of white US high school students in Fine *et al.*'s study (Chapter 4, this volume). It also inverts the status usually attached to black and white people in British and US society into a hierarchy where black British boys and men of African Caribbean descent and African Americans are positioned as possessing culturally superior masculinities. This hierarchy places contestation about culture on the agenda for many young men. On the one hand, the performance of 'black masculinity' is clearly an important set of cultural practices for young men in schools and other social institutions. On the other hand, the racialisation of these cultural practices apparently places them out of the reach of white and Asian boys. Three sets of consequences follow from this. Some boys from all racialised/ethnicised groups repudiate such cultural practices and/or deny that they are the prerogative of black boys and men. Some white and Asian boys attempt to emulate what they see as 'blackness' in order to perform popular masculinities, and some black boys attempt to embody 'cool pose' as if it is an individually possessed identity. Given these differential positions and the different resources available to boys with which to produce masculinity, it is not surprising that the racialisation of masculinities produces many contradictions and conflicts. In relation to the ambiguities of 'cool pose', for example, Sewell (1997) found that many black boys resented being 'Othered' by teachers, being perceived as threatening and being picked upon for no reason they could see other than because they were black. However, for some, the knowledge that teachers were afraid of them was a source of power and provided an incentive to perform in ways which signified threat.

In Sewell's study, boys' accounts indicated that masculinities were racialised in two ways: through differential treatment from teachers and others; and because black, white and Asian boys were differentially positioned in terms of 'popular' masculinity. This was also the case in our study, where it was clear that the dynamism of culture in British multi-ethnic schools includes a range of cultural repertoires. The following example is notable not only for the racialisation of black boys as popular, but for the differential production of Asian boys as not popular – a racialisation that was common among the boys we interviewed, as in Sewell's group. The context is a group interview with four white boys from Year 8 (12 to 13-year-olds).[2]

Des: Don't know, I think the black boys are more popular.
Rob Pattman (RP): Are they?
Des: Hmhm.
RP: Why's that?
Des: Don't know it's just (.) black boys seem to get friends easier (.) and they're more popular I suppose.
RP: Yeah, (.) they get friends more easy yeh.
Des: Mm (3)
RP: But I was just wondering 'cos you said that black boys tend to be quite popular and I was wondering if it was the same with Asian boys (3). What about in your class, are Asian boys as popular as black boys?
Des: No I shouldn't think so.
Jason: No.
RP: They're not no.
Des: No (2)
RP: Why's that? (3)
Des: Don't really know (sigh) (3) black boys urn Asian boys just go round with (.) like who they want (.) but they don't they don't go out picking, they wait for them come to them (1) they've only got a few friends (2)

Black boys were commonly constructed as more likely than other boys to embody the characteristics of popular masculinity, particularly sporting ability, coolness and toughness:

RP: So they tend to be more interested in football then?
David: Well, black people are good at athletics, they're very good at running and everything, and high jump.
                          (11-year-old white boy, individual interview)

This familiar notion of the in-built superior physicality of black people, which coincides with visions of 'ideal' masculinity but which is also racist in its strong connotations of 'animality', recurs frequently in the descriptions of racialised difference given by young white boys. These descriptions racialise black boys' bodies and their cultural practices, adopting the rhetoric of traditional, 'scientific' racism.

    Although these accounts often leave whiteness unmarked, they also implicitly racialise it in opposition to blackness. The following extract, from an interview with a group of six 12 to 14-year-old white boys, demonstrates their contestation of black boys' perceived cultural dominance and their explicit normalising of 'white style' in comparison with 'black style'.

Gary: =White people have their own styles so do black people (.) sometimes Moroccans have theirs (1) but Somalis just copy.
RP: What's the white style then?
Joe: Kind of normal innit (G: tracksuit) (.) normal clothes (2) no flashness no nothing.
RP: No flashness.
Adam: Casual clothes.
RP: So black boys are more flash are they than white boys?
Adam: Yeah they like showing off.
          /. . ./
RP: Why do the Somalis and Moroccans try and copy the black boys and not the white boys? (3)
Gary   It's just that (1) they learn that (.) the clothes that look (1) the (.) top innit?
Adam: I – I wouldn't wear them=
Joe: =Black people they wear like like design designer wear (2)
RP: Right.
Joe: And like they (Adam: more expensive) yeah much more expensive.
RP: More expensive yeh?
Joe: Yeh (Adam: inaudible)
Gary: =Doesn't mean they've got more money or nothing it's just that (.) they like (.) they like to show what they've got and everything but (1) (RP: Right) they're just spending their money just on clothes.

As will be seen in the following dialogue, the racialisation of black boys' bodies and cultural practices is often hedged around with uncertainties, like noting that 'people say' black people are characterisable in certain ways but some white boys are also tough. This qualified racialisation also links with the ambivalent way in which some white youngsters want to 'be' black in order to achieve the cultural trappings of 'cool pose'.

RP: Right. Does, does it make a difference being, being white, d'you think?
Paul: No. People that finks like black people might be stronger, like, most black people are better than white people at basketball 'cos (1) they like (.) play it a lot.
RP: Right (2) D'you think, d'you think black people are stronger than white people?
Paul: Don't know like, people like say (.) like boxers, most boxers are black. (*RP*: Yeah, yeah) 'Cos people say like (.) black people's bones are harder an' that. (*RP*: Right) But (1) . . . the strongest boy in our year's (1) somebody I don't like, there's a boy called ——. He's white but like (1) there's four strongest boys, three of them are black, one of them are white. (*RP*: Mmm, mmm.) But most people they're just like (1) mixed who's the hardest an' that.
RP: D'you think some white boys then envy black boys (1) 'cos they think they're stronger?

Paul: Yeah like, they wanna like, some people wanna be black 'cos (1) they might like be more popular. Like, black people like, don't like really cool. Black people have like black slang don't they an' they call people (.) bro an' that. Like white people don't call each other (.) names like that an' black people call some people some. And sometimes people wanna be black an' that.

(11-year-old white boy, individual interview)

Not all boys, black or white, accepted that black boys are automatically more representative of an 'ideal' masculinity. It was, however, a pervasive narrative which partially defined cultures of masculinity and against which boys positioned themselves as they attempted to embody, appropriate or repudiate it. Many boys in our study expended a great deal of energy in this racialised 'jockeying for position' (Edley and Wetherell, 1997). For example, as Paul mentioned in the above dialogue, some white boys were reported to be adopting the cultural practices they considered central to 'black masculinity'. In such accounts it is always other white boys, not the speaker, who are reported to want to be black:

RP: Do you think of yourself as being English, or white?
Ben: Um, I do fink of myself as a British person, a British citizen but I, I don't fink of myself as any other race because I was born in England which makes me English so I'm not nofing else, I wouldn't try and be nofing else.
RP: Right. Do you think some boys do they try and be something else?
Ben: Yeah. Yeah, try and act hard or try and talk in a, like some people like try talkin' like a Jamaican accent or=
RP: =Do they?
Ben: Yeah and like kiss their teeth like Africans, like Afro-Caribbean do, try and copy them.
RP: This is English boys tryin' to be like that. White English boys?
Ben: Yeah. Some do. Yeah.
RP: So why is that then? Why do they try and be like that?
Ben: Dunno because they look as . . . quite hard people and if they try and, if they act like that then they're gonna, people are gonna fink 'oh look they look hard. Don't look at them else they're gonna start trouble'. So that's probably why.

(14-year-old white boy, individual interview)

Racialised Otherness: constructing masculine identities through racist cultural discourses

The racialisation of masculinities discussed above produced ambivalence in those white boys who resented being excluded from cultural practices seen as representing 'ideal' or 'popular' masculinity. The racialisation of masculinity thus involved contestation over access to the cultural resources available for the performance of masculinity. Among white boys, this contest produced both attraction and aversion to black masculine cultural practices, an ambivalence which sometimes generalised to all black people, as in the following example.

RP: Are these people at school? (*Luke*: Yeh) Is your school quite ethnically mixed?

Luke: Yeh (.) It's quite sort of equally mixed I would say.

RP: Is there any reason why you have Asian friends but not black friends?

Luke: Um (4) 'cos I suppose because most of the (.) black boys (2) again are like (1) think they're like sort of (1) rude boys and well hard and they like (.) music I don't like I don't know they just (.) I don't get on with them.

RP: Do they tend to stick together, the black boys or do they mix?

Luke: They mix with other people as well but (*RP*: With similar kinds of interests?) Yes (1) it's just (.) it's not (.) I don't think it's 'cos they're black it's just 'cos (.) they're (.) not the type of people I'd get on with most of them (.) relate to other groups.

RP: Have you ever thought you'd rather not be white?

Luke: Um (2), nah actually um (6) 'cos (3) I don't like most of the black women not 'cos they're black (.) but just not 'cos (1) they relate to the group that I don't like so I wouldn't want (1), no I've never wanted to be black actually.

RP: Are there any things that you admire about black people?

Luke: Um (8), they seem more confident in a way they're sort of (5), they act sort of bigger and louder and more confident (.) and I sort of admire that.

RP: Do you wish you were more like that then?

Luke: Sometimes (1) but not like (2) inaudible. It's not like I don't think about it a lot (.) I don't think, 'Oh I really want to be black' (.) or, 'I really want to be like that'.

(14-year-old white boy, individual interview)

Alongside the ambivalent positioning of black masculinities described above, a variety of racisms appear in our interviews, particularly among those with white boys. As will be seen, straightforward assumptions of racist identities are resisted by the boys – perhaps not surprisingly, as racist discourses are currently recognised to be socially proscribed among British people and in British schools (Back, 1996; Billig, 1991; Tizard and Phoenix, 1993; Troyna and Hatcher, 1992). But this proscription does not prevent numerous long-established racist ideologies from appearing in the boys' narratives, in many instances connected to exactly the same elements of 'coolness' and physicality which excite envy and admiration. The following dialogue ascribes black boys' concern with style and appearance to their having 'a chip on their shoulder'. The speaker told to 'go home' by black boys flips the meaning from what is presumably a dismissive admonition to go away, to a discourse of racialised exclusion from the nation – a discourse he is afraid to voice to the black boys who antagonise him.

Alan: Seems to be all black boys have a chip on their shoulder. Er, you do get white bullies – I'm not sayin' that, but half of the school here, erm, half the black boys – all of them walk around walkin' like that, brand names, lookin' down at people, like Year 7s, the little girls. They look at you and stare at you as if you're lower than them. (.) And the worst bit is and then they say 'What you doin' ruckin' up my clothes' and you're like, 'pardon? Ruckin' up your clothes – what's that?' And they say – 'you're juggin' my clothes, you're ripping them, you're touchin' them' and you're like, 'Sorry, we're in a corridor' and you're bound to bump into them, especially when they're walkin' in a line. And they're lookin' at you as if to say, 'What you doin' here? Why are you here?'

RP: Mmm.

Alan: Not being racist, but they come over here. Mean I have no problem with black people. Most of my friends are coloured and foreign but sometimes it really annoys me especially when they say, 'What are you doin' – why are you here. Go home' and all of dis. I'm like, I am home, this is England. And I say in my mind, why have I got to go home – I live here. This is my home. Sometimes I feel like sayin' 'Go back to your home, Jamaica' – somewhere like that and then think about sayin' most of my friends are coloured, be upsettin' them as well.

(12-year-old white boy, individual interview)

For this boy, Alan, an element in his construction of his everyday experience of school is the black boys swaggering and looking down on him, as if to say to him, 'What you doin' here? Why are you here?' They take up all the space and in so doing push him out: it is literally the case, in his account, that there is no room for him. His interpretation of this corridor jostling is a racialised perception of contestation of space and cultural practices. Black boys are constructed as 'coloured and foreign' outsiders who usurp what is rightfully his – they tell him to go home. In his vision, the black boys are constantly asserting their superiority and pose a cogent threat based on their capacity to undermine his sense of location and identity: they treat the place as home, when he sees it as his own home: '*I live here. This is my home.*' They have taken it away from him; his wish is that all of them, from wherever they might have come, should go back to their home, which he calls 'Jamaica – somewhere like that'.

This 'Jamaica' is an important place in British racism's psychic geography. It is one of the places from which it is imagined that all these 'coloured and foreign' others come to invade and take up all the space. In Alan's mind, it is the immediate association – 'my home England, their home Jamaica' – which racialises black and white boys in relation to each other. As described above, many of the boys we have interviewed share Alan's conviction that African Caribbean boys are 'hard', stylish and to be admired, but they also carry an image of aggression and disdain for others. Alan makes it clear just how much antagonism is attached to this construction. The black boys' reported airs – superiority, disdain and 'lookin' down at people', their '[staring] at you as if you are lower than them' – are markers of cultural as well as racialised Otherness and are deeply resented. For Alan, it is as if his home has been invaded and taken from him; conflict and cultural usurpation is evoked, difference is thoroughly racialised.

In keeping with the findings of a number of studies, many of the boys whom we have interviewed see black and white boys as being more like one another than they are like Asians, whose difference is marked out by their tight culture, strong family ties, and in particular, their language (Back, 1996; Boulton and Smith, 1992; Cohen, 1997).

Angus: That's what most people don't like about (3) the Bengali people 'cos they speak in their own language and you can't really understand what they are saying but when you are speaking in English you can you can understand what they are saying (*RP*: Yeah) right and . . .
RP: Is that something you don't like about them?
Angus: Yeah 'cos you don't even have to say anything about you (*RP*: Right) (2)
RP: Do you think they might be saying things about you then?
Angus: I don't know.

                                                    (14-year-old white boy, individual interview)

Extracted from the uncertainties of 'you' and 'they' in this boy's talk, the theme again seems to be that the white boy feels excluded, with this exclusion carrying a paranoid charge. The Bengali-speaking boys could be saying anything to one another, and this is automatically excluding because it is hidden in their own language. Very centrally for this boy and for many others, 'culture' becomes something bound up with envy, in all the ambivalent senses of the word. An explicit bond, expressed through shared language and 'sticking together', is valued; it is also antisocial, dangerous, promoting antagonism and a wish to destroy. This boy and the others whom we have quoted clearly demonstrate how their identities are constructed in relation to who or what they are *not* – in this case they are racialised as white in contradistinction from black and Asian people. What perhaps can be seen here are the seeds of an attitude towards 'culture' which is deeply emotional: the strong investment that these boys have in placing themselves inside or outside particular 'ethnic' or racialised masculine cultures suggests that racialised constructions of difference are central to the production of identity positions.

Conclusion

Our argument in this chapter is that 'culture' is a key element in the formation of identity positions of all kinds, and that it is best understood as a set of lived practices and imagined encounters embodying a variety of tensions and codes of difference. Here we have focused on the intersection between masculinities and 'race', using the versions of blackness and otherness invoked by white boys in London as they reflect on their lives. It is hardly surprising that the cultures of masculinity explored in this age group are diverse and at times contradictory, but what particularly interests us here is the way in which they are perpetually racialised, with 'us' and 'them' becoming the coding images and differentiating discourses around which culture is experienced. However, despite our emphasis on 'race', racism and ethnicity in this chapter, we are not arguing that 'culture' is reducible to racialised and ethnicised differences. Rather, 'race' and ethnicity are particularly potent instances of how, more generally, the construction of identities arises out of a whirlpool of forces (which also include, for example, sexuality and class), with which each of us has to engage in establishing our 'subject positions'. For the London boys we have interviewed, this is no easy task: their masculinities, like all other identity positions, are embodied versions of discursive cultural practices. Cultures, whether constructed as national, religious or youth cultures, are a resource in the construction of masculinities. They are, however, also *produced* in boys' everyday practices of contestation or compliance. This means that culture itself, as well as the individuals who stand within it, is full of the contradictions and anxieties which these 'everyday practices' entail.

Notes

1 This study is funded by the British Economic and Social Research Council, grant number L129251015.
2 Names of all participants except the interviewer, Rob Pattman, have been changed. (.) indicates brief pause; longer pauses are timed – for example, (2) means 'two-second pause'. = signifies overlapping speech. Comments in brackets are brief interruptions to continuing speech.

References

Anthias, F. and Yuval-Davis, N. (1992) *Racialised Boundaries: Race, Gender, Colour and Class and the Anti-racist Struggle*, London: Routledge.

Back, L. (1996) *New Ethnicities and Urban Culture*, London: UCL Press.

Billig, M. (1991) *Ideology and Opinions*, London: Sage.

Boulton, M. and Smith, P. (1992) 'Ethnic preferences and perceptions among Asian and white British school children', *Social Development* 1: 55–66.

Brah, A. (1996) *Cartographies of Diaspora: Contesting Identities*, London: Routledge.

Clifford, J. and Marcus, G. (eds) (1986) *Writing Culture: The Poetics and Politics of Ethnography*, Cambridge, MA: Harvard University Press.

Cohen, P. (1997) *Rethinking the Youth Question: Education, Labour and Cultural Studies*, London: Macmillan.

Connell, R. (1987) *Gender and Power*, Cambridge: Polity Press.

—— (1995) *Masculinities*, Cambridge: Polity Press.

—— (1996) 'Teaching the boys: new research on masculinity, and gender strategies for schools', *Teachers College Record* 98(2): 206–35.

Edley, N. and Wetherell, M. (1997) 'Jockeying for position: the construction of masculine identities', *Discourse and Society* 8(2): 203–17.

Farrington, D. (1995) 'The development of offending and antisocial behaviour from childhood', *Journal of Child Psychology and Psychiatry* 36: 929–64.

Hall, S. and du Gay, P. (eds) (1996) *Questions of Cultural Identity*, London: Sage.

Mac an Ghaill, M. (1988) *Young, Gifted and Black: Student Teacher Relations in the Schooling of Black Youth*, Milton Keynes: Open University Press.

Majors, R. and Billson, J. (1992) *Cool Pose: The Dilemmas of Black Manhood in America*, New York: Lexington.

Omi, M. and Winant, H. (1986) *Racial Formation in the United States: From the 1960s to the 1980s*, New York: Routledge & Kegan Paul.

Pattman, R., Frosh, S. and Phoenix, A. (1998) 'Lads, machos and others: developing "boy-centred" research', *Journal of Youth Studies* 1(2): 125–42.

Sewell, T. (1997) *Black Masculinities and Schooling: How Black Boys Survive Modern Schooling*, Stoke-on-Trent: Trentham Books.

Tizard, B. and Phoenix, A. (1993) *Black, White or Mixed Race? Race and Racism in the Lives of Young People of Mixed-Parentage*, London: Routledge.

Troyna, B. and Hatcher, R. (1992) *Racism in Children's Lives: A Study of Mainly-White Primary Schools*, London: Routledge.

Vizard, E., Monck, E. and Misch, P. (1995) 'Child and adolescent sex abuse perpetrators', *Journal of Child Psychology and Psychiatry* 36: 731–56.

Wetherell, M. (ed.) (1996) *Identities Groups and Social Issues*, London: Sage/Open University.

4 White girls and women in the contemporary United States

Supporting or subverting race and gender domination?

Michelle Fine, Abigail J. Stewart and Alyssa N. Zucker

There is a growing literature on what Lipsitz (1995) has called the 'possessive investment in whiteness', and Harris (1993) has theorised as 'whiteness as property'. These and other social theorists contest the view of whiteness as essential, and instead articulate the material 'worth' of whiteness 'for gaining access to a whole set of public and private privileges that materially and permanently guaranteed basic subsistence needs and therefore survival' (Harris, 1993: 1713; see also Ignatiev, 1995; Morrison, 1992). Whiteness is most evident, ironically, when it is denied or obfuscated as if only 'normal'. It is at once constituted by exclusivity and privilege and premised on innocence and deservingness. This innocence is maintained by Americans' preference for individual rather than structural explanations for social problems, including explanations that demonise 'people of color for being victimized . . . while hiding the privileges of Whiteness by attributing them to family values, fatherhood and foresight – rather than to favoritism' (Lipsitz, 1995: 379).

If US culture is organised in part through racialised, classed and gendered structures, relations and practices of domination that are justified in a language of freedom, choice and equal opportunity, then we ask the question, 'What about white women?' What about girls and women who sit at the always contingent nexus of privilege and subordination – white girls and women who see too much, sometimes speak too loudly, or more often remain too silent and complicit at critical moments of domination?

Hill Collins (1990) theorises that the knowledge and experiences available to us as individuals are determined, in part, by the positions in which we are situated within social power hierarchies. Drawing on the writings of Hartsock (1983), Hurtado (1996) and Hill Collins (1990), we find standpoint theory useful for understanding the analytic constrictions and possibilities available to white girls and women now and in the past (for a revealing analysis of the standpoints of white slave-holding women in the South, see Faust, 1996; for an analysis of the construction of masculinity from the standpoint of white English boys, see Frosh *et al.*, Chapter 3, this volume). In this chapter we discuss the complex forces defining both postwar American white girls'/women's position with respect to patriarchy and racism, and their choices to support or undermine them. We argue that white girls and women perform an important role in sustaining or subverting the material and discursive hierarchies that organise cultural domination in America.

We present this story as if about white girls and women in US culture. But the analysis may apply to others in American structural arrangements who occupy positions of privilege and subordination within the same (contested) cultural space, including, perhaps, middle-class or advantaged racial minorities, successful black immigrants, and middle-class white gay men (see Guinier *et al.*, 1997). In a larger sense we may be discussing those men, women and children with one foot in the swamps of cultural subordination (see Apfelbaum, Chapter 11, this volume) and one foot in the stirrups of potential domination, torn by biography, loyalties and rewards. As post-structuralism has enabled us to understand that we all occupy many positions at once, we ask, 'Under what conditions do such liminal subjects – in this case white girls and women – collude in or subvert cultural domination?'

Almost twenty years ago Michelle Fine (1981) conducted an experimental study that provides interesting leads. In her study, sixty groups of three women (a victim, a non-victim and a victimiser) were situated in a context of 'social injustice'. The three engaged in a discussion and rewards were distributed unfairly, with the victim the clear undeserving loser, the judge the clear undeserving winner, and the non-victim privileged compared to the victim, but a loser compared to the victimiser/judge. All women were asked to rate the fairness of the distributions. Across conditions victims were most likely to challenge the distributions as unfair. Victimisers challenged least, and non-victims, *depending on the context in which they were placed*, selectively read the very same allocations as fair or unfair, deserving or not. When there was structural opportunity to appeal against the distributions, non-victims considered the victims' portion to be unfair; with no options for appeal, non-victims blamed victims. Non-victims, however, never challenged the allocations given to the judge/victimiser, while victims were most willing to challenge allocations to all three players; that is, to see and speak out about structural injustice top to bottom. In short, non-victims – those with contingent power and more to lose by a redistribution of the chits – were sometimes willing to 'help' or speak out against unfair treatment of the victim, but they never challenged the structural hierarchy of the distribution systems.

With two decades of hindsight, it now appears that non-victims occupied a position similar to that of white girls/women in the USA today: liminal political players; relatively (dis)advantaged; contingent on and providing comfort to the structures of domination; benefiting and benefed only relative to others at a greater loss; privileged and subordinated in the same sweep. While white women (like 'non-victims') often 'help', they rarely challenge the institutions of racialised domination *per se*.

We use the 'case' of white women to interrogate how our particular position of relative privilege and subordination operates in the racialised, classed and gendered hierarchies of the United States. This interrogation requires us temporarily to suspend attention to heterogeneity within the category of 'white women', though we recognise of course that it exists.

Frankenberg (1993) identified a set of discursive moves engaged by white women when addressing race. One of Frankenberg's discourses is most pertinent to our argument here: 'colour blindness', which she recasts as colour evasiveness and, more pointedly, as power evasiveness. By adopting this discourse white women promote notions of sameness and 'equality' in profoundly unequal times, flattening questions of power and injustice (see also Hollway (1989); MacPherson and Fine (1995); Miller (1976) for related arguments). This 'discourse of equality' may have offered radical possibilities in the 1960s when civil rights and feminism were (re)emergent in the USA, but in today's cultural shift to the Right it takes on a quite conservatising, blaming significance.

We have extracted from two studies – one qualitative and one quantitative – a set of critical commitments within this discourse of equality, in order to reveal how white girls and women can uphold or, alternatively, subvert deeply racialised cultural formations. We present data from one ethnographic study of a contemporary group of early adolescents (Fine) to document those practices (see Griffin, Chapter 1, this volume) in talk and relationships that constitute a discourse of equality in integrated conversations. We then document these same dynamics within responses to a survey of political attitudes of adult white women (Stewart and Zucker). This blend of methods and generations allows us to bridge a large methodological divide, while documenting how different groups of white girls and women understand their political positions and responsibilities for disabling or enabling racialised social justice.

Study 1: White girls patrolling the borders of race

In 1991, in New Jersey, the Montclair High School English faculty voted to offer an academically ambitious, multicultural world literature course – heterogeneous by gender, race, ethnicity, social class and academic history – in an untracked or unstreamed ninth-grade classroom, where pupils are around 14 years old. Michelle Fine engaged in an ethnographic study of this set of public high school classrooms from 1996 to 1998. Fine began observation in four classes of the world literatures course, one to two mornings a week,[1] met with the faculty every other week, and worked with a group of students who were writing over the course of two years (see Fine *et al.*, 1997a).

As we will see in the selected fragments from this classroom, educators are contesting dominant constructions of race, class and gender, attempting to decentre whiteness, and inviting youths to explore questions of 'difference' (see Fine *et al.*, 1997b). This is a classroom dedicated to intellectual rigour *and* racial justice. In reading a broad range of multicultural texts and genres, these young men and women – ranging from very poor to very rich, including whites, African Americans, Asians and Latinos – practise voices long sanctioned and those long smothered. Some listen to others, not always easily, not always gracefully. In the early months many of the white boys resist the multicultural core of the course, typically through silence. Many of the often very articulate white girls carry the torch of whiteness, often against African American girls. Fine extracts a set of discursive practices engaged in by the white girls in this contested, stormy cultural space.

The cultural context: hierarchies of gender and race

It is October. Five students have been preselected by race and gender, forming an inner circle of conversation: one white female, one white male, two African American females and one African American male. The remaining fourteen students form a circle around them, and are asked to analyse how the 'group works together'. The observing students craft a joint analyses on the board:

> The white male student sat at the head of the table, had the clearest and loudest voice, often tried to direct the discussion, frequently jumped in or even interrupted other students. . . . The white female vied for power over the discussion, often challenging statements made by other members and taking over the conversation when silences fell. Both the white male and the white female aligned with each other . . . when there was dissension with African American students. Both African American females made attempts to contribute to the conversation with one asserting her opinions, often arguing with the others, while the other was soft-spoken, seemingly uncertain about her own ideas. Their ideas were frequently challenged.

Jean Baker Miller (1976) named the gendered portion of this dynamic over two decades ago – that it is (white) woman's work to serve the patriarchy, know its weaknesses, keep the secrets and demonstrate loyalty – pretending, as Nell Painter (1995) writes, 'not to notice' the race politics. We share Baker Miller's (1976) view that women are assumed responsible not only for the maintenance of cultural hierarchies and the repair of cultural fractures, but also for keeping silent about the extent to which men depend on women, at home, work and on the street (see also Fine and Carney, forthcoming; Flax, 1990). And we share Painter's recognition that white women keep the secrets of patriarchy and racism.

If white women told the secrets of privilege, sexuality, danger, terror, violence and oppression, then the dependencies and fears that sustain the culture would be unmasked. But a substantial research literature shows that we generally do not tell (see Bertram *et al.*, forthcoming; Fine *et al.*, 1996; Gilligan *et al.*, 1990). In this class, as in the culture, white girls did not, for the most part, tell about the fall-out of racism, sexism or classism. But women and girls of colour more often, as in this class, did speak the critique (see Collins, 1990; Fordham, 1996). And as we have seen so often in US culture, these girls and women were, in turn, hated, demonised, silenced or banished for revealing hypocrisies, domination and injustices (see Espin, 1998; Morrison, 1992). It is in this cultural context of domination that we can witness the discursive practices that sustain and, less so, subvert.

A discursive move repeated throughout the year may be categorised as *declaring universals and whiting out inequity*. Throughout the year, in this class-room comprising largely white and black students, ranging from poor to very wealthy (with the black range enormous and the white range from middle-class to elite), there were many moments when African American girls spoke through a kind of critical conversation about social oppression and 'difference', or interrupted a smooth conversation about social relations. Such comments were typically followed by a white girl domesticating (making 'nice') the original comment, removing the sting, with what may be a 'relational' (*à la* Carol Gilligan) universal, which actually occludes the original comment, often intended to sting, to critique, to challenge.

To illustrate: Three-quarters of the way through the term, the students and their teacher, Dana, are discussing *Two Old Women* (Wallis, 1994). Dana raises the issue of social power directly:

Dana:	Is society really based on a hierarchy? Do we define ourselves hierarchically in relation to others? What if I said there is no such thing as better, less than or equal?
Joanna (white girl):	*We were taught all our life we should be the best.*
Nefertiti (black girl):	**Not everyone.**

(MF: **Here's the challenge to universalism**).

Joanna:	*Everyone* wants an A in school.
Serge (Asian boy):	It's how **a lot of people** see things. But **it's a superiority complex.**
Sharon (black girl):	**I** have to disagree with Joanna. **Not everyone** is taught to be all you can be. Some are raised to grow up and try as hard as you can. Most parents don't talk to kids about getting an A. Half the time parents don't care.
Nina (white girl):	*Everyone* is taught being the best even though no one really taught us. It's there. *Everybody* gets it. And then there are those who acknowledge they are not going to be the best, but they know everybody thinks they should be.

A critical feature of the *equality discourse* (note the italics above) is its insistence upon universals. While Serge, Nefertiti and Sharon **challenge** (in bold) the universal claims, Joanna and Nina (in italics) elaborate declarations of universality. A decree for sameness both marks and unmarks the standard as the white self. A flattening of power inequities is attempted by a muting of 'difference' and, as you will see below, an assertion that everyone has 'choices'.

Within the same classroom, a second discursive move for 'equality' is the *insistence on everyone's 'choice' and therefore 'my innocence'*. In a discussion of the text *La Llorona* (Anaya, 1984), the story of Cortes colonising Mexico, partnering with the princess Malinche, the birth of their sons and Malinche's ultimate murder of the boys out of her belief that such an act would save her people, a small but vocal group of white girls rise quickly to blame Malinche. They insist that 'everyone has choices'. While Cortes' responsibility evaporates, students question why Malinche conspired with Cortes against her people (small

historic fact: Malinche was a 14-year-old princess who 'fell in love' with the
Captain from Spain).

Dana (teacher):   Maybe we need to recharacterise their relationship for a
                           minute. She does have her forms of resistance – why does
                           she go with the plan?
Paul (white boy):   She's submissive because she loves him. She honours him.
                           If *you're* in a relationship, *you need to be submissive.*
Laura (white girl):   *She's a sell-out.* Like when bands trade in their sound to
                           become more corporate. She sells out her people.
Natasha (black girl):   She sells out her village, goes to new places with gold, but
                           she **realises she's wrong.** Do you **understand? She
                           realises it's a mistake.**
Cherie (white girl):   *Everyone has choices – even then.*

While Dana (white teacher) and Natasha try to insert an analysis through power,
Cherie resolves the conversation with a conclusion that everyone has choices. As
Harris (1993) and Lipsitz (1995) asserted, the power of whiteness is not only in its
material advantage but in its posture of innocence (see also MacPherson and Fine,
1995). The move to innocence and individualism severs its narrators, in this case
white girls, from history, responsibility and cross-race solidarity.

Moving further into the semester, we can hear, from some, a *muting of racialised
social critique*, replaced by a gender analysis. The class read widely internationally,
globally, critically; now it wanders into India, late 1950s, with *Nectar in the Sieve*
(Markandaya, 1954). Rykmani, an Indian mother who lives by dharma, fate, and
asks few questions about why or what could be, befriends Kenny, the white,
western-trained physician. Kenny prods Rykmani about what he sees as the
ignorance and patience of her people.

Amid intense discussion about Rykmani and Kenny, Sondra – a young woman
who calls herself African American but then explains, 'really part Puerto Rican,
black, and part Native American' – pipes up, crawling out of her often silent mode,
and says, 'Sometimes I think I would like to be white. I mean to have your' – she
points to Steven – 'your house and cars and stuff.' Steven, the implied white boy,
turns and assures her, 'If you try, you can have what I have.' Kito, a first-
generation Dominican American, challenges notions of individualism and choice
in a barely audible voice, after years in special education: 'But I do try hard. I try
hard all the time. And I don't have what you have.'

Many African Americans in the class chime in to turn on Sondra. 'You should
be proud of who you are.' 'You don't really want to be white. That's ignorant to
want to be what you ain't.' Sondra tries to explain: 'It ain't about bein' white. It's
about having what he has. Like if I was sittin' in a soft chair and you're in a hard
uncomfortable one, you'd want to be switchin' seats. That's it.' She degenerates
into apology: 'I'm not being clear.'

Chelsea enters the conversation with, 'You think it's easy being a white girl?
Getting called white bitch in the hallway?' She speaks for a long time – over seven

minutes – responding in part to Sondra's muffled 'It's not easy being black and female.'

Again an African American girl in this class has opened a conversation about power and racism; again we hear a white girl insist upon an equality of oppressions, effectively shutting down the conversation.

In both fiction and non-fiction, we can find the power and courage through which women of colour articulate social critique, as in Audre Lorde's writing, Gloria Anzaldua's (1987) 'tongues of fire', and Signithia Fordham's (1996) essay 'Those loud black girls'. And yet in this class, a practice of white girl etiquette is the rapid-fire rephrasing, softening or 'correcting' of what a black girl has just said. This strategy, aimed at alliance building, is often received as a form of discursive violence. The intervention whitens the original critique, converting it into a misunderstanding and/or a question of gender alone.

As we noted in our introduction, the pivotal white girl seat can both reflect and refract – in talk and in social practice – relations of domination. Thus it is important to close our ethnographic musings with an observation that it is also often white feminist girls in this classroom who pose powerful and direct critique around gender, and stretch to form a coalition with African American girls. Maya, in an interview about the course, admits, 'There are lots of ways to be smart. I went to school with so many of the people in this class and I never heard their voices. Maybe they're just not as comfortable speaking, or not a loudmouth like me . . . but now I realise there are ways to connect where I never saw them before.'

In this strategic move, a small set of white girls practised and articulated a sometimes hesitant, perhaps naive *sense that change is possible*, desirable, to be grabbed and reachable. No cynicism here. The white girl *equality discourse* views change as good and achievable, and for this, feminist white girls pay a price to almost everyone for their optimism. To white boys and men they sound 'naive' or 'unrealistic'; and to boys and girls of colour they sound naive about the real 'micro-aggressions' (Franklin, 1998) and structural obstacles. This small set of girls are dreamers. They dare to call themselves feminist in high school. They know that something is wrong. The possibilities for multiracial activism sit, delicately and uncomfortably, in their hands.

Study 2: Surveying white women: documenting the power of feminism

Abby Stewart and Alyssa Zucker were poised to explore this issue in a different way, since we had collected survey data from adult women about their different views of activism, as well as race and gender inequities. Having discussed Michelle's findings with her, we were eager to assess whether signs of the responses she found might also be visible in survey data from white women. We also wondered whether different groups of white women could be identified, in terms of their views on the discourse of equality.

We had collected data from the University of Michigan alumnae for a study of three groups of women: those who identified themselves as feminists, those who held some 'feminist' beliefs, but did not identify themselves as feminists (we called them 'egalitarians'), and those who did not hold egalitarian beliefs and identified themselves as non-feminists. In this way we could examine whether actually identifying as feminist was 'daring' and consequential in some way beyond simply holding feminist beliefs. Women were considered 'feminists' if they chose to respond to a set of questions headed 'The questions on this page should be answered only by women who consider themselves feminists' (and not those headed 'These questions are to be answered by women who do *not* consider themselves feminists') *and* they endorsed at least two of the following items: 'Girls and women have not been treated as well as boys and men in this society'; 'Women and men should be paid equally for equal work' and 'Women's unpaid work should be more socially valued'. Women were considered egalitarians if they endorsed all three of the items reflecting egalitarian feminist beliefs, but responded to the questions for women who did not consider themselves feminists. Women were considered non-egalitarian if they did not respond as a feminist, and they rejected at least one of the egalitarian beliefs (see Zucker (1998) for a description of the development of these criteria).

Because we had collected so much data on these attitudes and beliefs about gender and race, we began with the themes Michelle had uncovered, and identified items that assessed them. We then examined whether women in these three groups differed in their expression or endorsement of these themes. It seemed, for example, that feminists would be least likely to *endorse universals*, or to *protect gender and race hierarchies* (among other ways, by *suppressing critique*), and most likely to *envision alternative possibilities*. It seemed that egalitarians would be most likely to *endorse universals and individualism*. It wasn't clear exactly where non-egalitarians would fall on the different themes, but it seemed possible that they would be most likely to *protect race and gender hierarchies*. For the purposes of these analyses, we restricted ourselves to data from white women ($N = 301$), but our hope was to illuminate one kind of difference among them by focusing on these three groups.

The sample was drawn to represent three generations of alumnae, with an overall mean age of 47.[2] Because in this study women responded to items written by others, we couldn't capture the spontaneous expressions recorded by Fine in girls' conversations. However, because they responded to each item separately, and to all of the items, women could – in others' words – express a range of potentially contradictory views. We could find out whether the different elements of discourse which Fine had identified actually cohered in the perspectives of women with different relationships to feminist ideas.

Most of the women were married (75 per cent), and many were mothers (68 per cent). They were, on average, well educated; 37 per cent of the sample completed their education with a bachelor's degree, and the remainder were either pursuing or had completed advanced degrees. They had considerable experience in the labour force; 73 per cent were currently employed at least part-time and 20 per cent had retired.

As we expected, our three groups differed in the degree to which they viewed the social landscape as including gender and racial inequality. (Except where specifically noted, all the differences we describe are statistically significant.) Feminists were most likely to rate white men as having more power than they should, and non-egalitarians least likely.[3] The women also differed in their perceptions of the legitimacy of discrimination based on sex and race (Gurin *et al.*, 1980). Non-egalitarians were less likely than both feminists and egalitarians to reject the legitimacy of sex-based discrimination.[4] They were also least likely to view race-based discrimination as unfair. In addition, egalitarians were less likely than feminists (though more likely than non-egalitarians) to question the legitimacy of racial inequality.[5] Specific items from these scales, such as 'In general, men [whites] are more qualified for jobs that have great responsibility', are good indicators of the type of complicity required to *protect these gendered and racialised hierarchies*. A poignant expression of the motivation for this complicity lies in the fact that both egalitarians and non-egalitarians rated the item 'It is especially important to me to feel accepted by the men in my life' more highly than did feminists.[6] In addition, both egalitarians and non-egalitarians also rated themselves as feeling more warmly towards white men than did feminists.[7] These warm feelings and need for approval may indeed work to limit or constrain some white women's capacity to acknowledge gender and racial injustices, particularly when combined with an individualistic understanding of the origins of different social positions.

As we expected, the feminists were not especially prone to *endorse universals*; it was particularly the egalitarians who did. For example, over 80 per cent of feminists indicated that the current social system does not protect universal justice, by endorsing the item 'We must work actively to change institutions in society to be fairer to women'.[8] Fewer than one-third of non-egalitarians endorsed this item, compared to fewer than two-thirds of egalitarians. Similarly, nearly one-third of the egalitarians and non-feminists suggested that universal principles do work well, by suggesting that the absence of discrimination against women was the reason for their lack of identification as feminists.[9] One item assessed the tendency to see the linkages among different forms of inequality: 'I presently experience a much greater understanding of the connectedness of the women's movement and other movements against injustice and oppression.' Non-egalitarians scored lowest on this item and feminists highest.[10]

Beyond the acceptance or rejection of the legitimacy of inequalities discussed above, there was limited evidence about how these adult white women viewed white responsibility or innocence. There was, though, some evidence that egalitarian and non-egalitarian white women were particularly prone to *individualistic evaluations*. For example, the egalitarian women most strongly endorsed the item 'As I have grown in my beliefs, I have realised that it is more important to value women as individuals than as members of a larger group of women'.[11]

Non-egalitarians most strongly endorsed an item blaming people of colour for their position in the social structure: 'People of colour may not have the same opportunities as whites, but many of them haven't prepared themselves enough to make use of the opportunities that come their way.' Feminists rated this item lowest, while egalitarians scored between the two.[12] The tendency to view those at the top and bottom of hierarchies as deserving their positions is a key element in a worldview that supports the status quo.

The survey contained only one item that seemed to address the dynamic of white women *translating conflict into 'misunderstanding'*; it was non-egalitarian women who most strongly endorsed this item. Specifically, they indicated significantly stronger agreement with the notion that 'People make too much out of things that aren't meant to be offensive' than both egalitarians and feminists.[13]

Overall, it is clear that the feminists in the sample were least likely to express the elements of the discourse of equality so prominent among white girls in the classroom which Fine studied. They were also most likely to *envision possibilities* for different social relations. For example, feminists were more likely than the other two groups of white women to report that they 'want to work to improve women's status',[14] to say that they want 'to make changes in society',[15] and they were also more likely to participate in activist pursuits.[16]

Interestingly, the feminists recall themselves as having had more visionary perspectives even as teenagers at the age of the students in the Fine study. The survey asked women to describe the way they viewed gender-linked possibilities when they were teenagers, in eight domains. There were significant differences between our three groups on three of these, and nearly significant trends on three more. Feminists tended to be most likely to recall believing that a girl could grow up and be president, and that men could be the main cooks for their families. They were significantly more likely than the other groups to recall believing that women could pursue careers and have happy families at the same time,[17] and least likely to believe that it was dangerous for mothers to leave their children in other people's care.[18] In contrast, egalitarians were least likely to recall believing that women could be doctors and that women and men could do the same jobs.[19]

Conclusion

We conclude with a set of reflections on our findings. First, we note with some trepidation that across methods and generations, there rings a rather consistent and chilling *discourse of equality* through which many white girls and women express a conviction that contemporary US culture affords social justice by offering equality of opportunity by race and class to those who work hard and make wise choices. Some white girls and women use this discourse to support the conservatising politics that attack affirmative action, welfare, and access to higher education – all steps out of poverty and racism that are being cut out from beneath the feet of poor and working-class Americans, particularly Americans of colour.

For the women of different ages whom we studied, these practices of whiteness have four distinct 'moves'. First, we find a willingness to clean up the hierarchy by explaining away social injustice as misunderstanding, insensitivity and lack of intentions. Second, we find an insistence on 'universals' (that is, 'we are all the same'), and a concomitant refusal to hear about difference or power discrepancies. Third, white girls and women seem committed to the not-at-all-evident position that 'we all have choices', allowing everyone to make a better life if she wants to. Fourth, white girls and women participate in an active muting of racialised critique such that when African American girls and women offer up their vibrant and often very critical analyses of racial and gendered relations, white girls and women often run to rescue the hierarchy. As culture is contested and domination challenged (even for only a moment), white girls and women may be the first to rebalance the status quo.

Beyond the shared discourse of equality, however, there is a second finding worthy of comment. Across the two studies, young and older white women who define themselves as feminist, those who avail themselves of feminist study and coursework and those who develop feminist consciousness may sometimes engage in this discourse of equality, but they do recognise the need for an ongoing struggle for both gender and racial justice, insist on the links between these forms of oppression, and endorse commitments to collective action. These adolescent girls and women are willing to see possibilities, and are ripe for multicultural coalition work. These women are, indeed, stretching the circle of 'we'.

It is important, in closing, to note that feminist consciousness is not only good for individual well-being – as several researchers have found (Ostrove *et al.*, under review; Tolman, forthcoming). Feminist analysis is also good for cultural well-being and global politics. Such consciousness provides white girls and women tools not only for analysing their own (potential and real) complicity in racial and class hierarchies, but also for moving from complicity to activism.

Notes

1 This work was generously funded by the Spencer and Carnegie Foundations.
2 The present sample is ninety-one women from the class of 1951 or 1952, 133 from the class of 1972, and seventy-seven from the class of 1992. The larger study included 333 women, with a response rate of 30 per cent; for detailed information about this study, see Zucker (1998).
3 Non-egalitarians (M=3.68; SD=0.84), Egalitarians (M=4.12; SD=0.79); Feminists (M=4.55, SD=0.62); $F(2,265)$=30.22, p<0.001. All three groups differed significantly from each other (p<0.05).
4 Non-egalitarians (M=5.52; SD=1.18), Egalitarians (M=6.15; SD=0.78); Feminists (M=6.43, SD=0.63); $F(2,268)$=25.18, p<0.001. Non-egalitarians were significantly lower than both other groups (p<0.05).
5 Non-egalitarians (M=4.56; SD=0.81), Egalitarians (M=5.07; SD=1.00); Feminists (M=5.49, SD=0.95); $F(2,268)$=20.57, p<0.001.
6 Non-egalitarians (M=2.54; SD=1.06), Egalitarians (M=2.59; SD=0.90); Feminists (M=2.06, SD=1.04); $F(2,267)$=8.47, p<0.001.
7 Non-egalitarians (M=70.21; SD=15.71), Egalitarians (M=71.78; SD=16.40); Feminists (M=59.25, SD=21.61); $F(2,260)$=12.11, p<0.001.
8 Eighty-three per cent of feminists; 62 per cent of egalitarians, 28 per cent of non-egalitarians; χ^2 (2, 271)=54.67, p<0.001.
9 Five per cent of feminists; 28 per cent of egalitarians, 31 per cent of non-egalitarians; χ^2 (2,264)=28.13, p<0.001.
10 Non-egalitarians (M=1.74; SD=0.98), Egalitarians (M=2.41; SD=1.09); Feminists (M=2.72, SD=1.05); $F(2,266)$=18.16, p<0.001.
11 Non-egalitarians (M=3.17; SD=0.99), Egalitarians (M=3.29; SD=0.81); Feminists

($M=2.96$; $SD=0.85$); $F(2,263)=3.59$; $p<0.05$. Egalitarians are significantly different from the Feminists ($p<0.05$).

12   Non-egalitarians ($M=4.72$; $SD=1.45$), Egalitarians ($M=4.10$; $SD=1.66$); Feminists ($M=3.61$, $SD=1.70$; $F(2,267)=9.66$, $p<0.001$.

13   Non-egalitarians ($M=5.07$; $SD=1.46$), Egalitarians ($M=4.18$; $SD=1.90$); Feminists ($M=3.61$, $SD=1.83$); $F(2,266)=14.02$, $p<0.001$.

14   Non-egalitarians ($M=2.02$; $SD=1.14$), Egalitarians ($M=2.23$; $SD=1.04$); Feminists ($M=3.05$, $SD=0.81$); $F(2,266)=30.77$, $p<0.001$. Feminists were significantly higher than both other groups.

15   Non-egalitarians ($M=1.90$; $SD=0.63$), Egalitarians ($M=2.08$; $SD=0.70$); Feminists ($M=2.37$, $SD=0.67$); $F(2,268)=11.64$, $p<0.001$. Feminists were significantly higher than both other groups.

16   Non-egalitarians ($M=12.28$; $SD=7.56$), Egalitarians ($M=13.64$; $SD=9.99$); Feminists ($M=20.35$, $SD=10.71$); $F(2,270)=18.85$, $p<0.001$. Feminists were significantly higher than both other groups.

17   President: 62 per cent of feminists; 47 per cent of egalitarians vs. 54 per cent of non-egalitarians; $\chi^2(2,262)=4.81$, $p<0.10$.
     Cooks: 47 per cent of feminists; 31 per cent of egalitarians vs. 38 per cent of non-egalitarians; $\chi^2(2,259)=4.87$, $p<0.10$.
     Career/family: 81 per cent of feminists; 64 per cent of egalitarians; 63 per cent of non-egalitarians; $\chi^2(2,257)=9.16$, $p<0.05$.

18   *Childcare*: 11 per cent of feminists; 25 per cent of egalitarians; 20 per cent of non-egalitarians; $\chi^2(2,255)=7.75$, $p<0.05$.

19   *Doctors*: 95 per cent of feminists; 83 per cent of egalitarians vs. 93 per cent of non-egalitarians; $\chi^2(2,262)=8.56$, $p<0.05$.
     Jobs: 73 per cent of feminists; 61 per cent of egalitarians vs. 79 per cent of non-egalitarians; $\chi^2(2,263)=5.63$, $p<0.10$.

References

Anaya, R.A. (1984) *The Legend of La Llorona: A Short Novel*, Berkeley, CA: Tonatiuh-Quinto-Sol.

Anzaldua, G. (1987) *Borderlands: La Frontera*, San Francisco, CA: Spinsters/Aunt Lute.

Apfelbaum, E. (1979) 'Relations of domination and movements for liberation: an analysis of power between groups', in W.G. Austin and S. Worchel (eds) *The Social Psychology of Intergroup Relations*, Belmont, CA: Wadsworth.

Bell, D.A. (1992) *Faces at the Bottom of the Well: The Permanence of Racism*, New York: Basic Books.

Bertram, C., Marusza, J., Fine, M. and Weis, L. (forthcoming) 'Where the girls are', *American Journal of Community Psychology*.

Bourdieu, P. (1984) *Distinction: A Social Critique of the Judgement of Taste*, Cambridge, MA: Harvard University Press.

Brodkin, K. (1998) *How Jews Became White Folks and What That Says about Race in America*, New Brunswick, NJ: Rutgers University Press.

Collins, P.H. (1990) *Black Feminist Thought: Knowledge, Consciousness, and the Politics of Empowerment*, Boston, MA: Unwin Hyman.

Espin, O. (1998) *Latina Realities: Essays on Healing, Migration, and Sexuality*, Boulder, CO: Westview Press.

Faust, D. (1996) *Mothers of Invention: Women of the Slaveholding South in the American Civil War*, Chapel Hill: University of North Carolina Press.

Fine, M. (1981) 'Options to injustice: seeing other lights', Unpublished doctoral dissertation, Columbia University.

Fine, M. and Carney, S. (forthcoming) 'Resisting responsibility and responsibly resisting: a feminist analysis of social psychology', in R. Unger (ed.) *Handbook of Gender*, New York: Wiley.

Fine, M., Genovese, T., Ingersoll, S., MacPherson, P. and Roberts, R. (1996) 'Insisting on innocence: accounts of accountability by abusive men', in M.B. Lykes (ed.) *Myths about the Powerless: Contesting Social Inequalities*, Philadelphia, PA: Temple University Press.

Fine, M., Weis, L. and Powell, L.C. (1997a) 'Communities of difference: a critical look at desegregated spaces created for and by youth', *Harvard Educational Review* 67(2): 247–84.

Fine, M., Weis, L., Powell, L.C. and Wong, L.M. (1997b) *Off White: Readings on Race, Power and Society*, New York: Routledge.

Flax, J. (1990) *Thinking Fragments: Psychoanalysis, Feminism, and Postmodernism in the Contemporary West*, Berkeley: University of California Press.

Fordham, S. (1996) *Blacked Out: Dilemmas of Race, Identity, and Success at Capital High*, Chicago, IL: University of Chicago Press.

Frankenberg, R. (1993) *White Women, Race Matters: The Social Construction of Whiteness*, Minneapolis: University of Minnesota Press.

Franklin, A.J. (1998) Personal communication.

Gilligan, C., Lyons, N.P. and Hammer, J. (1990) *Making Connections: The Relational Worlds of Adolescent Girls at Emma Willard School*, Cambridge, MA: Harvard University Press.

Guinier, L., Fine, M. and Balin, J. (1997) *Becoming Gentlemen: Women, Law School, and Institutional Change*, Boston, MA: Beacon Press.

Gurin, P., Miller, A. and Gurin, G. (1980) 'Stratum identification and consciousness', *Social Psychology Quarterly* 43: 30–47.

Harris, C.I. (1993) 'Whiteness as property', *Harvard Law Review* 106: 1709–91.

Hartsock, N.C.M. (1983) *Money, Sex and Power: Toward a Feminist Historical Materialism*, New York: Longman.

Hollway, W. (1989) *Subjectivity and Method in Psychology: Gender, Meaning and Science*, London: Sage.

hooks, b. (1988) *Talking Back: Thinking Feminist, Thinking Black*, Boston, MA: South End Press.

Hurtado, A. (1996) *The Color of Privilege: Three Blasphemies on Race and Feminism*, Ann Arbor: University of Michigan Press.

Ignatiev, N. (1995) *How the Irish Became White*, New York: Routledge.

Lipsitz, G. (1995) 'The possessive investment in whiteness: racialized social democracy and the "white" problem in American studies', *American Quarterly* 47(3): 369–87.

MacPherson, P. and Fine, M. (1995) 'Hungry for an us: adolescent girls and adult women negotiating territories of race, gender, class and difference', *Feminism and Psychology* 5(2): 181–200.

Markandaya, K. (1954) *Nectar in the Sieve, A Novel*, New York: J. Day.

Miller, J.B. (1976) *Toward a New Psychology of Women*, Boston, MA: Beacon Press.

Morrison, T. (1992) *Playing in the Dark: Whiteness and the Literary Imagination*. Cambridge, MA: Harvard University Press.

Ostrove, J., Deitch, S. and Stewart, A.J. 'Feminist identity and midlife women's well-being', under review.

Painter, N.I. (1995) 'Soul murder and slavery: toward a fully loaded cost accounting', in L.K. Kerber, A. Kessler-Harris and K.K. Sklar (eds) *US History as Women's History*, Chapel Hill: University of North Carolina Press.

Rollins, J. (1985) *Between Women: Domestics and Their Employers*, Philadelphia, PA: Temple University Press.

Taylor, J M., Gilligan, C. and Sullivan, M. (1995) *Between Voice and Silence: Women and Girls, Race and Relationship*, Cambridge, MA: Harvard University Press.

Tolman, D. (forthcoming) 'The ideology of femininity', Manuscript in preparation for Wellesley Center for Research on Women.

Wallis, V. (1994) *Two Old Women: An Alaska Legend of Betrayal, Courage and Survival*, New York: HarperPerennial.

Zucker, A.N. (1998) 'Understanding feminist identity in three generations of college-educated women', Unpublished doctoral dissertation, University of Michigan.

5 Constructing racism

Discourse, culture and subjectivity[1]

Bipasha Ahmed

The social psychology of racism has received considerable attention from researchers, largely since the Second World War. This work has been based mainly in theories of personality (Adorno *et al.*, 1950), attitude theory (Allport, 1954) and, more recently, social cognition and social identity theories (Hewstone and Brown, 1986; Hogg and Abrams, 1988; Tajfel, 1982; Tajfel and Turner, 1986; Turner, 1987). However, these theories have been extensively criticised by authors from within a perspective which views racism and 'race' as socially and culturally constructed (Billig *et al.*, 1988; Henriques *et al.*, 1984; Potter and Wetherell, 1987). Such critics accuse mainstream psychological theories of racism for falling into the trap of an 'individual–society dualism' and concentrating on 'the individual' as their site of investigation (Henriques *et al.*, 1984). This concentration reduces the problem of prejudice to one of 'natural cognitive error' within the individual (Billig, 1985), thus suggesting that it is an unfortunate yet inevitable part of human thinking (Ahmed *et al.*, 2000).

Even social identity theory (SIT) (Tajfel, 1982; Tajfel and Turner, 1986), which demonstrates how social action is achieved when individuals locate themselves within a pattern of wider social relationships (Henwood, 1994: 43), is oversimplistic in its explanation of racism. 'Race' is reduced to a static and therefore measurable 'independent variable', favouring experimental methods (Ahmed *et al.*, 1994; Henwood, 1994) which do not take into account how social life is culturally constituted (Henwood, 1994).

Socio-cognitive and social identity theories have been criticised for failing to problematise the very notion of 'race' as a category for study, implying acceptance of race as a 'natural kind' and hence perpetuating 'metalevel racism' (Condor, 1988). In other words, 'race' itself is taken as given, an already existing, taken-for-granted natural category, rather than being seen as a rhetorical, cultural construction.

There has also been a neglect in psychology of the experiences of those who encounter racism with the exception of studies of 'inter-ethnic' friendship among adolescents and children (Davey and Mullin, 1982; Denscombe, 1983; Husband, 1982), and studies which measure the formation of 'ethnic identities' in terms of 'acculturation' and 'adaptation' (e.g. Berry and Annis, 1988; Weinreich, 1988a and b). This neglect of the experiences of potential victims of racism leads to an incomplete and distorted account (Billig, 1988; Condor, 1988; Henwood, 1994); these approaches fail to take into account the points of view of all those involved. They also fail, again, to analyse how people understand such concepts and how they are socially and culturally constructed. In addition, such studies view 'culture', like 'race', as a fixed category or factor which can be measured. In this context, 'social' refers to how we construct such concepts in social groups and communities and not, for example, individually as mere cognitions; 'culture' refers to how such social constructions are effected by certain kinds of shared (often taken-for-granted) knowledge within those same social groups and communities.

Using a discursive social constructionist approach (Billig *et al*., 1988; Hall, 1988; Henriques *et al*., 1984; Parker, 1992; Wetherell and Potter, 1992),[2] this chapter explores the ways in which individuals describe their experiences of racism. I will draw upon a 'critical realist' definition of discourse similar to that of Parker (1992 – see Ahmed *et al*., 2000) In this definition, discourses are systems of statements which construct an object (such as racism). The discursive and cultural practices within which discourses are (re)produced can have the ideological effect of reproducing power relations characteristic of the dominant culture. Critical realists are concerned with processes of social construction, but they are not relativist; they privilege a version of reality within which certain power asymmetries exist. Thus, for example, they believe we live within a culture where racism has a reality that is partly though not completely independent of discourse. The term 'discursive practice' is emphasised (see Ahmed *et al*., 2000; Griffin, Chapter 1, this volume), because it is important to stress not only *what* the discourses are, but *how* and *when* they are used and how effects are achieved due to this variation.

What will also be demonstrated in this chapter is a tension around the issue of subjectivity when using discourse-analytic techniques. The types of discourse analysis which take a more relativist stance view subjectivities as methods of self-construction (as with any other constructions) available at a particular historical and cultural time. Yet the focus in these analyses is only on the functional and rhetorical nature of talk and text (Edwards and Potter, 1992; Potter and Wetherell, 1987, 1988). They give no sufficient explication of how the particular historical and cultural time impacts on constructions of subjectivity. Indeed, the relativist view would suggest that by focusing on the functional nature of discourse, we need not even consider who the discourses are coming from. This analysis will demonstrate that not only is racism constructed from certain cultural discourses, but these discourses need to be understood as coming from specific participants, in this case from middle-class second-generation Bangladeshis. Such participants have cultural discourses available to them which may not be available to others within the same cultural and historical time, and which impart different meanings and effects even for discourses of racism that are apparently held in common between them and the wider community.

The study

The data for this study came from thirteen male and female second-generation, middle-class Bangladeshis aged between 18 and 32, in the form of six discussion sessions where three or more participants (including myself – also a second-generation Bangladeshi) were present. All sessions lasted between forty-five minutes and two hours. The structure within each discussion session was flexible but at times focused on issues concerning racism, identity and the participants' experiences of living in Britain as second-generation Bangladeshis within a so-called 'multicultural' society. There was no interview schedule; rather, the conversations developed of their own accord around the broad themes described above, and for as long as the participants wished. This strategy was preferred as a way of promoting the natural development of the conversations, allowing participants to explore relevant issues as and when they arose. Therefore many of the topics raised in the sessions related to the main theme (our experiences of living in 'multicultural' Britain), but were raised by the participants. All sessions were tape-recorded, transcribed[3] and analysed (see Ahmed *et al.*, 2000, for details). All names have been changed to ensure the anonymity of the participants.

The analysis presented here concentrates on some of the discourses and discursive practices which this particular group of middle-class second-generation Bangladeshis produced during the conversation sessions to describe their experiences of racism. The various ways in which participants account for the meaning and significance of racism and how racism is constructed as 'real' are examined. The justifications for the claims, and the ways explanations and solutions for racism are offered, are also examined.

The analysis is divided into two sections. The first explores the ways in which participants construct racism and probes their accounts of how and why it exists. On this basis I argue that these constructions of racism and its causes imply particular strategies and political interventions for dealing with racism. The second section looks at the participants' explanations of how racism could be dealt with. Within each section, discourses used to construct racism when describing racist experiences are identified. How these discourses function by establishing, sustaining or reinforcing certain kinds of power relations and how 'culture' and subjectivity impacts on such discourses are considered.

Theme 1: The nature of racism

Discourse 1: 'Improved present'

The following analysis will demonstrate how a discourse of an 'improved present' – where 'things are better than they used to be' – is used to talk about racism. This discourse constructs racism as a relatively minor problem at present.

Extract 1, session 5

Niki: I think it's more underground than it was then, it was more blatant but I think (.) if you, with education (.) I think there's more educated people around and occasionally I think (.) the root of racism is ignorance (.) and because most of us have gone to school with white people and hence white people have gone to school with us (.) they've realised that we're quite normal and all we are is (.) got a bit more pigment than they have (.) so a lot of people I don't think are racist, you just get the odd few, sheer ignorance I think, arrogance and ignorance.

Extract 2, session 3

Bipasha: Right, so do you think this prejudice, or whatever, has got worse since your parents first came here?

Cally: No, it's got better.

Bipasha: You think it's got better?

Cally: Yeah, I know stories of em (.) Asians (.) and even my dad, mum and dad's time (.) you couldn't get a (.) a flat you couldn't get living accommodation except from an Asian landlord, the minute they saw your face (.) they'd say 'excuse me is there room?' you know they've got a sign on their window saying 'to let' and they'd say 'no' and like shut the door in your face you know (.) even if you were polite and educated (.) it's, you'd still get the door slammed in your face left right and centre (.) but I think now (.) because more and more people are growing up (.) with (.) alongside Asians (.) they are a bit more accepting (.)

In these first examples, two women, 'Niki' and 'Cally', reproduce a familiar commonsense discourse that 'the root of racism is ignorance'. This is a popular cultural construction of racism in everyday discourse. It is often referred to in antiracist practice and forms the basis for some psychological theories (Henriques, 1984). This account constructs racism as due to a lack of knowledge and experience of certain groups. In extract 1, Niki suggests that if people knew the facts, namely that we are all the same under our skins and 'all we are is (.) got a bit more pigment than they have', then it would be just a matter of time until we become familiar to them: the 'contact hypothesis' (Henriques, 1984; Hewstone and Brown, 1986). Niki uses this discourse to describe things as better now than they were before. She says that over time, more people have been 'educated' and gained contact with groups they were previously unfamiliar with. Now there are only 'the odd few' left who are racist. Similarly, in extract 2, Cally describes her parents' experiences from the past and compares her experiences with theirs. She sees herself as more fortunate than they are and offers an explanation for this: 'more and more people are growing up . . . alongside Asians'. The 'fact' is that we are all the same, and so racism is constructed as merely a lack of understanding of this fact. This discourse suggests that there has been a change in people's attitudes due to increased contact and education and that therefore there is less racism at present, compared to the past.

This discourse, as Henriques (1984) says, allows for a strategy of doing nothing, waiting until people get used to those with whom they are unfamiliar through increased contact. However, this discourse could also be seen as implying a strategy for actively educating those who are ignorant of the facts, though who will actually take the responsibility for doing the educating is a moot point. This discourse can also be seen as one which does not acknowledge social difference (Henriques, 1984), as when Niki describes how ignorant racists, if educated, would understand that 'we're quite normal' apart from our skin colour. This suggests that there exists a 'norm' against which we must be compared, a white norm, from which our only difference is an incidental one of 'pigment'. Implied in the discourse, therefore, is a denial of difference, which must be seen as socially, culturally and historically produced. As Henriques suggests, this denial 'means that the conditions for successful intervention – the recognition of these differences and the analysis of their cause – cannot be achieved' (1984: 89).

Discourse 2: 'Racism as present but hidden'

What also emerges from these two extracts is another discourse that appears to contradict the 'improved present' discourse. As Niki puts it, racism is 'more underground than it was then, it was more blatant'. Racism is described as less conspicuous than it was in the past, and this is considered to be an improvement. This discourse implies that racism still exists and things have not in fact changed; rather, people are more cunning and keep their attitudes hidden. The following extracts demonstrate the point further.

Extract 3, session 4

Mash: . . . so a lot of it's ignorance.
Bipasha: Yeah.
Mash: From (.) well from people who don't know but from people within the university, other students (.) after a few pints you can hear their real (.) attitudes anyway . . .

Extract 5, session 5

Bipasha: So for you racism is is sort of blatant abusive stuff?
Pran: Yeah.
Niki: Not always blatant, it could be underlying as well, but (.) you can't really tell, when it's that, when it's sort of like underlying, you can't really tell can you? You can't really do a lot about it.

Not only is it taken for granted that people think in a racist way, it is also taken for granted that it will be something that is not made explicit, because of situational constraints. This inhibition allows people who are 'really' prejudiced to appear as if they are not. Therefore, to be considered as non-racist is just a matter of controlling how visible racism is. In extract 5, Niki constructs racism as present but hidden to the extent where she suggests it is something which cannot be changed. If it is blatant and therefore more visible it can be challenged, but if it is inconspicuous then 'you can't really do a lot about it'. In her own words, Niki has described how constructing racism as hidden but present means it is possibly something which will always exist.

Thus under a general theme of describing the nature of racism, we can see how participants reproduced, within specific conversational contexts, specific discourses which perpetuate the oppressive social relations involved in racism and racist discourse. The broad competing discourses of an 'improved present' and 'racism as present but hidden' construct racism as a problem of the past or a not-so-blatant problem of the present and trivialise it in various and contradictory ways. They function to develop an argument where racists can be commended for their efforts at 'getting used to' groups they are unfamiliar with, or for being able, at least, to be covert about the way they think. This implies that 'getting used to' unfamiliar groups and 'hiding' racist opinions work well enough as antiracist strategies. Such constructions obscure oppressive power relations. The participants position themselves as being fortunate that they do not suffer racism, or at least not to the same extent as their parents did before them, and as fortunate that racism is subtler now so they do not have to, and indeed cannot, challenge it.

Theme 2: Dealing with racism

Discourse 1: 'Being streetwise'

In the following extracts, participants describe how they have dealt or might deal with racism. A discourse of being 'streetwise' emerges which considers dealing with racism in terms of survival.

First, 'Jo' and 'Mo' describe their experiences of racism. Once more the description does not indicate any difficulties. Jo actually talks about how it has not hindered his progress, presumably in terms of his education and career.

Extract 6, session 2

Jo: . . . Well I've never experienced any myself (.) in getting anywhere.
Bipasha: What do you mean by getting anywhere?
Jo: Well like stopped to do (.) whatever (*Bipasha*: Oh right) to do whatever because of my supposed race.
Bipasha: Well have you been victims of racism at all then, rather than . . .
Mo: I've been called names.
Jo: Yeah, I've been called names, but never had any violence (*Mo*: No) you know the situations (.) that might occur and you just stay out of them (*Mo*: Yeah) don't go looking for trouble (.) yeah (.)

A racism which causes problems is constructed as something that hinders one's progress. It is also constructed as something which manifests itself blatantly, in violence. This construction is in stark contrast to the subtle ways in which it was constructed under Theme 1. Jo admits to being subject to name-calling but in doing so plays down the severity of the racism he feels he has experienced. He also says the reason he has not experienced racism is because 'you know the situations that might occur and you just stay out of them . . . don't go looking for trouble'. In other words, he is 'wise' to troublesome situations that might occur, so is always prepared to act accordingly by adopting a strategy of avoidance. Racism is perceived as part of real life, and therefore a person's ability to deal with it is seen in much the same way: a necessity if you are to be able to cope with the world.

In the following extract, 'Jim' denies that he has encountered any problems with racism, and again we can see that he does this by reproducing the discourse of the 'improved present', suggesting that 'things are better than they used to be' as he recounts how his only memories of being at the sharp end of racism are of events in his childhood. Again the idea of being streetwise is invoked, as in extract 6, but this time what is implied is that it would be wise not to go looking for trouble, rather than that you should have an instinct about potentially troublesome situations. It is not that racism should be avoided; rather, by actively seeking racism, it may be created in the imagination of those doing the seeking. So here, being 'streetwise' is possessing the ability to get on with things and not to go looking for or making trouble for yourself.

Extract 7, session 1

Jim: . . . But what I'm trying to say is if you don't look for it, you don't always notice it (*Bipasha*: Right) I mean, for instance, when I was very much younger eh (.) in Tooting, there was obvious em racism, I mean people would call you names and that (*Bipasha*: Yes) I mean like when I was at primary school, and one thing that I've noticed as I get older is that doesn't happen any more, nobody ever calls me a name (right) as they did when you were younger, but that doesn't happen. (.) You see the problem is, if you are asking somebody about their experiences, it's (.) I don't know what I'm trying to say it doesn't matter, but em something like racism and that, if you're looking for it, then you might find it or you think you might find it . . .

Extracts 6 and 7 both show how a broad discourse of survival and being 'streetwise' is produced when participants explain how racism should be dealt with. Overall, the discourse constructs racism as something that will always exist. It is up to the individual as a potential victim to do something about it; preferably, to avoid it. It may also be a matter of whether one is intuitive enough to know when to avoid situations which may be difficult. In the case of Jim, a variation of the discourse is produced, where racism only exists in the paranoid minds of those looking for it. This is a discourse which is all the more difficult to argue against when thinking, as, for instance, in Jo's case, about how not being 'streetwise' and 'looking for trouble' may hinder one's career. The discourse is also important in challenging the participants' status as victims. Rather than merely accepting racism as a fact of life about which they can do nothing, the participants position themselves as actively *not* being troubled by racism, not allowing it to get in the way of their personal progress and daily living. This particular discourse seems especially consistent with the discourses from the previous section which constructed racism either as having changed, with only a few people being racist, or as still present but hidden. In either case, the implication is that one is unlikely to encounter racism; there are either a few overt racists or many covert racists out there. Anyone who does encounter racism must therefore be paranoid. Overall, it is a discourse which places responsibility for dealing with racism on those who may be subjected to it. Strategies are suggested for working *around* racism as existing, though not for challenging the existence of racism itself.

Discourse 2: 'Being lucky'

In this final extract, 'Hal' and 'Jo' are both discussing their feelings about how their own experiences of racism compare to those of their parents. Here, a discourse of 'being lucky' can be identified. Hal and Jo deny that they have ever really experienced racism, not because there is less racism about but because they are lucky and privileged. The environment in which they have been brought up is simply not as bad as others; they are more fortunate than their parents and those who live in worse surroundings. Jo, Mo and Hal feel that they have had the good fortune to be in an environment where racism has not been a prominent issue for them.

Extract 8, session 2

Jo: . . . as far as I'm concerned (.) we're lucky that in the environment we've been brought up. If we were like in the East End or whatever (.) I'm sure . . .

Mo: We're more privileged than they are.

Hal: It depends on the area . . .

Jo: . . . the environment's not as racist or er (*Hal*: Tower Hamlets or whatever) the discrimination they might face . . .

This discourse functions by constructing racism as something which is ever-present, as the 'present but hidden' discourse of racism would suggest, but which can be avoided. Not experiencing it is a matter of privilege (rather than rights, say) and good fortune. Racism is seen as something which happens to other people, those in 'less privileged' areas such as the East End of London or Tower Hamlets – an area which is well known as having a large community of working-class Sylhetti Bangladeshis. This discourse implies that a possible antiracist strategy is to avoid racism, or areas where racism may be prevalent, thus following the examples of those who have been lucky enough not to encounter it. Racism is something which is area-specific, and those who have the good fortune to live in areas where it does not occur have demonstrated for us that it need not be a problem. However, what this extract also demonstrates is that these participants show an awareness of how racism *is* a problem, but for other people. On the one hand, the discourse avoids challenging the racism which exists in particular areas, but on the other, it shows that the participants do acknowledge that racism is a problem for others whom they see as from the same 'group' as themselves. They position themselves as luckier and more privileged than, say, Bangladeshis who live in the East End of London.

Conclusions

This chapter has demonstrated some of the ways in which racism and racist experiences are constructed by a group of middle-class second-generation Bangladeshis, and the dilemmas and contradictions which become apparent when talking about these experiences in everyday conversation. More importantly, I have speculated on the effects of these discourses in practice and how they perpetuate particular types of power relations. There seems to have been a shift from talking about the 'dreadfulness' of racism, to emphasising how 'things are better than they used to be' for this group of people. The overall function of such discourses is to suggest that either there is little that *needs* to be done to challenge racism, due to a change in people's attitudes, or that there is little that *can* be done, as racism is too subtle to deal with. There is a denial that racism is a real problem, and a sense that the situation regarding racism is satisfactory, at least more so than in the past. Although these discourses might be indicative of changes that have occurred in the forms of racism, they also function to blur the lack of change, the maintenance of oppressive social relations. This blurring is achieved by constructing racism as ignorance, and suggesting it has reduced (and can further be reduced in future) through increased education and contact. Or racism may be constructed as difficult to challenge, not because there is less of it, but because it is less blatant and more subtle than it used to be.

When participants talk about dealing with racism, they construct it as something which is only a problem if one makes it a problem. Being 'streetwise' is being able to deal with racism through, for instance, avoidance or not becoming unduly paranoid about it. This discourse positions the participants as dealing with racism actively, not being disturbed by it, and not allowing it to get in the way of their daily lives and personal progress. However, at the same time, the discourse suggests that racism should be recognised and avoided, or not looked for as it may be imaginary. With the 'being lucky' discourse we can also see how racist experiences can be attributed to 'bad' luck if one is fortunate enough to be in an environment where it is not a great problem.

One of the most commonly used strategies by this group of people is to refer to the past: either their own childhoods or the experiences of their parents before them. Many participants referred to their childhood as a time when they experienced racism most blatantly, and that reference functioned as a powerful way of substantiating the argument of an improved present. Another strategy was to compare their own experiences with those of their parents. As well as further substantiating their claim that 'things are better than they used to be', it also clearly positions participants in this study as being second-generation rather than first-generation Bangladeshis, with different and less unpleasant experiences than their parents. This highlights a particular tension among discourse analytic techniques regarding subjectivity, namely whether to see these discourses only in terms of their rhetorical function or as originating from specific participants. From the analysis it would appear that the kinds of strategies used are specifically available to this group of people (see also Frosh *et al.*, Chapter 3, this volume). In this case they show an awareness of their experiences as being different from another group of people – first-generation Bangladeshis such as their parents. A similar strategy used by some participants was exemplified in extract 6, in the 'being lucky' discourse. Here, the participants again positioned themselves as lucky and privileged compared to another group of people, those in less privileged areas – such as Tower Hamlets – where there is a large community of working-class Bangladeshis. Again they positioned themselves and their experiences as different, a rhetorical positioning that might be used by many speakers but has a specific functioning here, recognising both difference and commonality.

The participants in this study thus show a clear comprehension of their position in relation to the dominant culture, but also compared to others who are less privileged such as working-class Bengalis or those from their parents' generation. They display this understanding when describing how their experiences of racism have not been as great a problem as they have been for others in less privileged positions and those before them. I have argued that these discourses, wherein racism is not seen as a major problem, can have the function of obscuring racism in the present. However, the participants show they are aware that racism may be a problem for other people who are less privileged than they are, such as their parents in the past or working-class Bengalis today. Their constructions of their identities can therefore be understood as politicised by a reflexive self-awareness. They are aware of the differences that exist among members of their own community, yet also share an empathetic understanding that oppressions, such as racism, may be a problem for others who may be considered as being the same as them – Bangladeshis.

Discourses need to be understood in terms of who the speakers are. To theorise subjectivity as merely being positions in discourse does not account for the fact that not everybody has access to the same discourses. This group of second-generation middle-class Bangladeshis clearly have access to certain discourses that others do not. Discourse analysts would argue that culture itself is socially constructed. What this chapter has tried to demonstrate is that we need to appreciate how people 'do culture' in discourse (see Fine *et al.*, Chapter 4, this volume). The participants in this study reproduced discourses which perpetuate certain (oppressive) social relations of the dominant culture but also did so with specific reference to their subjectivities as second-generation, middle-class and Bangladeshi. It is not enough merely to refer to discursive practices as cultural without actually trying to understand how they are cultural and what that means for those speaking.

Notes

1 Parts of this chapter have appeared, in a different form, in Ahmed *et al.* (2000).
2 I have drawn selectively on all these authors, though I acknowledge that there are metatheoretical differences between their approaches. However, it would be inappropriate to enter into a discussion about these differences for the purposes of this chapter.
3 The transcription procedure used here stresses readability rather than accuracy in terms of detailing all the various features of talk, as the main concern here was the content of the broad discourses rather than 'moment-by-moment conversational coherence' (Wetherell and Potter, 1992). Therefore, a dot in parentheses marks pauses (.), overlapping speech is placed in round brackets – for example (*Mo*: Yeah), and omitted speech is marked by three ellipsis points.

References

Adorno, T., Frenkel-Brunswick, E., Levinson, D. and Sanford, R. (1950) *The Authoritarian Personality*, New York: Harper & Row.

Ahmed, B., Nicolson, P. and Spencer, C. (1994) 'The secrets of success: constructions of identity and inter-ethnic experiences in conversations with second generation Bangladeshis', British Psychological Society London Conference, Institute of Education, December.

—— (2000) 'The social construction of racism: the case of second generation Bangladeshis', *Journal of Community and Applied Social Psychology* 10: 33–48.

Allport, G. (1954) *The Nature of Prejudice*, Reading, MA: Addison-Wesley.

Berry, J. and Annis, R. (1988) *Ethnic Psychology: Research and Practice with Immigrants, Refugees, Native Peoples, Ethnic Groups and Sojourners*, Amsterdam: Swets & Zeitlinger.

Billig, M. (1985) 'Prejudice, categorisation and particularisation: from a perceptual to a rhetorical approach', *European Journal of Social Psychology* 15: 79–103.

—— (1988) 'The notion of "prejudice": some rhetorical and ideological aspects', *Text* 8: 91–110.

Billig, M., Condor, S., Edwards, D., Gane, M., Middleton, D. and Radley, A. (1988) *Ideological Dilemmas: A Social Psychology of Everyday Thinking*, London: Sage.

Condor, S. (1988) '"Race stereotypes" and racist discourse', *Text* 8: 69–91.

Davey, A. and Mullin, P. (1982) 'Inter-ethnic friendship in British school children', *Educational Research* 24: 83–92.

Denscombe, M. (1983) 'Ethnic group and friendship choice in the primary school', *Educational Research* 25: 184–90.

Edwards, D. and Potter, J. (1992) *Discursive Psychology*, London: Sage.

Hall, S. (1988) 'New ethnicities', in *Black Film, British Cinema, ICA Documents 7*, London: British Film Institute and Institute of Contemporary Arts.

Henriques, J. (1984) 'Social psychology and the politics of racism', in J. Henriques, W. Hollway, C. Urwin, C. Venn and V. Walkerdine (eds) *Changing the Subject: Psychology, Social Regulation and Subjectivity*, London: Methuen.

Henriques, J., Hollway, W., Urwin, C., Venn, C. and Walkerdine, V. (1984) *Changing the Subject: Psychology, Social Regulation and Subjectivity*, London: Methuen.

Henwood, K. (1994) 'Resisting racism and sexism in academic psychology: a personal/political view', in K.-K. Bhavnani and A. Phoenix (eds) *Shifting Identities Shifting Racisms*, London: Sage.

Hewstone, M. and Brown, R. (1986) *Contact and Conflict in Intergroup Encounters*, Oxford: Blackwell.

Hogg, M. and Abrams, D. (1988) *Social Identifications*, London: Routledge.

Husband, C. (1982) *Race in Britain: Continuity and Change*, London: Hutchinson University Library.

Parker, I. (1992) *Discourse Dynamics*, London: Routledge.

Potter, J. and Wetherell, M. (1987) *Discourse and Social Psychology: Beyond Attitudes and Behaviour*, London: Sage.

—— (1988) 'Accomplishing attitudes: fact and evaluation in racist discourse', *Text* 8: 51–68.

Tajfel, H. (1982) *Social Identity and Intergroup Relations*, Cambridge: Cambridge University Press.

Tajfel, H. and Turner, J. (1986) 'An integrative theory of intergroup conflict', in W. Austin and S. Worchel (eds) *The Social Psychology of Intergroup Relations*, Monterey, CA: Brooks/Cole.

Turner, J. (1987) 'A self-categorisation theory', in J. Turner, M. Hogg, P. Oakes, S. Reicher and M. Wetherell (eds) *Rediscovering the Social Group*, Oxford: Blackwell.

Weinreich, P. (1988a) *Manual for Identity Exploration using Personal Constructs*, Centre for Research in Ethnic Relations, University of Warwick.

—— (1988b) 'The operationalization of ethnic identity', in J. Berry and R. Annis (eds) *Ethnic Psychology: Research and Practice with Immigrants, Refugees, Native Peoples, Ethnic Groups and Sojourners*, Amsterdam: Swets & Zeitlinger.

Wetherell, M. and Potter, J. (1992) *Mapping the Language of Racism: Discourse and the Legitimation of Exploitation*, London: Harvester Wheatsheaf.

Part III

Culture and representations

Introduction

Culture includes not just established, stable values and practices, but also the more transient, less concretely 'lived' field of popular or mass culture. In this field, it is clear that specific systems of representation – visual representations, for instance – have their own rules, their own ways of coding meaning. The chapters that follow take on these issues, neglected within psychology although they have been key concerns for cultural studies.

In 'Good, bad or dangerous to know: representations of femininity in narrative accounts of PMS', Jane Ussher, Myra Hunter and Susannah Browne report on an interview study of 120 British women who met the diagnostic criteria for pre-menstrual syndrome. The chapter explores the relationship between the women's talk about their bodies, and culturally dominant discourses and narratives of femininity. It describes polarised representations of these bodies, in the women's talk as well as in popular media and the public sphere, as split between 'good' – in control, rational, happy, non-premenstrual, and 'bad' – excessive, pathological, failed, privatised, premenstrual. If this splitting is emblematic of representations of femininity, the authors argue, it is also emblematic of the western repre-sentations of health and illness with which concepts of femininity are implicated.

The next chapter in the section, 'The tyranny of the "six pack"? Understanding men's responses to representations of the male body in popular culture', is concerned with the complex relationships between cultural representations and individual psychologies. Here, Rosalind Gill, Karen Henwood and Carl McLean focus on the ways in which young men respond to the increasing numbers of idealised visual images of male bodies in various media, especially advertising. Drawing on 140 interviews with young men in different regional locations across the UK, the chapter rejects the notion that these new images are seen as straightforwardly aspirational. Instead, using what they call a socio-emotional approach, the authors argue that men respond in a multiplicity of different ways to these representations. They also explore how differences in men's orientation to imagery which constructs the male body as hard and muscular may be connected to age, 'race,' ethnicity, sexual orientation, class and regional identification.

In the final chapter in this section, 'Changing youth: an exploration of visual and textual cultural identifications', Harriette Marshall and Anne Woollett examine the ways in which a young woman of Asian origin uses the video diary format to define and discuss aspects of her identity, including her ethnicity. The diary was produced as part of a wider research project, 'Changing youth', which is looking at the transition to young adulthood. The chapter studies visual images, as well as verbal self-presentation and music, in explaining the complex set of referents, spanning 'cultures', ethnicities, religions and histories, that make up the video diary. The writers suggest that such representational practices, while they are not in themselves a politics, can open up psychological and political possibilities through the breadth of cultural resources they recruit. They argue for greater recognition of the ways in which women bring together aspects of the dominant culture in which they live and their own ethnic identities.

6 Good, bad or dangerous to know

Representations of femininity in narrative accounts of PMS

Jane M. Ussher, Myra Hunter and Susannah J. Browne

Introduction: Femininity and representation

Analyses of cultural representations of femininity have been central to feminist thinking for decades. Early critiques, located largely within a sociological tradition, argued that symbolic images of 'woman' act as a direct reflection of women's lives (Moore, 1975; Weibel, 1977). In recent years, largely due to the influence of post-structuralist theorising, there has been a growing acknowledgement that representations do not merely *reflect* the lives of women, but actively subjugate female subjectivity through creating and reinforcing the notion of 'woman' as lack, as absence, or as other to man. As the art historian Griselda Pollock has argued, 'representation is one of the many social processes by which specific orders of sexual difference are ceaselessly constructed, modified, resisted and reconstituted. . . . Representations articulate/produce meanings as well as re-presenting a world already meaningful' (Pollock, 1988: 206). This school of feminist criticism, drawing on both psychoanalytic theorising and analyses of semiotics, focuses not on reflection but on the *repression* of woman through representation: on the creation of conditions within which femininity is discursively constructed (Smith, 1988).

The focus here, perhaps even more than in the two following chapters by Gill and her co-writers and Marshall and Woollett, is on the regulatory power of discourse[1] – the power of images, of beliefs, of language and of thought. What we see and what we say about what it is to be 'woman', and what we 'know' about femininity, are the fictions and fantasies that come to be seen as facts or truths (Foucault, 1976). This is an analysis of what semiotic theorists would term 'woman as sign' – an analysis of what the term 'woman' signifies or symbolises at a mythical level.[2] To present an image of 'woman' is to communicate a whole set of meanings which are not reflective of what women are, or even what women might like to be, but which tell us what femininity stands for at the level of cultural representation. In this view, cultural representation plays a central role in the formation of women's subjectivity. Women understand themselves as 'woman' (and men as 'man') in relation to the cultural representations of what it means to be so; in relation to historically and culturally specific definitions and constructions of femininity and masculinity. As one critic comments, 'one becomes woman in the very practice of signs by which we write, speak, see. . . . This is neither an illusion nor a paradox. It is a real contradiction – women continue to become woman' (Blumm in de Lauretis, 1984: 335).

Women transgressing the boundaries of femininity

The move to the analysis of discourse and cultural representation in critical feminist and social psychology has facilitated an analysis of *how* women become 'woman'. This work has examined both the particular configuration of 'woman' as sign in language, visual representation and in material and discursive practice, and the way in which women are regulated and resist through negotiating hegemonic scripts of femininity (Ussher, 1997a; Walkerdine, 1990, 1996). The question I want to address here is: How do women account for themselves when they attempt to emulate these idealised representations of femininity we see in popular culture, but fail? More specifically, what are the ways in which women make sense of experiences, emotions or behaviours which are at odds with representations of the 'perfect woman', if that is what they are trying to be? In previous work I have examined this question in relation to sexuality, a sphere where popular culture provides women with pleasure and power, yet also serves to regulate femininity (Ussher, 1997a). In this instance I will look at the discursive construction of the transgressive woman as 'mad' and the positioning of experiences or emotions which fall short of the feminine ideal as 'symptoms' (see also Ussher, 1991). I will take one example, that of premenstrual syndrome (PMS), and draw on the results of a recently completed interview study which was conducted to examine women's subjective experiences of PMS. One can find similar patterns of transgressive femininity being pathologised if one looks at women who present with depression, eating disorders or self-injurious behaviour, among other 'disorders' (Ussher, 1991, 2000b). One can also find it in accounts of women merely talking about their lives. What makes PMS unique, though, is that for a certain proportion of the month women experience and give accounts of themselves as managing to live up to their own high expectations; of *becoming* the perfect 'woman'. Perhaps unsurprisingly, they can't keep it up. Who could – at least without great cost? But in women's accounts of their experiences, what we see is that it is not they who fail. It is 'PMS', or the premenstrual self, which is positioned as to blame.

PMS has been exposed to feminist scrutiny for decades, being seen as a socially constructed category that serves to pathologise and dismiss women's anger or discontent (Laws *et al.*, 1985; Ussher, 1989, 1996, 2000a). Before the 'discovery' of PMS in the 1930s, and its widespread discussion in medical, psychological and popular cultural texts, no woman (or her partner) would have adopted this particular discursive explanation for transgression or distress. Indeed, in other cultural contexts today, where representations of PMS do not circulate, symptoms are not attributed to 'PMS' (Ussher, 1989; Walker, 1997). My argument here will be that PMS partially functions for women as a discursive category which makes sense of emotions, behaviours or desires which are at odds with hegemonic cultural constructions of the perfect 'woman'.[3] For one of the most striking aspects about the interviews was the repeated contrasting of the self as good or bad/mad woman, drawing on hegemonic representations of good, bad and mad femininity. PMS thus positions women as split, the real me being the non-premenstrual self, and the non-me being the premenstrual self, as descriptions of the premenstrual self as imperfect, failing, difficult, were contrasted with descriptions of the non-premenstrual self as perfect, consistent and in control. The terms women used when they positioned themselves as suffering from PMS included selfish, angry, moody, difficult, depressed, over-sensitive, negative and generally feeling that they were horrible. In contrast, when they were *not* pre-menstrual, these women described themselves as competent, happy, energetic, outgoing, in control and sensitive to others; as living up to the expectations they laid down for themselves, expectations which are arguably deeply embedded in cultural representations of the perfect 'woman' which pervade western culture.

Method

One hundred and twenty British women who met DSM (the Diagnostic and Statistical Manual of the American Psychiatric Association) criteria for PMS, and who had a significant increase in premenstrual symptomatology on prospective diaries completed over three months, took part in a controlled clinical trial comparing medical and psychological intervention. The average age of the women was 38; middle- and working-class affiliation was evenly balanced, as was parity. The majority of women were in paid work. Narrative interviews were conducted before and after treatment, the aim being to examine women's subjective experience of PMS, and what PMS meant to each individual woman (Ussher *et al.*, forthcoming). In order to elicit narratives, an open-ended question was asked at the beginning of the interview: 'In this interview I'd like to explore some of the meaning PMS has for you, and the part it plays in your life. I'd like to start by asking "what does PMS mean to you?"' The interviewer, Susannah Browne, then followed the woman's lead, asking questions of clarification as and when necessary. The interview was thus framed as a dialogue between two people, rather than a question-and-answer situation. In this chapter I am drawing on the pre-treatment interviews, which were analysed within a framework of thematic narrative analysis. After transcription,[4] the interviews were coded thematically, line by line. Themes were grouped together, and then checked for emerging patterns, for variability and consistency, and for the function and effects of specific narratives. The interpretation of these themes was conducted by a process of reading and re-reading, as well as reference to relevant literature and consultation with colleagues.

This process follows what Paul Stenner (1987: 114) has termed a 'thematic decomposition', a close reading which attempts to separate a given text into coherent themes or stories which reflect subject positions allocated to or taken up by a person (Harre and Davies, 1990). It is based on the assumption, common to most discursive and narrative analysis, that stories told do not simply mirror a world 'out there', but are constructed, creatively authored, rhetorical, replete with assumptions and interpretive (Potter and Wetherell, 1987; Reissman, 1993: 5). In this study, drawing on post-structuralist theory, it was assumed that narratives act to construct subjectivity. Narratives provide interpretation or meaning for experience, but in the telling we make sense of phenomena (Young, 1989) and do particular 'identity work' through constructing subject positions for ourselves and others. The narratives were acting to construct an account which is consistent with wider cultural discourses about femininity, PMS or reproduction, as well as other factors such as bodily symptoms, age and social class. This analysis is conducted within a material-discursive-intrapsychic epistemological framework which assumes that cultural discourse is irrevocably interconnected with both materiality and the intrapsychic; one cannot be understood without reference to the other (Ussher, 1997b, 2000a and b; see also Frosh *et al.* (Chapter 3), and Yates and Day Sclater (Chapter 9), this volume). However, in this chapter I will focus on the relationship between cultural representations of 'woman' and women's presentation of their own symptomatology, through deconstructing three interconnected themes which position the PMS sufferer as split. These are: coping and control versus intolerance and inconsistency; woman in the public sphere versus woman at home; and woman in relation versus woman alone.[5] I have chosen to discuss these three themes here as they each contrast idealised femininity with transgressive or non-perfect femininity, both reflecting the splitting of 'woman' in cultural representation, and the way in which women position themselves as split in narratives about PMS.

The PMS sufferer as split: representations of femininity in narrative accounts of PMS

Coping and control versus intolerance and inconsistency

One of the most pervasive representations of idealised femininity we see in popular culture today is of 'woman' as always positive, in control, able to cope, and juggling competing tasks and demands with hardly a hair out of place. We see it in advertising, cinema, women's magazines – woman as object has been superseded by woman as agentic subject (Douglas, 1995). *Not* being able to cope, or feeling out of control, were the most commonly reported 'symptoms' in these interviews. Failing to cope is positioned as pathology or transgression, caused by PMS.

Helen: (PMS) makes me feel as if I'm not in control (1) and that is quite an issue (1) it's not being in control of my own body and the way I behave and anything and ahmm I (1) find that quite worrying really

Paula: It's like it (PMS) *knocks* (you). Your self-esteem and your self-confidence and all that sort of (.) gets lowered. (1) I think you feel (.) you just feel less worthy or less (1) or less *capable* (and) (1) because you *are* less capable, 'cos you're not coping with things as well as you could or should normally.

What these women described themselves as coping with 'normally', when they weren't experiencing PMS, was invariably of considerable magnitude – difficult or pressurised paid work, complex social relations, the demands of children and families, as well as attempts to be attractive, slim and happy. Perhaps the most notable factor to emerge from these interviews was not that women *didn't* 'cope', but that the ideal of the controlled and coping woman was reported as being partially achieved, for a certain amount of time, or in certain contexts, until one final thing tipped the balance.

Julie: It might build up throughout a day and my, um, something might annoy me on (.) this day or (1) just get at me, and I'll feel like (.) reacting. I'll feel like (.) reacting aggressively. And I'll control it. And I'll think, 'No. It must be the time of the month.' And (.) I can control it to a certain extent. But it then might build (.) a bit, um, another thing might happen (and) another thing might happen. And then eventually one small thing will just (top) the whole lot off. That (.) is often the case.

This is a typical account of PMS as loss of control of emotion, in the face of competing demands or external problems. Rather than positioning emotional reactions as pathology, an alternative account could be that frustration, irritation or anger were understandable responses – yet this account was notable by its absence. What is evident here is that *no* reaction is positioned as the ideal. The Stepford Wives are made flesh. For in these accounts the perfect non-PMS 'woman' is represented as consistent; as calm, capable, tolerant, and nice to live with, *at all times*.

Ann: What annoys me is that I can't be all right *all the time* and that's the frustration that you, you almost plan out the (.) the *year* around these times and you *know* that for a couple of months, a couple of weeks you're not going to be very nice to live with (.) and you're not going to perform as well (.) in your (.) job (.) because of it. (Emphasis added)

If women expect themselves to be positive at all times, it is not surprising that intolerance becomes a sign of irrationality or pathology. Many women reported that they were told by their husbands that they were irrational (or that they must 'have PMS'), and while they wanted to resist this ascription, they appeared to have no other way of making sense of their uncontrolled feelings or behaviours, as we see below.

Debbie: I start to get intolerant (1) um, or short-tempered. Things that perhaps I would normally not react to or do and (1) in his words, he would probably say I become irrational, although I wouldn't (1) say that (.) (although I'm sure it's probably the case).

Here we see women positioning themselves (or being positioned) as ill because they fail to be the consistently confident, positive, optimistic creature who is represented in popular culture (Douglas, 1995), the smiling woman we see contrasted with the woman of misery in advertisements for anti-depressants put out by pharmaceutical companies (Vines, 1992). A number of women commented that if they didn't 'have' PMS, they would be this perfect woman.

Interviewer: What do you think your life would be like if you didn't have PMS?
Linda: (2) Um? (4) Um (1) more balanced. (1) Um, I'd be on more of an (even keel. (1) My moods wouldn't (1) swing so much (1) and so I'd be (1) more stable). Oh! I don't like saying that, but yeah. (2) Um, (I could) be more (1) optimistic. (1) More confident. (1) All those kind of things. (2) I think! [Laughs]

In many of the interviews there were also discussions of the fantasy that *other* women, women without PMS, were able to be consistent, positive and in control of their lives.

Interviewer: How does it feel to you?
Linda: That I'm really *horrible*. But, you know, um (1) being a horrible person who's moody and (1) people won't want to be around me. (1) That (1) lonely, lonely (again). It feels (.) it feels different to everybody else. (1) That they all seem to be getting on with their lives and doing things and I'm (thinking, 'Oh) (1) I wish I could *feel* like that, but I don't.' I think, I look at their lives as well and think, 'What's the point of it?' as well. It's not like I want their lives. At that time [laughs] I don't want anybody's life really!
Jane: It was (.) everybody else seems to be getting on with everything and (1) I don't feel like getting on with (anything). (2)

These accounts of the idealised other woman draw on cultural discourses which represent women as being in competition with each other, always comparing, always looking for the flaws in others in order to elevate themselves – take Snow White and her wicked stepmother, or Julia Roberts and Cameron Diaz in the film *My Best Friend's Wedding*. It is these representations which provide a discursive framework for women looking at the inadequacies in themselves in comparison with the perceived perfection of others (Berger, 1972; Chernin, 1981; Ussher, 1997a). This mythical discourse of womanly perfection is documented in feminist critiques of fashion, beauty, and the regimes of body management. It acts to regulate femininity and make individual women dissatisfied with themselves (or their bodies) because they can't emulate the mythical ideal (Bordo, 1990; Bartky, 1988; Craik, 1993; Malson, 1996). It also functions in the sphere of mental health, where women are reluctant to voice their anger, discontent or distress for fear that they will be positioned as one who is weak or who fails in contrast to all those *other* women who are consistently strong, successful and positive.

Woman in the public sphere versus woman at home

A second related theme within which women positioned themselves as split contrasted the idealised woman in the public sphere with the transgressive woman at home. Many women described themselves as being able to cope with the demands which were placed on them at work because they 'have to', then letting down, or losing control, when they got home – at least when they were pre-menstrual. This is arguably tied to newly emerging representations of the rational and unemotional super-woman, who can take up an equal place with men in the public sphere, where femininity and emotionality are traditionally aligned and positioned as alien or other (Nicolson, 1996). Here, it is contrasted with representations of the emotional, irrational woman who is out of control.

Amy: It *often* happens with my husband. I, um (1) it (never I) (.) always manage to control it in work. (1) Um, I think it's almost as though (1) because it's my husband, I *can* let (.) go. I can have a tantrum. Um, perhaps because I can't it's weird that I can control it (.) in work where you *have* to control it. I still feel it. I still feel tense and what will often happen then is that when I get home perhaps (I let go).

The fact that control is contrasted with 'a tantrum' is significant; 'woman' as responsible and rational is contrasted with 'woman' as child. This notion draws on broader representations of woman as childlike or immature, representations that were used to maintain women's exclusion from positions of authority in the public sphere for centuries. Women and children were categorised together, neither being able to vote or own property, both needing to be protected from violence and pornography because of their supposed immaturity and vulnerability (Ehrenreich and English, 1978; Kendrick, 1987; Sayers, 1982). Open displays of emotionality, fragility or vulnerability are thus signs of immaturity, and need to be repressed as they threaten the legitimacy of woman in the public sphere.

Amy: Um, but it's (2) it's (1) it's mental but it's (2) um, it's almost as though I'm going to explode. Um (1) with the frustration. Almost like a child. Um (1) and (1) it's either going to come out as aggression, or in tears or (1) um, I just want to go into the corner of the room and (curl) away. Um (1) and just sort of (.) stop, really (1) the thought process. (2)

Positioning these feelings as childlike, and as 'PMS', allows the woman to maintain a sense of herself as public, coping and competent – it is her PMS that lets her down. At the same time the mantle of PMS gives women permission to express private, forbidden emotions, as they can simultaneously disown these feelings. In addition, as PMS is positioned as a thing which is outside, acting to *cause* the problems which women experience, it also serves to unite the woman and her husband against a common domestic foe.

Sharon: We *live* with it but we're (.) (distraught) about it and, and it's (.) My God, you know, is this (1) is this sort of something we've got to live with? And it's just worn us out. (1) Utterly worn us out. Um (1) and it's (1) (devastating in a traumatic way I suppose). We hate it.

Thus both the woman and her husband are positioned as private victims of PMS. Both are exonerated from responsibility. Neither is to blame.

Woman in relation versus woman alone

Always being in relation, attending to the needs of others, and putting other people first is central to traditional representations of femininity (Snitow, 1983). The ideal woman is always happy and successful in relationships; the transgressive woman is not, or is alone. This has been put forward as an explanation for why women are attracted to 'caring' professions, such as nursing or teaching, and as a reason why women experience higher rates of depression when relationships go wrong – women experience it as *their* failure (Bebbington, 1996). It's hard work playing this part of the 'good woman' to perfection. PMS gives women permission to step off the stage. But this is at a price – the price of positioning their desire for solitude, for not wanting to perform, not wanting to put others first, as a symptom, rather than a perfectly normal and acceptable way of being.

Marie: I become very with*drawn*, which again is *not* me. It's quite interesting that one of the questions in (.) the diary was, 'Do you want to spend time alone?' and I thought (.) 'That's exactly it.' You know, I, I just *don't* want to be with anybody else. U::m it's (.) and you don't want to discuss it, you just want to sort of retreat almost into your shell. U::m, I find (.) I think that's stopping me develop my life.

In talk about PMS, the ideal woman was always positioned in relation to others – to man, to family, to work colleagues, friends or children. This positioning recalls the hegemonic cultural constructions of 'woman' alone as signifying something sad or as suspect – Cinderella without her prince (Leiberman, 1986); or Helen Mirren in *Prime Suspect*, and Amanda Burton in *Silent Witness*, two British-made television programmes showing strong 'career women' who solve crimes in a masculine world, yet are represented as sadly eating their supper alone, their solitude the price for their worldly success. Given this cultural pattern, it isn't surprising that wanting to 'get under the quilt cover and hibernate', as one interviewee put it, was positioned as a sign of pathology. An alternative account was to position the desire for solitude as an impossible luxury.

Interviewer: Hmm. (1) Have you made any, sort of, effort to (1) be on your own [inaudible] (when) you're feeling like that?

Nina: U::m? (1) I mean not to an extreme level. Not to actually to sort of pick myself up and sort of and go away. U::m (.) it's (.) I [sighs] you know there's never enough *time* (.) to, to do that. You know, to (.) you know, that's almost a sort of a, a *luxury*. Um (1) I suppose (1) when I say also (.) you know, (of *wanting*) to be on my own, it's also (.) not *relating* (.) on a (.) a deeper level with people around me. You know, I keep it sort of quite superficial. I'll do what I *have* to do. U::m (.) but (.) (I won't take it any further). (1) Um (1) you know, that's, that's as far as it goes. (2)

This account draws on alternative cultural representations of the woman alone as indulgent or narcissistic – as in British television advertisements showing a woman lying in her bath seductively eating chocolate, with surrounding connotations of illicit pleasure and hedonism. A related theme which emerged in many of the interviews was 'I have it all – why aren't I happy?' Women talked of having good relationships, good jobs, being able to *be* the perfect woman, yet still feeling that something was missing from life, feeling sad and, as they wanted to be alone, concluding that something must be wrong with them.

Tara: You know, I want to sort of (.) *lock* myself away. I do. I mean I, I can *function* properly. U::m, but it is (.) I feel *sad*. Really sort of sad and sort of (.) fed up and *everything* (.) instead of sort of looking at the *positive* aspects of my life (.) and all the good that I do and sort of (.) I can do, it's just the negatives are *high*lighted to such a degree. U::m (1) and that shouldn't be the case (.) 'cos I, I had nothing (.) you know, there's nothing (.) *in* my life that sort of (1) should make me want to feel that way. (1) You know I have, (you know) (1) you know, a *wonderful* partner. I have a sort of, I have a *job* that people would give their right arms for. U::m, you know, I *go* to (wonder..) (.) there's no *reason* (1) in my life for that, so it feels as though something else is sort of taking me over.

This account demonstrates the way in which women we see in popular culture whose lives apparently conform to the representations of success – in women's magazines, romantic fiction or film (McMahon, 1990; Modleski, 1984; Radway, 1987; Winship, 1987) – account for their unhappiness. Again, the explanation that is adopted is that the problem must be within. The body is to blame.

Conclusion

In this chapter I have argued that women come to understand themselves as 'woman' in relation to cultural representations of what it means to be so; in relation to historically and culturally specific definitions and constructions of femininity. In narrative accounts women give of themselves when they are premenstrual, we see representations of what the ideal 'woman' is *not*. The premenstrual self is 'woman' outside of the boundaries of acceptability. Woman is excess; the monstrous feminine made flesh. Fecund, bleeding flesh at that. PMS thus stands as a successor to disorders such as hysteria and neurasthenia, pathologies centred in femininity, mantles that women themselves take on. In defining what 'PMS' means to them, we see how women negotiate both representations of femininity, and representations of madness or pathology. They slip from good to bad (or mad), from ideal 'woman' to 'PMS sufferer'. There doesn't seem to be any space in between.

Drawing on cultural representations of 'woman' as split – the mother/madonna/whore split being the most common (Kaplan, 1991; Nead, 1992; Ussher, 1997a) – women position themselves as split when talking about PMS. The transgressive PMS self is contrasted with the idealised non-PMS self: the PMS self contains all that is not wanted, or is positioned as 'bad', whereas the non-PMS self is idealised femininity personified. Yet while PMS may explain unacceptable feelings, behaviours or thoughts, it also reinforces a dissociation between the woman and her emotions. Splitting thus moves women away from looking at the feelings which they experience in the premenstrual phase of the cycle – the anger, the vulnerability, the desire to be alone – and taking these feelings seriously, or attempting to resolve them. In this way PMS does not provide us with a progressive or empowering narrative to explain the conflict or difficulty in women's lives. It perpetuates the age-old ties between woman and the body, medicalising distress, when we might see more plausible explanations in the daily conditions of women's lives.

Representations of PMS in popular culture, self-help books and bio-medical literature reinforce this splitting (Rittenhouse, 1991; Walker, 1997). Here the premenstrual woman is represented as mad, bad or dangerous to know. Such representations do not exist in an existential vacuum, separate from materiality or the intrapsychic (Ussher, 1997b). Post-structuralism may have provided us with a plausible account of the cultural construction of subjectivity, explaining the particular configuration of femininity (and masculinity) in specific cultures, at particular points of time. But this is not to deny the importance of factors such as the body, material inequalities or social structures, factors such as age, ethnicity or social class, or the myriad forms of intrapsychic experience – defence mechanisms, projections, desires, fears or anxieties. In understanding PMS, or indeed subjectivity in general, we have to recognise that discursive representations are irrevocably interconnected with these other phenomena. 'Woman' as signifier may be central to women's subjective experience of themselves as *having* PMS; it may provide the context in which certain experiences become 'symptoms'. Equally, cultural representations of PMS act to provide a set of meanings for these 'symptoms' so that they come to be associated with the female body, with reproduction. But cultural representation is not the only factor in operation here. PMS is a construction produced by the interrelationship between the material, discursive and intrapsychic, a constantly shifting, fluid relationship in which feelings and experiences which are inconsistent with notions of idealised femininity become 'symptoms', or PMS (see, similarly, Gill *et al.* on masculinities, Chapter 7, this volume).

As raging hormones have been posited as the root cause of women's supposed irrational inconsistency of mood for centuries (Foucault, 1976; Martin, 1985;

Sayers, 1982; Ussher, 1989), we should not be surprised that women adopt a biological discourse themselves and categorise mood 'inconsistency' as a symptom caused by PMS. However, the issue of emotional inconsistency as a sign of pathology is not simply a gendered issue. The equation of mental health and positive mood has been described as one of the core myths of a western view of mental health (Epstein, 1996; see also Malik, Chapter 10, this volume). It is antithetical to other cultural traditions, such as those associated with Buddhism, where variability and inconsistency are expected, and fluctuations in mood, sensation, reactions to others, or in bodily experiences, are accepted as a normal part of life experience (Ussher, 1999). So it isn't simply a gendered discourse that women are drawing on here, it is one which underpins a western cultural representation of good mental health. This critical deconstruction of the meaning of PMS to women thus has far broader implications than at first might appear, challenging the very meaning of madness, of symptomatology, and of our cultural construction of mental health.

Acknowledgements

Thanks are offered to Helen Malson for discussions and comments on this chapter, and to Margaret Cariss for collaborating on the research project on which this chapter is based. The research was funded by the North Thames Health Authority, London.

Notes

1 This control is through what Foucault termed the 'intelligible body'. The term 'discourse' is here used in its post-structuralist sense, to refer to cultural representations in the broadest form.
2 Barthes has argued that myths are presented as 'natural' as a means of disguising their historical origins and social meaning (1972: 11).
3 I am not arguing here that PMS can be completely explained in this way. See Ussher (1996, 1999) for further discussion of PMS.
4 Transcription conventions were (.) pauses of less than a second; (1) timed pauses; italics for emphasis. The emphasis was on readability, following Marshall and Wetherell (1989).
5 In more detailed analysis of the interviews presented elsewhere (Ussher *et al.*, forthcoming) these themes are elaborated, with other examples, and a number of other themes arising from the interviews are explored.

References

Barthes, R. (1972) *Mythologies*, New York: Hill & Wang.
Bartky, S. (1988) 'Foucault, femininity and the modernisation of patriarchal power', in I. Diamond and L. Quinby (eds) *Feminism and Foucault: Reflections on Resistance*, Boston, MA: Northeastern University Press.
Bebbington, P. (1996) 'The origins of sex differences in depression: bridging the gap', *International Review of Psychiatry* 8: 295–332.

Berger, J. (1972) *Ways of Seeing*, London: Penguin.

Bordo, S. (1990) 'Reading the slender body', in M. Jacobs, E. Fox Keller and S. Shuttleworth (eds) *Body Politics: Women and the Discourses of Science*, London: Routledge.

Chernin, K. (1981) *The Obsession: Reflections on the Tyranny of Slenderness*, New York: Harper & Row.

Craik, J. (1993) *The Face of Fashion: Cultural Studies in Fashion*, London: Routledge.

De Lauretis, T. (1984) *Alice Doesn't: Feminism, Semiotics, Cinema*, London: Macmillian.

Douglas, S. (1995) *Where the Girls Are: Growing up Female with the Mass Media*, London: Penguin.

Ehrenreich, B. and English, D. (1978) *For her Own Good: 150 Years of Experts' Advice to Women*, New York: Anchor Doubleday.

Epstein, M. (1996) *Thoughts without a Thinker: Psychotherapy from a Buddhist Perspective*, London: Duckworth.

Foucault, M. (1976) *The History of Sexuality*, Volume 1, London: Penguin.

Harre, R. and Davies, B. (1990) 'Positioning: the discursive production of selves', *Journal for the Theory of Social Behaviour* 20: 43–63.

Kaplan, L.J. (1991) *Female Perversions*, London: Penguin.

Kendrick, W. (1987) *The Secret Museum*, London: Viking.

Laws, S. (1990) *Issues of Blood*, London: Macmillan.

Laws, S., Hey, V. and Eagen, A. (1985) *Seeing Red: The Politics of Premenstrual Tension*, London: Hutchinson.

Leiberman, M.K. (1986) '"Some day my prince will come": female acculturation through the fairy tale', in J. Zipes (ed.) *Don't Bet on the Prince: Contemporary Fairy Tales in North America and England*, Aldershot, Hants: Gower.

McMahon, K. (1990) 'The cosmopolitan ideology and the management of desire', *Journal of Sex Research* 27(3): 381–96.

Malson, H. (1996) *The Thin Body*, London: Routledge.

Marshall, H. and Wetherell, M. (1989) 'Talking about careers and gender identity: a discourse on performance', in S. Skevington and D. Barker (eds) *The Social Identity of Women*, London: Sage.

Martin, E. (1985) *The Woman in the Body: A Cultural Analysis of Reproduction*, Milton Keynes: Open University Press.

Modleski, T. (1984) *Loving with a Vengeance: Mass Produced Fantasies for Women*, New York: Routledge.

Moore, R. (1975) 'From rags to riches: stereotypes, distortion and anti-humanism in fairy tales', *Interracial Books for Children* 6: 1–3.

Nead, L. (1992) *The Female Nude: Art, Obscenity and Sexuality*, London: Routledge.

Nicolson, P. (1996) *Women, Power and Organisations*, London: Routledge.

Pollock, G. (1988) *Vision and Difference: Femininity, Feminism and Histories of Art*, London: Routledge.

Potter, J. and Wetherell, M. (1987) *Discourse and Social Psychology*, London: Routledge.

Radway, J. (1987) *Reading the Romance: Women, Patriarchy and Popular Literature*, London: Verso.

Reissman, C.K. (1993) *Narrative Analysis. Qualitative Research Methods*, Volume 30, London: Sage.

Rittenhouse, C.A. (1991) 'The emergence of PMS as a social problem', *Social Problems* 38: 412–25.

Sayers, J. (1982) *Biological Politics*, London: Methuen.

Smith, D. (1988) 'Femininity as discourse', in L. Roman and L.K. Christian Smith (eds) *Becoming Feminine: The Politics of Popular Culture*, Brighton: Falmer Press.

Snitow, A.B. (1983) 'Mass market romance: pornography for women is different', in A. Snitow, C. Stansell and S. Thompson (eds) *Desire: The Politics of Sexuality*, London: The Women's Press.

Stenner, P. (1987) 'Discoursing jealousy', in E. Burman and I. Parker (eds) *Discourse Analytic Research*, London: Routledge.

Ussher, J.M. (1989) *The Psychology of the Female Body*, London: Routledge.

—— (1991) *Women's Madness: Misogyny or Mental Illness?*, Hemel Hempstead: Harvester Wheatsheaf.

—— (1996) 'Premenstrual Syndrome: reconciling disciplinary divides through the adoption of a material-discursive epistemological standpoint', *Annual Review of Sex Research* 7: 218–52.

—— (1997a) *Fantasies of Femininity: Reframing the Boundaries of Sex*, London: Penguin.

—— (1997b) *Body Talk: The Material and Discursive Regulation of Sexuality, Madness and Reproduction*, London: Routledge.

—— (1999) 'Spirituality and psychotherapy: the case of Premenstrual Syndrome', paper presented at the ISTP conference, April 1999, Sydney, Australia.

—— (2000a) 'Women's madness: a material-discursive-intrapsychic approach', in D. Fee (ed.) *Psychology and the Postmodern: Mental Illness as Discourse and Experience*, London: Sage.

—— (2000b) 'Women and mental illness', in L. Sherr and J. St Lawrence (eds) *Women, Health and the Mind*, London: Wiley.

Ussher, J.M., Hunter, M., Browne, S. and Cariss, M. (forthcoming) 'Women's subjective experiences of PMS'.

Vines, G. (1992) *Raging Hormones*, London: Macmillan.

Walker, A. (1995) 'Theory and methodology in premenstrual syndrome research', *Social Science and Medicine* 41(6): 793–800.

—— (1997) *The Menstrual Cycle*, London: Routledge.

Walkerdine, V. (1990) *Schoolgirl Fictions*, London: Verso.

—— (1996) *Daddy's Girl: Young Girls and Popular Culture*, London: Macmillan.

Weibel, K. (1977) *Mirror, Mirror: Images of Women Reflected in Popular Culture*, New York: Anchor Books.

Winship, J. (1987) *Inside Women's Magazines*, London: Pandora.

Young, K.G. (1989) 'Narrative embodiments: enclaves of self in the realm of medicine', in J. Shotter and K.J. Gergen (eds) *Texts of Identity*, London: Sage.

7   The tyranny of the 'six-pack'?

Understanding men's responses to
representations of the male body
in popular culture

*Rosalind Gill, Karen Henwood and
Carl McLean*

Introduction: Changing representations of men?

Over the past decade there has been a dramatic increase in the numbers of images
of men in popular culture. Where once images of women dominated advertising
and magazines, increasingly men's bodies are taking their place alongside
women's on billboards, in fashion shoots, entertainment troupes like The
Chippendales and large-circulation magazines. However, it is not simply that there
are now more images of men circulating, but that a specific kind of representational practice has emerged for depicting the male body: namely an idealised and
eroticised aesthetic showing a toned, young body. This, we will argue, is a *new*
phenomenon, which is culturally and historically specific, although we are not
suggesting that male bodies have not been presented as desirable before. Clearly
they have, and heterosexual women and gay men have swooned over the years
about Fred Astaire, Cary Grant, James Dean and a hundred matinée idols. What *is*
new, however, is the ways in which the male body is being presented: specifically,
the coding of this body in ways that give permission for it to be looked at and
desired. Men's bodies, it has been argued, are now coded – like women's – as 'to
be looked at', to use the awkward but insightful phrase current in film studies
(Cohan and Hark, 1993; Jeffords, 1994; Mulvey, 1975; Screen, 1992). That is, the
ways that men's bodies have begun to be represented over the past ten years
constitutes a disruption of conventional patterns of looking in which, in John
Berger's famous phrase, 'men look at women and women watch themselves being
looked at' (1972: 47).

This chapter does two things. First, it explores the reasons for this change in
cultural representations of masculinity, discussing a range of factors that have
converged to produce this shift. Second, it examines men's responses to the
emergence of this new representational practice, drawing on a large-scale
qualitative study conducted by the authors during 1998 and 1989, based on
interviews with 140 men.

Reasons for the emergence of new representations of masculinity

In this section, we consider both *what* has changed in the ways in which men's bodies are represented in popular culture, and *why* these changes have occurred. We reject any single or unitary explanation, and instead argue that there are multiple factors involved, which have combined to produce a new generic style for representing masculinity.

Feminism and new social movements

Clearly, one key influence upon the way in which masculinity is regarded and presented is feminism. Feminists' interrogation of conventional assumptions about gender relations and their problematisation of 'traditional masculinity' have had a seismic effect upon popular culture and social relations. Through the influence of feminism many taken-for-granted aspects of masculinity have been questioned, with forums as diverse as women's magazines and talk shows echoing feminist criticisms of traditional masculinity as distant, uninvolved, unemotional and uncommunicative. Since the 1970s these critiques have given rise to a great appetite for a new kind of masculinity, which would encompass many traits previously thought of as feminine – emotionality, intimacy, nurturing and caring (Chapman and Rutherford, 1988; Connell, 1987; Hearn and Morgan, 1990; Kimmel, 1987; Seidler, 1989, 1992).

More weight to feminist campaigns to reinvent gender and the relations between women and men came from the rise of a particular style of humanist psychology in the late 1970s and 1980s. This popular psychology took as its focus the notion of the 'whole person', and was concerned with good communication and with validating different parts of the person and different styles of interaction. Assertiveness was promoted above aggressiveness or passivity and there was an increase in interest in personal therapy, and in a range of alternative or complementary approaches to medicine or healing. Taken together, these movements put the idea of the *whole person* or the *self-actualised person* (Maslow, 1970) on the cultural agenda. The whole person was seen as the *androgynous* person, as extreme masculinity and extreme femininity came to be seen not simply as socially restricting or damaging, but also as unhealthy.

Linked to this trend was the rise of what have been called New Social Movements. Included in this category alongside feminism are the peace movement, antiracist organisations, environmental movements, movements for sexual liberation, and a variety of identity-based political organisations focusing on, for instance, disability rights and postcolonial struggles. What this loose categorisation of groups shares is both a disillusion with conventional class-based party politics, and a commitment to new forms of organisation and struggle, based less upon representation and more upon direct action. Taken together, the New Social Movements disrupted the very understanding of what politics meant, showing that everyday life was irredeemably political. They also promoted a different model of the individual, as someone connected not simply to a family, but to wider communities and to the environment. In doing so, we would argue, they sowed the seeds for a revisioning of traditional masculinity, and helped to create a cultural milieu in which a 'new man' could emerge and flourish. The nature of that 'new man' is highly contested. He represented, for some, a shift to a more emotionally and domestically involved, pro-feminist nurturing man. For others, he was a more individualistic and narcissistic man whose bathroom shelves groaned under the weight of skincare and fragrance products; and for others still he was the 'great pretender', a wolf in sheep's clothing, a way for men to hold on to their power while appearing to have changed (see Chapman and Rutherford (1988); Mort (1996); Nixon (1996) for discussions and comparisons with the rise of the 'new lad').

The rise of the style press

A different kind of influence came from the rise of the style magazines in the 1980s. For years, within the fashion, magazine, advertising and retailing industries people had fantasised about the creation of a magazine which could be targeted at affluent male consumers. Such a product was seen as an impossible dream because men did not define themselves *as* men in the same way that women defined themselves as women. Men lacked self-consciousness about their sex, and while they bought magazines about cars or fishing or cameras there was scepticism about whether they would buy a title organised around *being a man* rather than a specific hobby. A second problem concerned the tone such a magazine should adopt. Women's magazines had long adopted the formula of treating their readers like friends, with an intimate tone, but this was seen as potentially threatening to men.

In terms of understanding the rise of discourses of new masculinity one magazine is key: *The Face*, launched by Nick Logan in 1982. It promoted itself as a style magazine rather than as a men's magazine, although the vast majority of its readers were male, and it was organised around fashion and music and any kind of social commentary deemed chic enough to fit in its pages. Sean Nixon (1996) argues that *The Face* developed a new aesthetic: it was not just about style, but it was emblematic of stylishness itself, creating a new vocabulary for fashion photography. This vocabulary, significantly, extended the notion of style to include fashion spreads of menswear and advertising for body products targeted at men as well as women.

The rise of retailing: masculinity goes to the mall

The rise of the style magazines can in turn be understood in terms of massive changes in the economy that were taking place in the 1980s. There was a dramatic decline in manufacturing and a rise in the service sector and retailing. The employment of increasing numbers of people within the retail sector was, however, just one of a number of factors that were changing the structure and meaning of shopping and consumerism (Mort, 1996). There was a significant trend towards conglomeration, with five or six companies controlling the high street by the end of the 1980s, a growth in out-of-town shopping, and a new sense in which shopping was promoted as a major cultural or leisure activity with the opening of large themed shopping centres with provision of crèches and restaurants, and the promotion of trips to large out-of-town stores as a relaxing day out. Indeed, studies consistently find that shopping is the main leisure activity of the British (*Cultural Trends*, 1998; Miles, 1996; Miller, 1995).

In the 1980s the 'New Man' became a new target for fashion companies – men were the new market (Edwards, 1997; Hession, 1997). This was heralded as a quiet revolution in fashion companies as men had been considered a market that was difficult to crack, and shopping had always been seen as traditionally female. The move was associated with the meteoric rise of a few companies – most notably Next and the Burton Group. Next, in particular, launched in 1986, traded images of the city and of share dealing and city gents in its clothes – striped shirts, brogues, double-breasted suits. It was trading on images that were circulating elsewhere through the privatisation campaigns, the Big Bang, as well as in major *Zeitgeist* films like *Wall Street*. Frank Mort (1988) argues that Next allowed people to play with these images without commitment. Where once clothes had been powerful and stable signifiers of social location, they were increasingly worn in more flexible and playful ways, such that people could 'try on' new identities through their apparel – perhaps working as a labourer throughout the week, but dressing like a share-room dealer to go out in the evening, and wearing the apparel of a 'country gentlemen' (corduroy trousers and a Barbour jacket) to visit the garden centre at weekends.

New musical trends

Mort (1996) argues that this new playful relationship between clothes and identity is the result of a series of changes provoked by punk in the 1970s. With its emphasis on bricolage, the putting together of things that are normally kept apart – for example, Doc Martens and ballet dresses – punk created a space for men and women to be able to play with different self-presentations, and broke down stable chains of signification.

Surprisingly, punk is the only musical movement to have been seriously discussed in relation to questions about masculinity and identity (but see also Hebdige, 1979; Thornton, 1995). Yet it would seem obvious that musical styles have had a profound effect upon masculinity and upon the ways in which men live and experience what it means to be male. The kind of codification of masculinity in heavy metal, for example, is a world away from the gender meanings encoded in glam rock, which itself differs from the masculinities on offer in reggae, techno, Britpop or ska, to name but a few. The significance of musical cultures and subcultures upon men's experience is seriously under-researched and would repay detailed study.

The rise of the gay community

Another factor that is crucial to our understanding of the emergence of new representational practices for depicting masculinities is the rise of the gay liberation movement from the late 1960s onwards. In the UK there has recently been a proliferation of magazines aimed at gay men which are no longer only targeted at a gay activist audience. These magazines offer new and pleasurable representations, not simply representations deemed politically sound. This change reflects the rising confidence of the gay community, at least in metropolitan areas, as well as increasing corporate recognition of the power of the 'pink pound'. These magazines, together with gay pornography, pin-ups, and particular subcultural styles within the club scene, have had a profound effect upon representations of masculinity, through a routing that has gone from gay porn through art house photography to advertising (Parsi, 1997). Notably, they have served to prise apart the association of masculinity with heterosexuality, and the elision of masculinity with activity, by showing men not simply as active sexual subjects, but also as *objects of desire* (Creekmuir and Doty, 1993; Mercer and Julien, 1988; Simpson, 1994). In other words, it is within the gay media that representations of men as erotic objects to be looked at were first produced, and, arguably, what has happened over the past decade is that this genre has gone mainstream.

The marketing of women's desire

If indeed gay images of men have gone mainstream, this has been the result of a realisation that representations of men previously confined to the gay subculture were enormously desirable to some heterosexual women. Suzanne Moore (1988) has argued that it was precisely the growing visibility of eroticised representations of men outside the gay media that facilitated, or gave permission for, a new kind of gaze among women. She suggests that this constituted a major disruption to the scopic order – the politics of looking. Rather than simply being objects of the gaze, women have become active subjects who can look as well as being looked at, as Marshall and Woollett demonstrate (Chapter 8, this volume) in their account of a young Asian woman's video self-presentation. This trend is also evident in contemporary culture in the new, confident tone of women's magazines, and models in advertisements (McRobbie, 1991) who now look and talk back, rather than simply being passive objects (Gill, 2000). It is humorously depicted in advertisements like that for Diet Coke in which women queue up for an '11 o'clock appointment' in order to gaze at the toned body of the labourer outside the window. The choice of the labourer is interesting because it highlights the reversal that has taken place: where once building contractors ogled and whistled at women, now women ogle them! (We would obviously not want to overstate this point, and it should be noted that the politics of looking still take their traditional form in many advertisements and many situations.)

What, then, are the characteristics of this kind of representation? One thing seems clear: rather than a diversity or variety of different representations of masculinity we seem to be confronting a very specific generic style. The models are generally white (with black models still mainly confined to sports product/ sportswear imagery); they are young (usually 30 or under); they are muscular and slim; they are usually clean-shaven – with perhaps the exception of a little designer stubble; and they have particular facial features which connote a combination of softness and strength – strong jaw, large lips and eyes, soft, clear skin (Edwards, 1997).

In the second section of this chapter, we will examine the ways in which young men in the UK experience and respond to such imagery.

Understanding men's reactions to idealised representations of the male body

This section draws on a study concerned with the interrelationships between cultural, social and economic changes and the changing psychologies of men. A total of 140 men were interviewed, in one of two ways: in individual life history interviews, or in focus groups comprising four or five men. The men in the study were drawn from four regional locations in the UK – Bangor, London, Manchester and Newcastle – and attempts were made to recruit as diverse a sample as possible in terms of 'race' and ethnicity, class and sexuality. All the men interviewed were aged between 15 and 35, because we were interested in the experiences of men who had grown up or were approaching adulthood against the backdrop of these changes.

We have discussed the design of the study, our methodology and the theoretical approach we adopted, which we characterised as a socio-emotional approach, in detail elsewhere (Henwood *et al.*, 1999). Here it is sufficient to note that the interviews were semi-structured, generally lasted between one and two hours, and focused upon a range of topics deemed pertinent to being a young male in the UK in the late 1990s: childhood; relationships with parents, family and friends; love and sex; education; shops and careers; hobbies and interests; music and fashion; aspirations for the future, and so on. In general, the individual life history interviews aimed to elicit more personal, biographical information, while the focus groups complemented these with an address to general themes. A particular focus of the study was the significance of embodiment, and thus there were also a range of questions in both kinds of interview concerned with health, diet, bodily practices and body culture. Men were asked a series of general questions about the increasing use of the male body in advertising and other popular cultural forms, and they were also shown – as prompts – representations of the male body which were taken from current editions of men's magazines. This strategy proved to be a highly effective one, and the concrete images in front of them elicited a great deal of talk and discussion about the meaning and significance of these types of representations for men.

All the men interviewed had noticed the increase in the number of images of idealised or eroticised male bodies in advertising and the wider culture. This was especially true of the older men (those in their late twenties and early thirties), who had observed the change during their adult life. The vast majority of the men believed that advertisers employed such images in order to encourage *aspirational identification*: as one young man put it, 'if you buy their perfume, you'll look like that'.

Despite their belief that the advertisements were designed to be aspirational, few of the men responded to them in a straightforward manner. In fact, the men expressed feelings ranging from desire and identification to anger and resentment when asked about the representations and confronted with specific examples. In the remainder of this chapter we provide a systematic analysis of the different types of reaction to these images, highlighting eight clusters of response, and exploring their significance for understanding male psychologies. The analysis is a thematic one, grouping together similar styles of reaction. The eight clusters were defined as follows, depending upon whether the images were perceived as:

1   Aspirational
2   Pressurising
3   Generating resentment
4   Body culture as shallow
5   Narcissistic representations
6   Uniform
7   Irrelevant
8   Desirable.

It is worth noting that these reactions were not mutually exclusive; in fact, men often drew upon and moved between different types of response, indicating the importance of theorising subject positions in mobile terms (see Gill, forthcoming).

Aspirational reactions

Although the vast majority of the men accepted that contemporary representations of the male body in advertisements and in many magazines were designed to be aspirational, surprisingly few claimed to aspire to the kind of look or body depicted in an aftershave advertisement or on the cover of *Men's Health*. Those who did were more likely to come from metropolitan environments. Indeed, the Bangor-based men frequently identified the representations as 'townie' and as appealing to men in cities, who were perceived to be overly concerned with their image. 'Aspirational' men were also likely to be in their mid-twenties rather than in their teens or thirties, suggesting that aspiring to this look has clearly defined lifestyle correlates. Men in their thirties suggested that it was too late to try to achieve that kind of body, while teenage boys lacked the resources to join a gym, and were also, of course, more likely to be physically immature and thus unable to obtain the look by body-work alone.

As significant as these demographic and social factors, however, was a *psycho-logical* one: those men who saw these images as aspirational were also those who saw them as achievable. That is, we found no evidence of men inhabiting a clearly aspirational subject position without also believing that they could achieve the body to which they aspired. This is interesting because it downplays the significance of fantasy and unconscious desire and suggests that men are – in this area at least – tailoring their desires to what they believe is achievable.

Respondent: Yeah, it looks good. I think it's achievable, you know, getting that toned kind of body.

Such expressions of straightforward aspiration, it should be noted, were quite unusual. While many men were members of a gym and worked out on a regular basis, few had such an unambivalent response to representations of the idealised, toned masculine body.

Feeling under pressure

By far the most common way of talking about the representations of the male body was in terms of feeling under pressure. The words 'pressure' and 'stressful' were spontaneously used by approximately half of the interviewees, who were not readily distinguishable by age, class, sexuality or region.

A typical response came from a 24-year-old student from Newcastle. Talking generally about representations of men, he argued:

Respondent: I think blokes are starting to get paranoid, you know, about how they look and stuff.

When shown an advert for Calvin Klein fragrance Escape for Men, he went on:

Respondent: I think that a bloke would look at that and, well I would look at that and I think I'm a bloke and I'm supposed to look like that am I.

A similar response was given by a London-based gay man who worked in the media. He talked about his desire to 'block out' all the images of male toned bodies because of the pressure they put on him:

Respondent: I tend to screen a lot of those out because I think it's too stressful to think I'm pudgy and and they're not really. Um, I, to be perfectly honest, this is a very. That Escape advert for example, I'd probably pay far more attention to it if he was dressed.
Interviewer: Why do you think that would be?
Respondent: Because that's quite stressful, as someone who hasn't got a body like that, um, and has stopped working out and all that malarkey. I tend to . . . lots of filters in your head. I tend to go 'Oh, go away! Stop it!'

Some men commented explicitly on how *recent* the experience of being bombarded with images of idealised male bodies is and described the pressure engendered as something *new*. Several drew comparisons with their fathers' experiences; others drew parallels with the pressures women have been under for much longer in relation to their appearance.

Unlike some of the men discussed below, these men did not entirely reject the representations on offer in many contemporary adverts and magazines. Indeed, they felt stressed precisely because they perceived the images as representing a desirable goal against which their own bodies fell short. Many of them were working out, taking other forms of exercise, and/or modifying their diet in order to achieve something which more closely approximated to the desirable body. However, they differed from the aspirational group in that they felt theirs was not a freely made choice, but rather something that was imposed upon them to which they were supposed to aspire.

Generating resentment

Some men expressed outright hostility towards the representations or towards the men represented. One London student in his mid-twenties expressed a feeling of outraged injustice about the toned, muscular and attractive bodies he saw all around him. Rather than feeling pressurised, he felt a mixture of anger and despair.

Respondent: Yeah. It's a sort of desirability thing, isn't it. You know, I mean, the adverts. I mean, these people are obviously going to appeal to the opposite sex. I mean that's what the advert's saying, isn't it? I mean that's what it's basically, that's its basic message. So saying, on a superficial level, that if you buy Escape, then you're going to, you're going to be as desirable as this person here. Although obviously it's not the case unfortunately. God, I hate these people! I do hate these men because it's not fair, it's not fair.
Interviewer: What's not fair?
Respondent: Well, look at them. I mean, as much as I try hard to work out, it just, you know, it's never going to happen.

Here, the resentment is engendered by a sense of unfairness about the speaker's ability ever to achieve a body like that of the model – however hard he tries. It offends against the dominant individualist and meritocratic notion of 'natural justice' because the speaker recognises that good looks are not equally distributed and are not achievable through hard work alone.

In recent years, research by advertising agencies, marketing companies and academics interested in the media has highlighted a significant degree of resentment among women about being addressed in terms of idealised and unattainable images (Goldman, 1992). In response to this, many companies have altered their advertising targeted at women to avoid or confront this hostility. Pantene, example, ran a campaign for its hair products using the slogan 'Don't hate me just because I am beautiful', tackling head-on women's anger and fatigue with bombardment by idealised representations of femininity. Its more recent campaign, 'L'Oreal – because you're worth it', is part of a major shift in advertising to women which tells them how good and valuable they should feel, rather than presenting an ideal to which they should aspire. A slightly different tack has been taken by Nike and other sportswear companies whose advertisements have taken as their explicit focus women's insecurity about how they look, and have included direct critiques of 'unrealistic media images'. However cynical these campaigns are, they have clearly been effective in picking up on and redirecting popular anger. To date, such strategies have been employed predominantly in advertising women's body products; the findings presented here, however, suggest that the mixture of resentment, anger and despair in relation to such representations is not exclusive to women.

Body culture as shallow

A small number of interviewees believed that concern with how one's body looked denoted superficiality or shallowness. Some expressed the view that one's appearance should be irrelevant, and that people should relate to each other in different terms. The men holding this belief tended to be gay and/or to have been influenced by feminist thinking, and they rejected what they saw as the increasing objectification of both women's and men's bodies. However, the fact that they believed this strongly did not prevent them from holding other views, and from being as immersed in body culture as anybody else. Frequently, though, they reported feeling 'conflicted' – torn between how they thought they should feel about representations of the idealised male body, and how they actually felt. Another source of conflict was having views which were perceived to be at variance with the dominant cultural values. Rich explains his struggle over his attitude to his own body:

Respondent: Obviously I do work out, well swim and go to circuit training to try and keep a fairly decent body.
Interviewer: Is that quite, is that important to you?
Respondent: I wish it wasn't, but yeah.
Interviewer: Why do you say you wish it wasn't?
Respondent: Well, because it is shallow.
Interviewer: In what way?
Respondent: Um, well, people should take me as I am. And I shouldn't be worried about, if I've got a gut, you know, they won't like me. They should just fuck off if they don't like it. But unfortunately, that's, that's the rules of the game.

Here, the fact that the 'rules of the game' were not as non-judgemental about appearance as he would like explains his insecurity and continual need to keep working on his body, while also making him feel that he is shallow for pursuing the goal of a toned body.

A similar view was expressed by a member of a gay focus group in London:

Respondent: Yeah, I mean it's that whole attitude that makes me a bit suspicious about that kind of advertising. But slightly resentful even. Because I am aware that I have been, that my attitudes to attractiveness had been, have been influenced by this kind of advertising. You can't escape it. And it annoys me a bit. You know, I would like people just to take me as I am, and I would like to take other people as they are as well. I don't like looking at people and thinking, yeah, you know, he or she looks all right, but, shame they haven't got slightly bigger pectorals or it's a shame she hasn't got more make-up on or whatever. I think it's bad, it's wrong.

This passage has a strong moral tone, about the unethical nature of judging people by their appearance. It also conveys a sense of personal discomfiture at the sense of having been influenced against one's own will. The speaker argues that he finds himself occupying the dominant cultural subject position of evaluating people because of how they look, but that he occupies it reluctantly: it is as if this ideological position has seeped into him without his consent.

Narcissistic representations

A more commonly held view among the interviewees was that the models represented in many magazines and advertisements were overly vain and self-loving. Several men professed a repulsion for the men represented, criticising their postures and facial expressions as narcissistic. Interestingly, the two groups most likely to hold this view were those from the sample in Bangor, who, as we have seen, were also more likely to perceive the representations as metropolitan, and the younger teenage boys in all areas. The phrase which cropped up repeatedly was 'He just loves himself, doesn't he?'

Interviewer: I mean what do you make of adverts like this? I mean what do they say? I don't know if they mean anything. What do they say to you? Or is it just something that don't. Just what is your opinion of these ones actually?
Respondent: Um a bit cheesy.
Interviewer: Yeah. What do you mean by cheesy?
Respondent: Well, stupid really. It's the only word that I can think of that comes to mind.
Interviewer: What kind of makes them stupid for you?
Respondent: The way he is standing there like that really. Looking like a poser.
Interviewer: Do you think he is quite up on himself?
Respondent: Yeah they all look like they think they are a bit special do you know what I mean? Just because they use a kind of aftershave they think they are better than everyone else.

This kind of reading was frequently correlated with a rejection of the product being advertised. It was connected to a *discomfort* with male concerns about appearance, rather than the more moral or politicised rejection evidenced by description of body culture as shallow. Those who saw the representations as uncomfortably narcissistic were more likely to hold traditional views about masculinity and to see the images as unduly feminine or homoerotic. Frequently, remarks about how 'up on himself' the model was were accompanied by implicitly homophobic comments. This may be seen in the dialogue below among a group of teenagers from Bangor:

Interviewer: And what do you think the focus of these is?
Respondent 1: I think they're facing a, like ponces that really are up on their image and really should get a [inaudible] (laughter)
Respondent 2: This grooming is excessive.
Respondent 1: Yes it is a bit over the top really.
Respondent 3: I think Boss adverts actually put me off wanting to buy.
Interviewer: Why do you say that?
Respondent 1: Because he's got a dodgy pair of underpants on.
Respondent 3: Yeah (laughter) I don't know. I don't like in a magazine it would just put me off having like this ponce posing in his underwear. Just no.
Respondent 2: I don't like this one at all. It's like, I don't like his face and everything.
Respondent 1: He looks like a dodgy, seedy little bloke, doesn't he (laughter).

Here connections are made between 'excessive grooming', a particular facial expression, being 'up on himself', being a 'ponce', and looking 'dodgy' and 'seedy'. Together, these attributions constitute a wholesale rejection of the image, and they are accompanied by the assertion that the image would actively deter the men from buying the products.

Criticising uniformity

A different critique focused upon the sameness or uniformity of contemporary representations of masculinity. The notion that the male fragrance advertisements were virtually indistinguishable from each other was frequently voiced, along with the suggestion that one could alter the product identifier in each of these advertisements without the meaning changing at all. A concern was raised about the similarity of the cultural repertoire of images of men. One respondent, only half joking, suggested that it was in fact only one man who was being photographed time and time again!

Respondent: I mean there definitely is something in the media, in TV programmes and in the people who are public public people, people in the public eye. You know, if all those people are of a certain shape and design, then there is pressure there to be felt, for the rest of us to think 'that's how we should be and we're not'. It shouldn't be like that.

Interviewer: I mean, do you think it would work if they used, I don't know, average people in these adverts?

Respondent: Probably not. That's why it's a vicious circle, isn't it? I suspect it would be better for them to use these.

Interviewer: Yeah, yeah.

Respondent: But maybe they could have several men in an advert and have, go for a variety. You know, short, tall, slim, long hair, short hair, whatever. But instead they tend to go for dark features, short hair, broad. Just the one man. So I don't know what the thinking is.

Some men believed that an increasingly narrow notion of beauty was being promoted by advertisers and magazine editors. Men talked of the images promoting one single particular kind of beauty, and of creating problems for any man who did not fit the mould.

Respondent: I think society's kind of going sort of uniformity of what we should be attracted to and what everybody should look like, as opposed to everybody being individual in the way they look.

Representations as irrelevant

Up to one-third of the men claimed that the representations had no significance for them at all, suggesting that they were a complete irrelevance to their lives and sense of self. The men who advanced this view neither aspired to the look, nor felt pressured, resentful or critical of the images; they simply imbued them with little significance.

All the men holding this view were heterosexual and two kinds of argument were put forward: either that they were 'insulated' from this imagery by being in a long-term relationship, or, alternatively, that the look presented was unappealing to women and thus of little significance to them.

Respondent: Christ, I don't know. Don't look like too many people I know. I don't know, I suppose it's one of those things. Perhaps. I don't know, I'm just looking at them and thinking, do I really want a body that looks like that? And I don't really know, I mean, it's kind it's kind of hard to say for me, you know, 'cos I've been seeing my girlfriend for five years and stuff, so like it tends to. Were you single you perhaps have a different perspective on it and stuff. And I assume they're aiming it at sort of young, free single men and stuff and just trying to reinforce this is the image what women find attractive.

In this extract, Dave argues that the security of a stable, long-term relationship prevents him from being affected by imagery like this, since, by implication, he does not feel the need to impress anyone (a woman). The relationship thus represents a safe haven from unwanted pressures that single men are assumed to face – the more significant connection/intimacy eroding the need to have a particularly toned or worked out body.

However, a different explanation was offered by some single men who argued that the representations were irrelevant to them because women were uninterested in men's bodies:

Respondent 1:   I don't think that women are really that bothered what the body is like. I mean, they're more bothered about what sort of person you are.

Respondent 2:   If you are confident in how you are and how you look, you don't really have to exercise, you don't have to have a six-pack to get a girlfriend and stuff like that. There are some girls that look for things like that, but a lot look for personality, and clothes and that are just a bonus really, aren't they. It depends, you know, if you like someone if you can relax round them and stuff like that. Whereas if you like someone but you can't relax with them there is no point in planning with them for like the future and stuff is there. If you can't relax round them then there is no point there is something missing isn't there.

Both these men suggest that women have other more important priorities in selecting a boyfriend than what their bodies look like. They are more interested in men's personalities than in their bodies. The second speaker, a 15-year-old from Manchester's Moss Side, also implies that this is his concern too; in selecting a partner, being able to relax with them is of paramount importance. Many of the men who argued that the images were irrelevant did so on the basis that there remains little pressure on men to look a particular way.

Respondent: The pressure on men is not really the same, you know, men don't necessarily have to look pretty, you know, they can get by looking all rugged, you know, women don't look at the guy and just look at his appearance, you know or how pretty he is or whatever other you know, women can find a man attractive if he's you know looking all scruffy and rugged and looking like he's just got up.

Clearly, this represents a significant disjuncture with the kinds of responses discussed earlier, indicating that men's perceived need to conform to a particular idealised look and body shape is unevenly distributed through the male population. Further research is needed to discern the patterns and causes of this variation.

Desire and inaccessibility

The final cluster of responses articulated feelings of desire in relation to the representations. Perhaps not surprisingly, most of the men expressing feelings of attraction towards the models represented defined themselves as gay.

Interviewer: What is the thing that immediately strikes you about them? Or is it just the whole package?
Respondent 2: Well, I suppose it's just that they, they're good-looking. They're sexy, yeah, it's erotic.
Respondent 1: Oh, I have never seen this one. I quite like that.
Respondent 2: Oh, this one is well known for being homoerotic.
Respondent 1: It's lovely.

However, a small number of heterosexual-identified men did admit to finding the representations attractive too.

Respondent: Because, I mean, obviously they're, you know, they're attractive. But there's something quite, I don't know. It something quite, what's the word I'm looking for? There's something quite appealing about them, you know. That's not the right word. But there is, you know, so I suppose
Interviewer: Kind of an aesthetic?
Respondent: Yeah, yeah. I suppose there's a homosexual thing about it as well, because you can't help but find them, well I find them anyway, attractive, you know. It's difficult not to, because they are so. I don't know, there's that aspect to it as well.

Many other heterosexual-identified men indirectly communicated the notion that the representations were attractive or desirable to them. This was largely done through exaggerated denial of their appeal, or, in focus groups, through humorous banter along the lines of 'You fancy him, don't you?', which showed that the representations were read as homoerotic, even if this was something which was too threatening to admit directly.

Conclusion

One of our aims in this chapter is to have exemplified how it is possible to bring together the questions, analytical concerns and methodological strategies of cultural studies and psychological research within a single study of contemporary men's psychologies. Our general theoretical orientation has much in common with recent projects that have sought to consider the *materiality* of cultural discourses (of sexuality, reproduction, madness, health and illness: Ussher, 1997; Yardley, 1997) and the *phenomenology* of subjection and resistance to power–discourse relations (Davis, 1997; Nettleton and Watson, 1998). In Chapter 1 of this volume

Chris Griffin has suggested that discursive social and cultural analyses in psychology should connect with wider cultural studies approaches that engage with cultural practices and so do not rest with analyses of talk and text alone. Our chapter makes the case for also including the study of socio-emotional issues such as embodiment, emotional expression and shifts with social positioning across the life span under the remit of cultural psychology's concern for practices, talk and text (see also Malik, Chapter 10, this volume). In particular, we have sought to explain a generic shift in the popular visual depiction of men alongside a systematic analysis of men's socio-emotional responses to this representational practice.

One of the main analytic gains to be made from combined cultural studies and psychology research of this kind is in grappling with the so-called 'crisis' of masculinity affecting contemporary boys and men. Some analyses have explored the discursive construction of this crisis, pointing out, for example, how it can serve to rehabilitate previously problematised definitions of traditionally defined strong, active, dominant and autonomous men (Coyle and Morgan-Sykes, 1998). Other analyses have addressed the issue of whether 'real' vulnerabilities, anxieties or discomfitures might be following from the cultural fragmentation or deconstruction of such masculine identity, in either a critical (Norton, 1997) or a more supportive way (Frosh, 1995). In this chapter we have gone down a third analytic pathway, while addressing the same web of 'crisis concerns'. Using our own analysis of men's firsthand accounts of their thoughts and feelings about male embodiment when prompted by images of other men's (exemplary) bodies, we can begin to explore the different kinds of subject positions that are being taken up by men and how they can carry quite disparate and incompletely known cultural, political and psychological implications. For instance, there are occasions where men apparently construct commonalities between their own embodied experiences and those that have previously been culturally associated only with women; where they view themselves as inoculated from threats of harm by secure, intimate relationships and the desires of women; where they personally reject emotional reactions and experiences while projecting them on to other men. Efforts to reflect upon the implications of such different types of socio-emotional positioning among boys and men are in their infancy, but are now being taken forward in the field of narrative and constructivist psychotherapy (McQueen, 1998). Future developments in this vein are likely to benefit by establishing synergies with some of the other perspectives advocated in this volume. For example, what are the implications for our own analysis of men's embodied subject positions of asking questions about the reflective or alienating possibilities opened up by late-modern risk, consumer, media and communications culture (as discussed by Yates and Day Sclater, Chapter 9, this volume)? What racialising dimensions might there be to the statements we found about men's embodied subjectivity (as analysed in Frosh *et al.*, Chapter 3, this volume)? Why have barriers to the take-up of discourses and subject positions not been considered, and what might this tell us about the relationship between privilege, embodiment and masculinities (following ideas introduced by Ahmed, Chapter 5, this volume)?

This chapter also highlights the complexity of men's reactions to contemporary representations of the idealised male body, and how men's responses are not limited to seeing representations in a singular or exclusive way, such as aspirational or pressurising. It shows how men have eight different ways available to them of making sense of these images, and how men can have not a single reaction but a combination of several responses. They can feel stressed, angry and aroused, with these responses combining to constitute a far more complicated and contradictory male subjectivity than analyses have previously suggested. The mobility and fluidity of men's subjectivities or identities now needs to be explored further so that men can be addressed as complex, embodied and relational beings whose ways of interpreting their cultural context, and their consequences, are bound up with a range of different social values and positionings.

Acknowledgements

We are grateful to Pip Austin and Dilys Hughes for their work in transcribing the interviews discussed in this chapter, and to the Critical Psychology Seminar at the University of Western Sydney for helpful comments on the analysis.

References

Berger, J. (1972) *Ways of Seeing*, London: BBC/Pelican.

Chapman, R. and Rutherford, J. (1988) *Male Order: Unwrapping Masculinity*, London: Lawrence & Wishart.

Cohan, S. and Hark, I.R. (1993) *Screening the Male: Exploring Masculinities in Hollywood Cinema*, London and New York: Routledge.

Connell, R. (1987) *Gender and Power: Society, the Person and Sexual Politics*, Cambridge: Polity Press.

—— (1995) *Masculinities*, Cambridge: Polity Press.

Coyle, A. and Morgan-Sykes, C. (1998) 'Troubled men and threatening women: the construction of the crisis in men's mental health', *Feminism and Psychology* 8(3): 262–84.

Creekmuir, C. and Doty, A. (eds) (1993) *Out in Culture: Gay, Lesbian and Queer Essays on Popular Culture*, London: Cassell.

Cultural Trends (1998) London: Policy Studies Institute.

Davis, K. (ed.) (1997) *Embodied Practices: Feminist Perspectives on the Body*, London: Sage.

Edwards, T. (1997) *Men in the Mirror: Men's Fashion, Masculinity and Consumer Society*, London: Cassell.

Frosh, S. (1995) 'Unpacking masculinity: from rationality to fragmentation', in C. Burck and B. Speed (eds) *Gender, Power and Relationships*, London: Routledge.

Gill, R. (2000) *Gender, Media Representations and Cultural Politics*, Cambridge: Polity Press.

—— (forthcoming) 'Mobile positionings in audience responses: not just a matter of gender, "race" and class', *Media, Culture and Society*.

Goldman, R. (1992) *Reading Ads Socially*, London: Routledge.

Hearn, J. and Morgan, D.H. (1990) *Men, Masculinities and Social Theory*, London: Unwin & Hyman.

Hebdige, D. (1979) *Subculture: The Meaning of Style*, London: Methuen.

Henwood, K., Gill, R. and McLean, C. (1999) *Masculinities and the Body: Mapping Men's Psychologies*, report prepared for Unilever.

Hession, C. (1997) 'Men's grooming: the next growth category', *happi*: 57–60.

Jeffords, S. (1994) *Hard Bodies: Hollywood Masculinity in the Reagan Years*, New Brunswick, NJ: Rutgers Unversity Press.

Kimmel, M. (1987) *Changing Men: New Directions on Research on Men and Masculinity*, Newbury Park, CA: Sage.

McQueen, C. (1998) 'A study of the multiple ways in which boys talk about their admission to a regional mental health unit', Unpublished D.Clin.Psy. thesis, University of Wales, Bangor.

McRobbie, A. (1991) *Feminism and Youth Culture: From 'Jackie' to 'Just 17'*, London: Macmillan.

Maslow, A. (1970) *Motivation and Personality*, London: Harper & Row.

Mercer, K. and Julien, I. (1988) 'Race, sexual politics and black masculinity', in R. Chapman and J. Rutherford (eds) *Male Order: Unwrapping Masculinity*, London: Lawrence & Wishart.

Miles, S. (1996) 'The cultural capital of consumption', *Culture and Psychology* 12(3): 139–58.

Miller, D. (ed.) (1995) *Acknowledging Consumption*, London: Routledge.

Moore, S. (1988) 'Here's looking at you kid!', in L. Gamman and M. Marshment (eds) *The Female Gaze: Women as Viewers of Popular Culture*, London: The Women's Press.

Mort, F. (1988) 'Boys own? Masculinity, style and popular culture', in R. Chapman and J. Rutherford (eds) *Male Order: Unwrapping Masculinity*, London: Routledge.

—— (1996) *Cultures of Consumption: Masculinities and Social Space in Late Twentieth Century Britain*, London: Routledge.

Mulvey, L. (1975) 'Visual pleasure and narrative cinema', *Screen* 16(3): 6–18.

Nettleton, S. and Watson, J. (eds) (1998) *The Body in Everyday Life*, London: Routledge.

Nixon, S. (1996) *Hard Looks: Masculinities, Spectatorship and Contemporary Consumption*, London: University College London Press.

Norton, J. (1997) 'Deconstructing the fear of femininity', *Feminism and Psychology* 7(3): 441–7.

Parsi, N. (1997) 'Don't worry Sam, you're not alone: bodybuilding is *so* queer', in P. Moore (ed.) *Building Bodies*, New Brunswick, NJ: Rutgers University Press.

Screen (1992) *The 'Screen' Reader in Sexuality*, London: Routledge.

Seidler, V. (1989) *Rediscovering Masculinity: Reason, Language and Sexuality*, London: Routledge.

—— (1992) *Men, Sex and Relationship: Writings from 'Achilles Heel'*, London: Routledge.

Simpson, M. (1994) *Male Impersonators: Men Performing Masculinity*, London: Cassell.

Thornton, S. (1995) *Club Cultures*, Cambridge: Polity Press.

Ussher, J. (ed.) (1997) *Body Talk: The Material and Discursive Regulation of Sexuality, Madness and Reproduction*, London: Routledge.

White, P. and Gillett, J. (1994) 'Reading the muscular body – a critical decoding of advertisements in *Flex* magazine', *Sociology of Sport Journal* 11(1): 18–39.

Yardley, L. (ed.) (1997) *Material Discourses of Health and Illness*, London: Routledge.

8 Changing youth

An exploration of visual and textual cultural identifications

Harriette Marshall and Anne Woollett

Critical psychologists have turned their attention to the consideration of culture with an agenda that in many respects mirrors the reconfiguration of culture throughout the humanities. Issues of cultural politics and the examination of relationships between culture, power and subjectivity are key to this agenda (hooks, 1991; Mirza, 1997; Said, 1993). A body of research studies now exist which share a concern for understanding culture as structures of shared knowledge, experience, beliefs and meaning, in their subtlety and range of variation, and the ways in which these find public and accessible expression through not only speech, but also music, the arts and other communicative forms (Hannerz, 1992).

Mainstream psychology and culture

Psychologists working in the mainstream have called also for an examination of 'culture' and 'cultural elements' and their influence on individuals (Betancourt and Lopez, 1993; Segall *et al.*, 1998). In attempting to formulate how research might proceed, various definitions of 'culture' have been presented. These range from learned 'designs and ways of life', shared by an identifiable segment of a population (Rohner, 1984), to more detailed formulations which specify 'subjective culture', taken to comprise norms, roles, attitudes, practices and values that are culturally associated (Kagitcibasi, 1997; Triandis, 1995). In these definitions the focus is placed on intrapsychic consistencies (knowledge, beliefs), with less concern for broader contexts within which 'culture' is variously expressed and within which intercultural contacts are increasingly evident.

Mainstream psychological concern with pinning down a definition of culture is in order to make 'culture' amenable to measurement. Varied uses are advocated for cultural measures. These include the assessment of *differences* in culturally informed behaviours and values within a culturally diverse population, including between minority/majority ethnic groupings (Betancourt and Lopez, 1993). Acculturation scales have also been developed, to measure an individual's level of identification with a particular culture (Berry *et al.*, 1986). The preoccupation of mainstream psychologists with cultural *measurement* is with a concern to establish the relationship between particular cultural elements and psychological phenomena. The aim is to inform mainstream psychological theories through the identification of cultural specificities which enable modifications to theory, and/or the confirmation of psychological universalities. Poortinga *et al*. (1987) refer to the investigation of cultural variables in terms of peeling an onion so as to reveal the 'psychic unity of mankind' which they assume lies at the core of culture. (See Lynne Segal, Chapter 2, this volume, on the renewed interest in mainstream psychology in evolutionary theory, viewed as a means of unifying the discipline in its search for universals of human behaviour.)

But the focus on the development of cultural scales and measures, and the rendering of culture in terms of an independent parents variable, implicates and reproduces a static and homogenised conceptualisation of culture. We have criticised the use of acculturation scales elsewhere, including their lack of engagement with the complex interactions and identifications between individuals, and especially those belonging to minority ethnic communities with the broader culture (Woollett *et al*., 1994). In addition, once measured, cultural content is assumed to exert a consistent influence on an individual's behaviour and sense of cultural belonging. Such a conceptualisation veils individuals' diverse and fluid commitments to cultures according to contextual considerations and takes no account of, for example, the intersections of gender and/or socio-economic class with culture (Yuval-Davis, 1997).

A concept much used by cross-cultural psychologists, and related to the association of X culture with X behaviours and values, is that of 'culture clash'. This refers to those individuals who are multiply positioned in terms of identifications and who are assumed to experience conflict, discomfort, cognitive dissonance or stress. 'Culture clash' explanations have been readily used in psychological research on minority ethnic young people, especially young Asian women and men, living in a UK context. But, as Brah (1996) argues, such explanations are problematic, in part because they make assumptions that people belong to either 'Asian' *or* 'British' culture.

Similar notions of 'culture clash' can also be found in mainstream developmental psychological research. Early psychological examples include formulations of adolescent culture as storm and stress, rebellion against parents and a propensity for more reckless and antisocial behaviour (Hall, 1904), through to more recent ideas that a young person's desire for greater independence will create conflict situations with parents (Laursen *et al*., 1998). These explanations prevail despite a growing body of research findings which suggest that intergenerational conflict has been overstated (Arnett, 1999). But Arnett's caution against over-generalisations of shared adolescent characteristics uses broad distinctions between 'traditional' and 'western' cultures, associating individualistic values with the latter, to suggest that young people's conflict with their parents is more likely to be found in western cultures. In so doing he equates particular values (individualism) with broad cultural groups (western), as criticised above. His argument produces the familiar prediction that young people from non-western cultures living in a western culture will be especially susceptible to intergenerational conflict. However, recent research is inconsistent. Some report that young Asian women and men living in the UK show no greater tensions with parents than do their white peers (Brah,

1996). What is interesting about the formulations of Hall, Laursen *et al.* and Arnett is that in each case the focus is on shared cultural values, on the one hand within ethnic group, on the other within generation.

Reconfiguring culture

If we move from mainstream psychological treatments of culture and turn instead to analyses developed in critical psychology, culture can be conceptualised as complex, relational and diverse: inclusive of 'a collection of customs and identifications that structure personal and community histories, as sometimes also structured by racism' (Burman *et al.*, 1998: 233). This definition of culture resembles that adopted by Frosh and his co-writers (Chapter 3, this volume). It draws attention to relations of power between cultures as shaping subjectivity, a consideration missing from mainstream psychological theories and research on culture.

Other researchers have argued for the need to contextualise culture with reference to processes of globalisation. They argue that growing intercultural contacts through, for example, migrations, pop culture, multinational corporations, the internet and new technologies have opened up the potential for cultural interchange (Hermans and Kempen, 1998). Given these social transformations, ideas about self-contained and easily differentiated cultures (such as 'western' and 'non-western') seem outdated. Instead, such changes call for conceptualisations of sociocultural identities and identifications as plural. Individuals' interaction with values and views associated with cultural groupings can then be seen as dynamic, capable of adapting to novel perspectives and ideas, and producing new and hybrid identities (Hall, 1989).

Hybrid identities, taken as emanating from globalisation, can be conceptualised in different ways, including as mixtures or fusions, and are themselves matters of debate. Some writers have emphasised fusions of cultures as creative and enabling new identities. This is Salman Rushdie's position in his characterisation of *The Satanic Verses* as celebrating 'hybridity, impurity, intermingling, the transformation that comes of new and unexpected combinations of human beings, cultures, ideas, politics, movies, songs. It rejoices in mongrelization and fears the absolutism of the Pure' (Rushdie, 1991: 394). Conversely, others take up Rushdie's terms of hybridity as 'impurity' and 'mongrelization' to argue its dangers and to call for a return to traditional cultural coherence. Others advance more cautious criticisms that to celebrate hybridity is to underestimate the power relations at stake in cultural differences (hooks, 1991).

Visual culture

The relation of cultural identifications to globalisation processes and technological advances should also draw attention to the recent and rapid growth of *visual* culture. Visual culture is argued to be a site of social interaction, where culture and sexual, gender and racialised identities are constructed, debated, contested and transformed (Mizoeff, 1998). Developing psychological treatments of culture as delineated above which permit the exploration of broad contextual considerations of gender, race and class necessitates the use of methods which are sensitive to such visual expressions of hybrid identifications. In addition, engaging with visual culture as central to identity construction calls for interdisciplinary methods that enable consideration of image making and cultural reception. Yet psychological engagement with the visual remains relatively rare even within recent feminist and critical research which places an emphasis on talk and texts, although interest in the visual is growing. (See Griffin's arguments for a broader range of methods (Chapter 1), and Gill *et al.* (Chapter 7, this volume).) In the introduction to a recent special issue on innovative methods in the *Psychology of Women Quarterly*, 'the visual as data' was included, with a mention of the uses of photography, drawings and films for feminist enquiry (Gergen *et al.*, 1999). The history of methods in psychology differs from that of disciplines such as anthropology where the use of ethnographic techniques is long-standing and where film and photography have been central in charting the organisation and practices of diverse cultural communities. However, methods which map the visual are a matter for debate (Mulvey, 1989), for reasons which resonate with feminist psychological discussions around representing the 'Other' (Wilkinson and Kitzinger, 1996). 'Looking' as 'reading' can be understood as a form of power as evidenced in analyses of art, film and photography where the 'capturing' of images of 'Other' cultures has centred around their representation as exotic and/or primitive, hence reiterating their constitution as different and 'Other' (Alcoff, 1991; Clifford and Marcus, 1986; Mercer, 1994).

In recent years research on youth has turned to issues of visual representation. Cohen (1997) reports action research which used stills photography because of its accessibility, low cost and technological simplicity. Cohen discusses the familiarity of photography as a popular form of *self*-representational and documentational cultural practice, as evidenced by long-standing widespread use of family albums and holiday snapshots. Archer (1998) reports her use of photographic diaries as a means of exploring young British Muslim women's identifications as multiple and fluid. She highlights their usefulness in permitting examination of the uses of discursive practices *and* visual symbols. The prevalence of camcorders means that this is also an increasingly familiar technology, easy to handle, and hence the use of video diaries in recent research projects concerned with issues of identifications (Holliday, 1999; Walkerdine, 1998). Programmes such as *Video Nation* and *Video Diaries*, broadcast on UK national television, have made familiar a genre whereby a person tells their story to the video camera. Video diaries have been hailed as a democratic methodology, in part because of their ready public access but also because representational issues reside largely with the diarist rather than being professionally mediated through, for example, voice-over narration. Similarly, when a video diary is used as a social scientific tool, the agenda for its content and contextualisation lies largely with participants. For these reasons, and in line with the work of researchers cited above, we take the visual as central to the representation of culture and cultural identifications.

Changing youth: the research project

In a project in progress, 'Changing youth', concerned with young people's accounts of various transitions to adulthood, we opted, as the three project leaders (Harriette Marshall, Anne Woollett and Helen Malson),[1] to use video diaries alongside other qualitative methods (interviews, written diaries) in working with (to date) fifteen young women and men from diverse backgrounds in terms of ethnicity, age (between 15 and 19 years old) and sexuality, all living in the UK, and predominantly in urban environments. The project is set up so that we have a team of research assistants (young women and men in their twenties, from diverse backgrounds), with each research assistant working with a research participant over a number of months. The research process entails several meetings with each participant, during which they are interviewed (six to eight interviews with each participant) and produce a video diary. This process allows for more exploration of complexity, variation and contradiction in views, values and identifications than permitted in a single interaction. Each participant chooses where (s)he wishes the interviews and video diary production to take place. To date, all research meetings have been conducted outside educational environments, sometimes in the participant's home, at other times in the researcher's home and occasionally in local meeting places such as cafés. Video diaries enable the examination of presentations of identities in talk, sound *and* image, as embodied through dress and physical appearance, and selves as 'distributed', displayed through, for example, relations with others, belongings and bedroom decoration.

Each participant works with their researcher to make a video diary lasting between forty-five minutes and an hour and a half. Participants are asked to consider in advance questions which include: How shall I tell a story about myself and my life? How can I represent myself and my story visually? What shall I include on the video in terms of things that make me what I am today? Participants are informed that if they find it useful, they can divide the filming into different 'scenes' and switch off the camera between scenes, to facilitate the display of different aspects of their lives.

We view the video diaries as socially constructed by participants, synthesised from familiar cultural resources, including cultural heuristics, that is, conventional and available biographical cultural forms (Gergen, 1993). In line with discursive analyses we consider both speech and image as text, not as simply reflective of the individual's identities and simply another route to intrapsychic realities (Parker and the Bolton Discourse Network, 1999). We take the video diaries as produced for particular purposes, including in the knowledge that they will be viewed and analysed by us as researchers and potentially made more public, through their presentation at conferences and in written publications.

In the analysis that follows we present material from the video diary made by one participant, Kavita, and some interview extracts. Kavita was the first participant to complete the project, including taking part in seven interviews (which have been fully transcribed) and making a video diary. She is 15 years old and introduces herself as a young Indian, Hindu woman living in Birmingham. Our reading of Kavita's video diary focuses on how she narrates issues of culture, 'race' and gender and contextualises various cultural identifications. We examine the organisation of Kavita's self-representational text, looking at spoken and visual elements included in the diary, and their interrelationships. We consider ways in which the video diary might be 'read'. In giving attention to alternative potential readings we also acknowledge our own part in the research process, presenting an analysis informed by our positions as researchers and academics, and our particular feminist and critical concerns. In this chapter the narrative of Kavita's video diary is structured by our interests in how her representation of issues of culture and cultural identifications relate to and pose challenges to mainstream psychological theorising.

Kavita's video diary

Kavita's diary includes numerous and varied presentations of her identifications with Indian, English, Hindu and youth culture. One section focuses on her clothes and appearance, which she presents by means of opening her wardrobe doors to the camera. She displays some of her favourite clothes, which include several T-shirts decorated with representations of Hindu gods.

I love tops with Hindu gods on them. I bought this top because no one else has it and you can't get any other clothes that show that, it [the T-shirt] shows what I am, it shows that I'm a Hindu. I like wearing it because I'm proud of being a Hindu. Even if it doesn't show that I'm Hindu it shows I'm influenced by India, or South Asia.

For Kavita, wearing her Hindu T-shirts signifies her identification with a Hindu collectivity. She discusses and puts on her favourite om pendant, again explaining that 'I wear this to show, so that people can see that I'm proud of being Hindu, I wear this quite a lot, a big fat thing round my neck. I'd wear this to school if they'd let me.'

In line with Yuval Davis's arguments, Kavita's diary at this point could be read as her embodied Hindu identification (Yuval Davis, 1997). Her Hindu identification extends beyond the body to the decor of her bedroom, as she explains when she displays the gold om decorations painted on her wardrobe door:

This is showing my Hindu culture, these are some oms which I've painted on to my wardrobe. I'm going to paint more on so they cover the whole wardrobe. You can see it's gold. Om represents, it's the symbol of Hinduism, it represents God. I've put lots of things that show my Hindu culture, stuff that affects me.

Simultaneous with Kavita's articulation of Hindu identification are alternative, unspoken cultural symbols. While Kavita's spoken narrative conjoins with her visual display of Hindu T-shirts and om pendant, she makes no mention of wearing jeans, a now somewhat classic symbol of US and long-term transnational marker of youth culture. In addition, as Kavita shows the viewer the oms on her wardrobe door, Madonna's 'Ray of Light' is playing in the background. There are three points of conceptual and methodological interest here. First, discursive analysts of written texts have argued the importance of using methods of data collection which do not restrict participants' responses to researchers' pre-existing concerns and which allow variation to emerge. Kavita's expression of identity by means of varied referents is evident here, including through music (although the use of music was unanticipated by us as researchers and not included in our video diary guidelines).

Second, these referents are simultaneously presented, in spoken, visual and music form, in Kavita's spoken narrative and display of Hindu cultural referents (oms/T-shirt), and her playing and display of an unspoken US culture (jeans, the pop diva Madonna). This unspokenness is unsurprising given the unmarked nature of dominant culture (Wong, 1994). While the simultaneity of the referents is particularly obvious in the video diary, it is less noticeable in the interviews, in which Kavita discusses frequently and in depth her identifications with Hindu and Indian culture but less often those with British culture. If we had relied on interviews in our research project they might have resulted in conclusions drawn from presence rather than absence; for example, that Kavita's identifications lie predominantly with Hindu and Indian culture. However, the variation in cultural identifications discussed above complicates conceptualisations of uni-cultural identification. Using methods which engage with the visual in exploring culture can therefore, as in this case, both support arguments for critical psychologists to broaden the range of methods they use, and serve as a critique of mainstream psychologists' reliance on scales and measures and their failure to consider culture and cultural identifications as subtly and variously expressed (Hannerz, 1992).

Third, elsewhere in the interviews Kavita 'justifies her love' of Madonna. She argues her approval of Madonna's recent spiritual awakening, her turn to alternative religion and understanding of Hinduism. Kavita's text here could be read as challenging notions that particular symbols can be mapped simply on to culture in a one-to-one fashion (Madonna = US icon) and taken as unambiguous markers of identifications. Instead, Kavita's text could be taken as an illustration of cultural referents' potential to be reconfigured. The point can be made in reverse with regard to clothing. Kavita articulates wearing Hindu T-shirts as being a message about Hinduism and Indian influences on her identity. However, the fashion industry has deemed clothing with eastern symbols of the Buddha and Chinese dragons as well as Hindu gods as in vogue, certainly in the UK in the late 1990s, hence appropriating 'eastern' images for a western market.

Multiple identifications can be read throughout Kavita's diary and seem more adequate than 'either/or' formulations of identity, as argued by psychologists critical of mainstream treatments of culture (Hermans and Kempen, 1998). Symbols that might be read as western, eastern, Indian, Hindu, English, European, black British, Mexican, Indian-American

can be read in Kavita's 'this is me', 'this is cool', 'I love this' presentation of Disney clothes and cartoons, GAP sweatshirt, photograph of Phoebe from *Friends*, Talvin Singh and Skunk Anansie cassettes, Chief White Cloud book, poster and poem, *Sugar Club Cookbook* and account of the six-course Mediterranean meal she cooked for her mother's birthday.

In terms of cultural identifications Kavita shows no single, consistent pattern. It might be possible to read her display of multiple identifications as evidence of

intrapsychic conflicts or confusion. Yet Kavita presents as meaningful and valuable her plural and changing selves, contextually located in her past, present and future lives. These formulations of identity are perhaps most vividly displayed in Kavita's painting in progress.

Kavita frames her presentation of her painting with reference to Frida Kahlo's painting *The Two Fridas* (1939), depicting her different selves. Hall's (1997) argument that cultural innovation is created intertextually through the accumulation of images, so that one image refers to another, is useful here in considering Kavita's identity constructions. Kavita's familiarity with various symbols is displayed in her use of them to narrate her present and future selves:

> She [Kahlo] did a picture like this showing the two sides of her. The side which is done in HB pencil, that's me and that's the English flag, showing my side now in the present and the candle is burning, representing that my life is burning this side. There's a Tudor rose which represents my school and a brain which represents the intellectual side and showing it's more intellectual than the other side which is the heart, the other side. That's a coffin to show how death this side doesn't just end. I don't know what to show on this side to show it's not ending, but it's going to carry on. The Nazi symbol is to show the conflicts on this side. Well this was going to be a split personality, but this, it's not me, but it's trying to be me, that's what I'm trying to be. The candle isn't lit, to show that my life isn't lit on this side. This side is India, it's more loving – the Indian flag is this side as hope.

The complexity and different meanings of Kavita's text are well illustrated here. Her spoken narrative references, her use of the Union Jack and Indian flag as national symbols, enable a reading of selves as nationally located. Kavita builds in another contrast between present and future selves, a temporal dimension, by means of a burning and an as yet unlit candle. Her depiction of her intellect and feelings – a brain and a heart – constitutes further contrast. These symbols are not unambiguous and the potential for other readings remains open. Although Kavita refers to her use of the Nazi symbol in her painting, this can be read as an Indian symbol reclaimed to signify goodwill. Her use of brain/heart to symbolise rationality/emotionality which she associates with west and non-west can be read as reiterating imperialist discourses used to justify the west's 'civilisation' of the primitive. The coffin as a symbol of death is not universal, but positions Kavita's visual self-construction as western. We include this extract partly to illustrate the possibility of different readings of Kavita's video diary. The text could be taken to argue the usefulness of conceptualisations of hybrid cultural identifications, of multiple identities/selves. Alternatively, it could be read as positioned in the west, shaped by Britain's colonial history.

Kavita herself construes her engagement with a complex of cultural iden-tifications as unproblematic, as in her account of her identification with the cultural fusion of Talvin Singh's music:

> I love this because it's Indian and it's western and I just love it and it's really cool and it's a mixture of my cultures and just cool. . . . The English side of me and the Indian side of me, and it's kind of both of them together and plus I love drum and bass music.

This reading strongly distinguishes her narrative from the 'equality' discourse dominating young white US women's talk (Fine *et al.*, Chapter 4, this volume) or the anxious exoticising of African-Caribbean Otherness expressed by young white British men (Frosh *et al.*, Chapter 3, this volume). Here, as elsewhere in her narrative, Kavita positions herself as liberal, open and appreciative of different cultures. Her use of discourses of multiculturalism could be taken as a 'pick-

and-mix' rendering of culture: a carnival of cultural diversity, but lacking in contextualised analyses of power relations between differ-ent cultural groupings. However, and more importantly, Kavita's identifications as Indian and Hindu are also contextualised in a UK and Birmingham context in relation to racism. This can be read from her inclusion in her painting of the Nazi swastika (see the photograph on the facing page) – part of her present, UK-located self – 'to show the conflict'. Elsewhere she relates being subjected to and resisting friends' racist comments, 'fighting back' as a member of a minority cultural grouping within dominant British culture. Kavita's formulations of culture and cultural identifications as resistant to racist discourses is narrated, for instance, with reference to her drawing of a Ku Klux Klan member:

> Basically this is a picture of a person from the Ku Klux Klan. I'll tell you what it's going to be. I'm trying to get an angry effect by scribble and then build up more texture. Then I'm going to do bars and blood running down. I need to do the sign better and I'm going to do HATE written across here. The message is that things like the Ku Klux Klan just disgust me. . . . It's what I'm about.

Kavita's representation of herself as Indian is from a position of belonging to an ethnic minority community subjected to racism. Her self-construal as Indian and Hindu yet as particular to Britain can also be read from her narrative of India and classical Indian music in nostalgic and romanticised terms as an imagined 'home'. For example, she contrasts classical Indian music, as 'true' India, with Bhangra, which 'wasn't there before', created in a UK context and lacking 'roots':

> I love classical Indian music because this is sort of like India, this is the roots of India . . . since like Krishna was roaming the land, that is really cool. I mean there is Indian music like Bhangra, but that wasn't there before. This is true roots of India.

Kavita's narrative and positioning of herself as living in the UK is also illustrated in her account of her involvement in various Birmingham-based youth activities. These include her drama group, a 'Balaji youth group' and Hindu youth camp where she attended a lecture from a swami 'who talks about Hindu position and state *in Great Britain*' and who 'relates to the youth *of Britain*' (emphases added). Here, the intersection of Hindu with youth culture is manifest.

Elsewhere, though, Kavita articulates an identification with youth culture that shares values of independence and 'openness' and is able to transcend cultural difference. In this respect Kavita's narrative can be read as in line with Gilroy's

(1993) arguments of youth cultures as often constituting sites for contesting nationalism and racial exclusivity. In her display of photographs of her friends pinned around her mirror, Kavita makes explicit their diverse cultural backgrounds.

Kavita renders youth as sharing values of cultural exchange again in her narrative of 'a get-together', 'one massive party' held in Birmingham for 'all the people in the grammar schools'. The party is narrated as 'wicked', 'really fun' and 'really cool', where 'everybody was dancing':

> Everybody, well loads of my friends came back to my house that night and we just stayed up all night. . . . And we were chatting, about, everything, just everything, about school friends, and the thing is, it was really cool, because it wasn't just like, one group of friends, it was like a few, from all the different types of groups.

The party can be read as an instance of youthful intercultural contact and communication across difference, although notable in the narrative here is a more specific grouping of 'youth', comprising 'all' Birmingham grammar school pupils. Of interest here, and related to our critique of psychological assumptions that such 'liberal' youth cultural values will most likely result in an intergenerational 'clash', is that Kavita accounts for her 'open' views by reference to her mother's influence:

> She's [mother] so open about everything. She's told me everything about sex and drugs and everything which I'm really happy about. . . . She's separated from my dad, and the fact that she's an Asian woman who's separated, that's quite a big thing.

So while Kavita's account could be read as endorsing 'youth culture' as progressive, contesting 'traditional' prejudices, she also construes these values as shaped by and in accord with those of her mother. In this respect, and by making reference to her parents as separated, Kavita directs attention to diversity within culture, both in 'youth' and in 'Asian' culture.

Conclusion

We have used extracts from a video diary to argue the usefulness of conceiving identifications as multiple, hybrid and constructed in relation to particular socio-historical, national and local circumstances. In turning attention to elements of visual culture and their relationships with spoken elements of self-representation, we have argued the complexity of culture and cultural identifications. We have also considered the prevalence in Kavita's video diary of illustrations of cultural interchange in spoken narrative and in visual display. Video diaries open up possibilities for exploring culture and cultural identifications as variably expressed, and cultural referents as changeable and affording the potential for innovation. They problematise notions that culture is a variable that is similarly experienced by all those designated as belonging to that culture.

Video diaries enable considerable flexibility in self-representation. Yet the requirement to make a diary implicates a particular narrative genre – one where the individual is made central. In addition, diary conventions are perhaps more likely to encourage coherence than fragmentation of self-representations. The interviews with Kavita, which direct attention at specific contextual considerations

– her identifications, values and investments at school, at home, her family and friends – show more disruptions and tensions than her video diary (Marshall *et al.*, 1999).

Working with video diaries, and engaging not only with issues of image making but also image analysis and reception, inevitably involves us in debates around representation, including issues of representational power relations between researcher and research participant. Our analysis of Kavita's diary has transformed it so as to highlight aspects of the representation of culture and cultural identifications for the purposes of this chapter. Our reproduction of certain images entailed a repositioning of images separated from the broader video diary narrative. We have also presented readings of the diary, in parallel to Kavita's narrative, to argue against the idea that cultural referents present a simple message about identity, acculturation or group membership. We share this research agenda with Archer (1998), Cohen (1997), Holliday (1999) and Walkerdine (1998), whose research with visual cultural methods stresses their emancipatory potential. However, by opening up previously unattended issues for investigation and arguing their potential for helping us rethink psychological treatments of culture, we have also pointed to visual texts as ambiguous. As Archer (1998) argues in relation to photographic diaries, there is no guarantee that viewers will read or see the diaries as do the image makers. This point is also applicable to mainstream psychologists viewing video diaries like Kavita's, or reading analyses presented by psychologists like us who are using the diaries to pose challenges to traditional conceptualisations of culture. The always existing possibility of alternative regressive readings of text is one of many problems in attempting to reconfigure culture in academic psychological theorising as a form of sociopolitical action.

Acknowledgement

We would like to acknowledge Aradhana Saxena Anand as the research assistant who conducted all interviews and worked with Kavita in producing the video diary discussed in this chapter.

Note

1   The three project leaders for the research project 'Changing youth' are Harriette Marshall, Staffordshire University, Anne Woollett, University of East London, and Helen Malson, previously at the University of East London and now at the University of Western Sydney, Nepean. The project has received funding from Staffordshire University and the University of East London.

References

Alcoff, L. (1991) 'The problem of speaking for others', *Cultural Critique* Winter: 5–32.

Archer, L. (1998) 'Constructing identities: British-Muslim young women's photographic diaries', paper presented at the British Psychological Society Conference, Brighton.

Arnett, J.J. (1999) 'Adolescent storm and stress, reconsidered', *American Psychologist* 54(5): 317–26.

Berry, J., Trimble, J. and Olmedo, E. (1986) 'Assessment of acculturation', in W. Lonner and J. Berry (eds) *Field Methods in Cross-cultural Research*, Newbury Park, CA: Sage.

Betancourt, H. and Lopez, S.R. (1993) 'The study of culture, ethnicity and race in American psychology', *American Psychologist* 48(6): 629–39.

Brah, A. (1996) *Cartographies of Diaspora: Contesting Identities*, London: Routledge.

Burman, E., Gowrisunkur, J. and Sangha, K. (1998) 'Conceptualising cultural and gendered identities in psychological therapies', *European Journal of Psychotherapy, Counselling and Health* 1(2): 231–56.

Clifford, J. and Marcus, G.E. (1986) *Writing Culture: The Politics and Poetics of Ethnography*, Berkeley, CA: University of California Press.

Cohen, P. (1997) *Rethinking the Youth Question, Education, Labour and Cultural Studies*, London: Macmillan.

Gergen, M. (1993) 'The social construction of personal histories', in T.R. Sarbin and J.I. Kitsuse (eds) *Constructing the Social*, London: Sage.

Gergen, M., Chrisler, J. and LoCicero, A. (1999) 'Innovative methods: resources for research, publishing and teaching', *Psychology of Women Quarterly* 23: 431–56.

Gilroy, P. (1993) 'Between Afro-centrism and Eurocentrism: youth culture and the problem of hybridity', *Young: Nordic Journal of Youth Research* 1, 2 May.

Hall, G.S. (1904) 'Adolescence: its psychology and its relation to physiology', in *Anthropology, Sociology, Sex, Crime, Religion and Education*, New York: D. Appleton.

Hall, S. (1989) *New Ethnicities*, ICA Documents 7, Black Film, Black Cinema.

—— (1997) 'The spectacle of the "Other"', in S. Hall (ed.) *Representation: Cultural Representations and Signifying Practices*, London: Sage.

Hannerz, U. (1992) *Cultural Complexity: Studies in the Social Organization of Meaning*, New York: Greenwood Press.

Hermans, H. and Kempen, H. (1998) 'Moving culture: the perilous problems of cultural dichotomies in a globalizing society', *American Psychologist* 53(10): 1111–20.

Holliday, R. (1999) 'The comfort of identity', *Sexualities* 2(4): 495–75.

hooks, B. (1991) *Yearning: Race, Gender and Cultural Politics*, London: Turnaround.

Kagitcibasi, C. (1997) 'Individualism and collectivism', in J. Berry, M.H. Segall and C. Kagitcibasi (eds) *Handbook of Cross-cultural Psychology: Social Behavior and Applications*, Needham Heights, MA: Allyn & Bacon.

Laursen, B., Coy, K.C. and Collins, W.A. (1998) 'Reconsidering changes in parent–child conflict across adolescence: a meta-analysis', *Child Development* 69: 817–32.

Marshall, H., Stenner, P. and Lee, H. (1999) 'Young people's accounts of personal relationships in a multi-cultural East London environment: questions of community, diversity and inequality', *Journal of Community and Applied Social Psychology* 9: 155–71.

Mercer, K. (1994) *Welcome to the Jungle*, London: Routledge.

Mirza, H.S. (1997) *Black British Feminism*, London: Routledge.

Mizoeff, N. (1998) 'What is visual culture?', in N. Mizoeff (ed.) *The Visual Culture Reader*, London: Routledge.

Mulvey, L. (1989) *Visual and Other Pleasures*, Bloomington: Indiana University Press.

Parker, I. and the Bolton Discourse Network (1999) *Critical Textwork: An Introduction to Varieties of Discourse and Analysis*, Buckingham: Open University Press.

Poortinga, Y.H., van de Vijver, F.L.R., Joe, R. and Van de Koppel, J. (1987) 'Peeling the onion called culture: a synopsis', in C. Kagitcibasi (ed.) *Growth and Progress in Cross-cultural Psychology*, Lisse, Netherlands: Swets & Zeitlinger.

Rohner, R. P. (1984) 'Toward a conception of culture for cross-cultural psychology', *Journal of Cross Cultural Psychology* 15: 111–38.

Rushdie, S. (1991) *Imagined Homelands*, London: Granta Books.

Said, E. (1993) *Culture and Imperialism*, London: Chatto & Windus.

Segall, M., Lonner, W. and Berry, J. (1998) 'Cross-cultural psychology as a scholarly discipline: on the flowering of culture in behavioral research', *American Psychologist* 53(10): 1101–10.

Triandis, H. (1995) *Individualism and Collectivism*, Boulder, CO: Westview Press.

Walkerdine, V. (1997) *Girls, Girls, Girls*, Video diaries Channel 4.

Wilkinson, S. and Kitzinger, C. (eds) (1996) 'Representing the Other', special feature, *Feminism and Psychology* 6(1 and 2).

Wong, L.M. (1994) Dis(s)-secting and dis(s)-closing 'Whiteness', *Feminism and Psychology* 4(1): 133–54.

Woollett, A., Marshall, H., Nicolson, P. and Dosanjh, N. (1994) 'Asian women's ethnic identity: the impact of gender and context in the accounts of women bringing up children in East London', *Feminism and Psychology* 4(1): 119–32.

Yuval-Davis, N. (1997) *Gender and Nation*, London: Sage.

Part IV

Culture and the emotions

Introduction

Cultural formations are highly meaningful to us, and it is only in psychology that their individual significance is taken into account, but cultural psychologists have tended to consign – or elevate – the emotional resonances of culture to biology. In evolutionary psychology, for instance, if we feel strongly about a certain cultural practice or representation, there is bound to be a reproductive advantage in being so invested. In Part IV the emotional meanings of culture, and the ways in which emotions themselves are culturally shaped, are explored in a less reductive and simplifying way. And while the contributors are interested in the way emotions imbue and drive culture, they are also concerned with how emotions inhabit, yet escape, the cultural matrix.

In Chapter 9, which makes an apt transition from Part III, 'Culture and representations', Candy Yates and Shelley Day Sclater argue that media narratives can be seen as Winnicottian 'transitional phenomena', in which subjectivities are formed, re-formed and transformed. Some media narratives allow the potential of transitionality to be realised, however, while some are too closed and singular to do so. 'Culture, psychology and transitional space' explores recent media representations of genetically modified (GM) foods, divided between idealised stories of scientific progress and demonising accounts of science as horrific and monstrous, and dealing in the highly emotionally salient material that 'food' always is. Yates and Day Sclater argue that in general, these polarised, closed representations do not permit transitional spaces to open up, though there are moments when they can and might.

Rabia Malik, in 'Culture and emotions: depression among Pakistanis', is interested in another, less universal aspect of the relationship between culture and the emotions: the extent to which we live emotions through culture. After a detailed analysis of the limitations of comparative psychological approaches to the emotions, and the value of a social-constructionist approach, she draws on her interview study with 120 indigenous and British Pakistanis about 'distress' to point up problems with psychological and psychiatric notions of depression, and the social construction of that category. She shows the resilience of some South Asian cultural formations; even interviewees who had lived most of their lives in Britain still conceptualised mental health in holistic, relational and religious frameworks derived from Hindu and Muslim health belief systems, and understood distress as part of culture, not the antithesis of it. This is not, though, the chapter emphasises, an excuse to relativise distress into a 'cultural' matter about which nothing need be done if its definition and expression are not congruent with those of the dominant culture.

Extending this concern with a social constructionism that allows for some limited universalism, Erika Apfelbaum examines the disturbing conditions of uprootedness which now mark most people's cultural lives, and focuses on the extreme case of genocide to emphasise that however inevitable the sense of loss, exile and unfamiliarity, it remains vital at the same time to retain narratives of cultural filiation and affiliation. In 'The impact of culture in the face of genocide: struggling between a silenced home culture and a foreign host culture', she argues that genocides go well beyond their primary goal of physically annihilating a social group in its entirety; ultimately, they also eradicate the very cultural roots by which this group has historically established and maintained its identity. Being a 'survivor' (or child of a survivor) of such a disaster thus means becoming a 'cultural orphan', violently separated from one culture now gone and silenced, who must attempt an existence and a reconstruction of identity on the sole basis of the 'host' culture; there is often no space in the latter to recapture the 'lost' roots. The chapter considers such extreme situations as test cases with which to begin to explore the way in which social identity is intimately embedded with culture. It draws on first-person narratives and literary sources to find parallels between data from genocide 'survivors', stories from other uprooted identities (for example, of exile), and accounts of struggles for entitlement of, for instance, women in leadership positions 'strangers in a strange land'.

9 Culture, psychology and transitional space

Candida Yates and Shelley Day Sclater

> If we look at our lives we shall probably find that we spend most of our time neither in behaviour nor in contemplation, but somewhere else. I ask: where?
>
> (Winnicott, 1971: 105)

Introduction

A recurrent theme in debates about the nature of contemporary culture is its ambivalent character. On the one hand, there are new possibilities for self-expression, and on the other, new risks to negotiate and a heightened potential for disappointment and confusion in all spheres of life (Bauman, 1990; Berman, 1983; Craib, 1994; Elliott, 1996; Frosh, 1991; Giddens, 1991; Nava and O'Shea, 1996). As cultural theorists have documented, today's uncertainties are related to a broader set of technological, social and political transformations associated with global capitalism and consumer culture (Featherstone, 1991; Foster, 1987; Giddens, 1991) and also to the loss of faith in the traditional 'grand narratives' and values associated with the Enlightenment and the old western patriarchal moral order (Lyotard, 1984).

Whether this changing cultural environment provides positive opportunities for new ways of being, and creative spaces for personal, political and social transformation, has been the subject of much debate in the social sciences (see, for example, Elliott, 1996; Elliott and Frosh, 1995; Minsky, 1998; Richards, 1989). Some in the sociological tradition of Max Weber and, later, the Frankfurt School (Adorno and Horkheimer, 1977) argued that the contemporary uncertainties engender a defensive cultural and psychological response, characterised by a fear of change, the wish for greater mastery over the unknown, and increased rationalisation in all spheres of life (Craib, 1994; Lasch, 1991). A more optimistic perspective, however, also prevails; it is argued that the paradoxical nature of contemporary culture facilitates new spaces for reflexive subjectivities, and ways of being that respond creatively to change and uncertainty (Berman, 1983; Elliott, 1996; Giddens, 1991, 1992; Nava and O'Shea, 1996).[1]

In this chapter[2] we explore the possibilities for different modes of subjectivity in the contemporary cultural setting of late modernity. The ongoing debate over genetically modified (GM) crops provides the focus for our discussion. The response to GM foods in the popular media (around which popular debate has polarised) provides a useful case study to examine the cultural and psychological response to broader transformations in the social sphere, and the fears engendered by the perceived risks of the late twentieth century (Beck, 1992; Giddens, 1991, 1999). We examine media narratives in which particular images of GM foods have been produced, and we use the psychoanalytic ideas of Donald Winnicott to discuss the psychological constellations implied by these narrative forms.[3] This chapter illustrates the ways in which culture and psychology interact, and develops a model, based on psychoanalysis, that challenges the conceptual fixities and dualities of more traditional psychology.

The cultural psyche

Identities are not constructed in a cultural vacuum, but rather are fashioned within the historically specific discourses and practices of everyday life (see Griffin, Chapter 1, this volume; also Burman, 1984; Henriques *et al.*, 1998; Parker, 1992). Following others working in the field of psycho-cultural theory (Craib, 1994; Elliott, 1996; Frosh, 1991; Minsky, 1998), it can be said that subjectivities and meanings are always in process, shaped in ongoing relationships of psyche and culture, between the inner and the outer worlds, and in the sphere of intersubjective relationships. Psychoanalytic theory provides a rich language for exploring the complexities of subjectivity and its relationship to culture because it also allows space for the contradictions and paradoxes that arise in relation to unconscious psychic processes that orthodox psychological accounts of subjectivity ignore (Henriques *et al.*, 1998).

The ideas of psychoanalyst Donald Winnicott (1965, 1971) are useful because they are able to capture the dialectic nature of subjectivity and cultural experience. Winnicott's ideas may be criticised for his universalising assumptions regarding the relationship between mother and child (see Malik, Chapter 10, this volume; Riley, 1983). But, as various authors have shown (Day Sclater, 1998; Elliott, 1996; Giddens, 1991; Phillips, 1988, 1995; Wieland, 1996), it is possible to apply his ideas to produce a model of subjectivity that escapes the reductive traps of an assumed biological basis (for example, as described by Segal, Chapter 2, this volume). Winnicott's ideas are useful because of the emphasis he placed on the importance of the wider environment and the subtlety with which he analysed its complex role in the construction of the relational self. He provides a paradoxical model of subjectivity, one that de-centres the traditional distinction between outer reality and the inner world (Winnicott, 1971; see also Phillips, 1988; Richards, 1996). He describes the ways in which social and psychological modes of experience continually intersect to produce what he calls the third area: a 'potential' or 'transitional space'. Here, meanings are continually created and re-created to produce our experience of cultural life and our sense of self. Winnicott (1965, 1971) argues that, given a 'good enough' environment, the dialectical interplay of social and psychic forces has an ongoing developmental role in the construction of self. For Winnicott, subjectivity is deeply imbued with cultural experience, just as our cultural experiences reflect our anxieties and desires.

Winnicott, cultural experience and the paradoxical self

Winnicott (1971: 99) emphasises the 'experience' of culture; he acknowledges the importance of cultural traditions but also pays attention to the interaction of subject and object in the continual creative production of experience, self and meaning.[4] We might say that Winnicott's view of the subject-in-culture is that of a *psychosocial process* in which subjectivities are inevitably bound into the matrices of cultural experience.

Winnicott (1951, 1971) explicitly links his description of cultural experience in adult life to the 'transitional phenomena' of infancy and to the space that emerges between the infant and the mother for play. He argues that the psychic significance of this space, in which subjectivity is constituted and reconstituted, remains throughout our lives. A central theme in Winnicott's work about our capacity for creative cultural experience is the need for a reliable 'facilitating' environment for the developing infant (1960, 1965). The child's first environment is its mother, and the imaginary spaces for play that are created form the crucial context in which the child's subjective identity is brought into being (1971: 47). Transitional phenomena are related to the progressive loss of infantile omnipotence and the gradual discovery of the independent existence of the external 'not-me' world.

At first the infant's experience is one of omnipotence; objects are subjectively rather than objectively perceived, and the mother is experienced as a part of the baby's own omnipotent orbit. In the transitional phase, however, the mother and the outside world increasingly take on an independent existence (Winnicott, 1971). Winnicott postulated a paradoxical state in which the infant's omnipotence coexisted with a developing sense of dependence upon the external environment. The central paradox is that the infant experiences the illusion of having created the maternal object even though she was already there waiting to be discovered. This illusory and creative process becomes the source of the infant's play and the basis of its potential for cultural experience.

Essential to this process of differentiation are what Winnicott called the 'transitional phenomena'; they mitigate the excessive anxiety that might otherwise accompany the dawning realisation of one's own separateness from the mother. Winnicott described the infant's relationship to a transitional object (for example, a treasured teddy bear or a piece of cloth) as playing a key function in building up trust in the environment and providing a bridging link to the material outside world. Gradually, as the infant separates from the mother and moves out into the world, this object ceases to hold meaning for the child. Instead, transitional phenomena become more 'diffused' as the subject learns to relate to culture on a daily basis (Winnicott, 1951, 1971). The capacity for moving in and out of transitional space remains and continues to mediate the subject's relationship to external reality and the broader cultural sphere in which meanings circulate (Winnicott, 1951). This transitional space is neither a subjective perception nor an objective reality, but is a third or intermediate zone. Winnicott puts it this way:

> We experience life in the area of transitional phenomena, in the exciting interweave of subjectivity and objective observation, and in an area that is intermediate between the inner reality of an individual and the shared reality of the world that is external to individuals.
>
> (1971: 64)

The experience of transitional phenomena continues to mediate our sense of reality throughout life and mitigates the 'shock of the new'. In adult life, transitional space is the realm of culture and creative activity, where meanings are made and remade. Throughout life, transitional phenomena assist the subject in the task of reality acceptance, which is never finally complete. In this way the subject is always in process and, like an artist, is able to use this space as a palette, to mix and creatively transform the potential colours and textures of existing symbols, fantasies, wishes and ideas into something new and different.

The narratives that abound in our culture, through which we routinely make sense of our experiences and fashion our sense of ourselves (see, for example, Rosenwald and Ochberg, 1992), can be conceptualised in terms of these 'transitional phenomena' (Day Sclater, 1998).[5] Here, the subject creates the world and the world creates the subject, in a space where the boundaried dualities of subject and object are dissolved only to be re-created, acknowledged only to be ignored, in a perpetual dialectic.

As in early childhood, the nature of the cultural environment is crucial for the emotional work that can be done in the transitional spaces. Where there is deficiency in the facilitating environment, disabling the kinds of spontaneity and symbolic modes of transformation described by Winnicott, the space can become filled with the desires and wishes of the other, leaving little room for the illusions of the subject.

Cultural life plays a central role in helping to create a 'good-enough' environment. In Winnicott's terms, a facilitating environment would seem imply a degree of social continuity and yet enough space to enable discursive contestation and struggle (Phillips, 1988). Whether contemporary culture provides this kind of necessary space continues to be a hotly contested topic, and we now turn to those debates to ascertain the possibilities for self in late modernity and to explore further the shifting relationship between self and culture.

Theories of cultural change: spaces for the self in late modernity

Psycho-cultural theorists agree that the kind of psyche needed to cope with the transformations of contemporary life, and to live creatively with its tensions, is ideally one that can exist with paradox and tolerate the experience of uncertainty (see, for example, Craib, 1994). However, there are disagreements as to whether, given the fragmented, multiple, risky and uncertain nature of our world, this is indeed possible.

Social theorists such as Anthony Giddens (1991, 1999) believe that it is. Giddens uses psychoanalytic object relations theory to inform sociology, and presents an optimistic vision of late modernity, in which the technological changes and innovations associated with the media and communications industries, and processes of globalisation, provide new possibilities for reflexive modes of being. His argument is that late-modern subjects can adapt to the contemporary risks by learning to live with paradox and uncertainty, rather than engaging in repressions and denials.

Others take a more pessimistic view. For example, Craib (1994) argues that life today is so fast-paced and uncertain that it has become difficult to form stable relationships and to retain a coherent and enduring sense of self. From this perspective, the transformation of traditional social structures and the expansion of the media and consumerism have contributed to an increased sense of social disorientation and personal alienation (see also Elliott, 1996).

Winnicott is insistent upon the need for an adequately facilitating environment in which the transitional phenomena can do their work. In Phillips' pessimistic reading (Phillips, 1988, 1995), it is argued that the experience of the late-modern world promotes a more 'primitive' psychological response which is defensive or, in the language of Klein, more split off and more 'paranoid schizoid'. This implies that people are not easily able to cope with paradox and emotional ambivalence but, in the face of uncertainty and change, are more likely to respond in more rigid and defensive ways.

The case of genetically modified crops

If we consider media representations of genetically modified (GM) crops as a contemporary example, we can see support for both sides of the debate. There has been a panic response, in certain sections of the media, which is no doubt related to a number of more general concerns about the perversion of the food chain (as, for example, in the BSE food scare) and the power of multinational companies that seem to care little about the environment. In Britain, where the reaction against GM food crops has been particularly strong, fears have reflected anxieties about nationhood, drawing on old rivalrous battles against the Americans, supported by a romantic belief in the identity of 'Britishness' and 'the countryside' (see Williams, 1993). Popular distrust[6] of those politicians, and the companies which advocate genetic modification in the name of economic freedom, scientific progress and food for all, has arisen and has been vociferously expressed.[7] Genetic science is, as Segal (Chapter 2, this volume) points out, fast achieving hegemonic status as the brave new science, best equipped to master the uncertainties of the millennium, promising plentiful bug-free crops with which to feed the world. The argument is seductive in its simplicity, but it clashes quite radically with 'green' politics, and perhaps people are now too jaded to believe that anything more than self-interest can motivate industrialised nations' aid to the developing world. Interestingly, though, the debate has polarised. Whereas the sceptics demonise genetic modification as something threatening in its perversion of nature, the pro-GM lobby draws on the altruistic counter-culture rhetoric of famine aid and equality to idealise it as the solution to world poverty and starvation.

What are we to make of these polarised responses? Food forms a real and imagined part of our environment and one that, for many people, has been largely taken for granted as safe. Food is one of the most material and symbolic of substances and one's relationship to it is closely bound up with the dialectic of psycho-cultural forces that shape subjectivity. Unless one lives in situations of extreme poverty, one's first relationship to food is hopefully one that is 'good enough' in Winnicottian terms; it becomes associated, from an early age, with experiences of plenitude, continuity and trust. Food can be seen as one of the first transitional objects that provides the bridge between the subject, the mother and the outside world. Seen from this perspective, the concept of a safe food chain is more than some abstract socio-economic or biological concept; rather, it resonates powerfully with the stuff with which our bodily subjectivities are made and remade. It is perhaps not surprising that the media narratives that have emerged around GM foods have been so split and defensive, allowing little space to think about change in a way that does not, on the one hand, deny and idealise or, on the other, condemn as the return of Frankenstein.

Science as saviour or destroyer: two narratives of GM crops

Considering the cultural scripts that frame media representations in the GM debate, we can see that the narratives fall into two main generic types. The first we might call the Enlightenment genre; here we see an idealisation of scientific progress, a denial of risk[8] (to the individual and to the environment), and an implicit assumption that science guarantees certainty, and therefore is worthy of our trust. The other prominent narrative form we might refer to as the Gothic Horror genre; here fantasies of science as out of control, and potentially damaging, find expression. Feelings of profound uncertainty and a sense of risk predominate; GM crops pose a threat both to citizens and to their environment. In recent media reports, these two narratives jostle with each other for dominance. Each represents a cultural processing of the profound social and personal anxieties generated by the so-called genetics revolution, in a society where new risks seem to be generated at every tick of the clock of 'progress', and where risks can threaten the integrity of nature and the sanctity of human life.

Science as saviour

> Everybody needs to calm down. There are good scientific answers to the questions that are being asked. What is needed is good scientific discussion to separate the truth from the myths. It has become a political issue and it should not be. It is sad that there is such hysteria. It creates an anti-science climate.
>
> (Dan Verakis, Monsanto, quoted in the *Evening Standard*,
> 16 February 1999: 10)

What we have called the Enlightenment narrative is exemplified in a short piece by Oxford professor Christopher Leaver FRS entitled 'Novel ways to feed the world' (*Guardian*, 17 February 1999: 8). Leaver draws on the language of science to describe the 'exciting potential of *transgenic* plants' (emphasis added). He reminds the reader of the benefits that gene transfer (the term 'genetic modification' is avoided) can bring. These benefits include feeding the world, in the light of a projected population increase; an environment less polluted by chemical insecticides and herbicides; the potential to produce useful compounds such as biodegradable plastic, vaccines and pharmaceuticals by 'natural' rather than industrial means; and a reduction of our dependence on fossil fuels.

Throughout, the reader is encouraged to equate science with progress and with the good of the global all. An attempt to assuage consumer anxiety is made through an invitation to trust a superior authority: science. The implicit message is that anxieties around genetic manipulation can be waved away by the magic wand of science. No reference is made to continuing scientific uncertainties or the ethical questions to which genetic modifications of individual organisms give rise.

Frankenfoods

Are we going to allow the industrialisation of Life itself, redesigning the natural world for the sake of convenience and embarking on an Orwellian future? . . . It will affect far more than the food we eat; it will determine the sort of world we, and our children, inhabit.

(HRH The Prince of Wales, *Daily Mail*, 1 June 1999: 11)

The other side of the story is represented by what we have called the Gothic Horror narrative. It appears strongly in a piece by Ed Harris and Peter Gruner in the *Evening Standard* of 18 February 1999 (pp. 10–11) entitled 'Stick to the facts on Frankenstein foods'. The piece is accompanied by a colour picture of a protester dressed as Frankenstein. The 'Frankenstein' metaphor in the title is not pursued in any detail; it doesn't need to be. The connotations of the word are sufficiently strong to carry the reader along in a state of fear, anger and indignation: 'We need GM products like we need a hole in the head.'

Similarly, a piece in the *Guardian* on 17 February 1999 by Paul Brown, the environment correspondent, carries a picture of 'mutant' fish that look like monsters. Horror is evoked by the spectre of GM crops producing 'monstrous Triffid-like plants', and the somewhat contradictory fantasy that agricultural land will turn into a 'biological desert'. GM crops, Brown says, will actually aggravate hunger and poverty in the developing world. On the same page Tim Radford, the science editor, reminds the reader that scientists themselves are divided and many believe that GM crops will damage British farming.[9]

As scientist Professor Don Grierson, quoted in an article in the *Guardian*, accurately states, 'If you label something "Frankenstein Foods" it does not encourage rational debate' (*Guardian* 'Higher', 11 May 1999: vi). The reference to Frankenstein is sufficient to evoke a whole range of connotations at the level of emotion, such that it is no longer possible to engage dispassionately with the issues. As the reader will know, Mary Shelley's *Frankenstein*[10] is a novel that explores the ethics of man's obsessional longing to conquer the unknown, and to tamper with the very stuff of life. The monster is created in a parody of scientific endeavour that serves to remind us of the dangers inherent in losing sight of fundamental moral values in the wake of technological advances. In the story, Mary Shelley tells us that such a compulsive enterprise is ultimately destructive of important human values, sensibilities and relationships.

In the novel, as in the GM foods scenario, the scientist is preoccupied by a heroic mission, standing aloof from the real anxieties of his fellow human beings, motivated by the hidden and demonic energy of the 'natural' artefact he is compelled to produce. In the GM debates, as in the novel, scientists appear callously indifferent to human anxieties, as though cut off from all feeling except that which drives them to master, or better, mother nature. The novel reminds us that technological manipulation is political – it is about the power of science – but the seeds of this power germinate in psychological soil, in the compulsion to control, and in the fantasy that men, as well as women, can create life. It is surely significant that the Frankenstein metaphor also appeared in commentaries during the heated debates over Steptoe and Edwards' development of IVF techniques in the 1970s.

As Wieland (1996) reminds us, too, Frankenstein is a central myth of our times; it links technological achievement to a masculine omnipotence and to the creation of a substitute world in which both nature and the mother are replaced. Our culture has both created the possibility of GM crops and disowned them as something alien. But, like Frankenstein, the crops themselves are not threatening until we imbue them with our own projections of destruction and harm. Modelled on our own repressed worlds, they face us with malice, as aliens to ourselves.

The other side of the story is our idealisation of that which we manufacture, technologies that render the self bigger, stronger, more potent than we can ever hope to be; the new god to whom we can all bow (Wieland, 1996). In the polarised debates around GM crops, what we see is our own creation being worshipped or, alternatively, facing us as a monster, out of control. The debates are difficult to resolve, because they represent the two sides of humanity: the good and the bad. The two opposing narratives reflect a psychological splitting that exemplifies the difficulties inherent in coming to terms with ambivalence, uncertainty and change.

They reflect, too, other late-modern concerns about democratic process and the nature of citizenship. The debate has polarised along the lines of commercial interests versus a lobby concerned with environmental conservation and the rights of citizens to knowledge, choice, good food and a voice that can be heard. The divisions in this debate reflect a changing political culture, far removed from the old left/right duality, and articulate a newer dimension of western democracy – the felt need for citizens to express their thoughts and feelings on matters affecting them. The debates also articulate a need to manage the risks of late modernity through open debate and publicly available information. The public can easily see that science itself is divided on the issue; it is no longer possible unproblematically to assume the trust that people may once have had in the old bastions of certainty and progress.[11] The Enlightenment narrative of certainty, most recently in the light of the BSE crisis, no longer has the power to contain anxieties about the risks of the contemporary world and, on the contrary, is likely to be read as risk-producing.

Conclusions

As we have seen, there is a sense in which the oppositional narratives around GM food that we have identified share some common ground. They both express anxieties about scientific progress in a world where science struggles to retain its authority and credibility as the promoter of general well-being. The very existence of such profound anxieties, on both sides of the debate, implies that there is a failure of adequate containment at a cultural level.

Psychologically speaking, the transitional spaces represented by the two dominant narratives are not 'good enough' to contain the anxieties around the risks of late modernity. When risk is framed in the rhetoric of science, we are faced with an omnipotent idealisation that demands compliance and presages closure, leaving no room for uncertainty, ambivalence and creative being. When, alternatively, it is framed in monstrous terms, we are faced with the prospect, as in Frankenstein, of the monster's revenge for our violation of the laws of nature and of the body of mother earth; perhaps nature will ultimately revenge herself, as she did in the novel, with death and misery. Here, the space created for subjectivity can be seen as a paranoid engagement, based on fear and projection.

It may be that a third, more constructive, space will emerge, which would better enable us creatively to cope with the transformations and uncertainties of late modernity. The suggested five-year moratorium on GM food trials, and the recent announcement that commercial planting of GM crops will be deferred by agreement between the British Government and commercial interests, for instance, would go some way towards containing current anxieties while permitting further exploration of the moral, economic and psychological issues which such a radical scientific departure inevitably raises.

However, at the moment, old cultural myths of vengeful monsters and stereotypes of mad scientists are being given new life, and are becoming potent symbols for a reactive culture that fears both doing something and doing nothing. The rhetoric of scientific certainty and safety appears exhausted when confronted with the stuff science fiction is made of.

Together, these opposing narratives create an impasse that negates the possibility of creative reflection and mitigates the possibilities of a positive potential space – the 'somewhere else' described by Winnicott in the opening quotation of this chapter. The debate has polarised around the omnipotence of Enlightenment science, on the one hand, and the persecutory fantasies of Gothic Horror on the other. These narratives are two sides of the same coin, and both preclude the kind of creative transitional space that Winnicott saw as necessary for the fulfilment of human potential.

In the transitional space as envisaged by Winnicott, there is the possibility that fantasies of either control or persecution can be recognised for what they are – mere fantasies – and narratives can be constructed that reflect the positive possibilities of late modernity and the transformative movement between self and other. In the climate of today's culture,[12] however, mutant monsters do not necessarily carry the negative connotations that Frankenstein did, but instead may embody transgressive potentials. In the postmodern world it is possible to transform commodified artefacts with the stamp of creativity and empowerment. Perhaps, then, the Frankenstein images that we have seen in the media similarly articulate an uncertainty about new technological developments. They embody both an acknowledgement of and a resistance to technological innovation, and, paradoxically perhaps, may uniquely offer the possibility of a more creative engagement with the realities of technological progress. Whether these images can constitute the kind of transitional space that Winnicott saw as so essential for the complex negotiations between the inner and the outer worlds depends upon not only the images, but also our capacity to live with the kind of psychological doubt that they depend upon and produce.

Notes

1 For further discussion of the history of these critiques of modernity, see Elliott (1996) and O'Shea (1996).
2 A previous version of this chapter was presented at the Centre for Family Research, University of Cambridge, in June 1999. We are grateful to participants there for their comments. We are also indebted to Corinne Squire; this chapter has benefited significantly from her editorial input.
3 For a discussion of the psychological significance of narrative from a Winnicottian perspective, see Day Sclater (1998).
4 Winnicott's description of culture as combining objective and subjective processes has much in common with Raymond Williams' (1993) definition of culture as a 'whole way of life', in which meanings are constantly subject to contestation and struggle (see Griffin, Chapter 1, this volume).
5 As Juliet Mitchell (1996) has argued in her paper 'Questioning the story', the first 'me–not me' transitional objects of infancy are the prototypes for later everyday creative activities such as story-telling.
6 Reflected, for example, in the 'not guilty' verdict in the fictional case of Tommy Archer, who destroyed a neighbouring farmer's GM crop, in the popular BBC Radio 4 programme *The Archers*.
7 In November 1999 it seems that the present British Government has capitulated to popular demand by securing the agreement of commercial interests that GM foods shall not be grown commercially for at least three years.
8 Or a conviction that science can effectively manage risk. There are parallels here with debates that have emerged around biomedical technologies, particularly genetic testing; see, for example, Hallowell (1999).
9 The idea that there might be 'damage' to British farming interests has, of course, profound rhetorical appeal in the context of the crisis in beef production occasioned by the BSE crisis.
10 First published in 1818.
11 Of course, it is true to say that science has never, in fact, been able to provide all the answers to the vicissitudes of human life (we are grateful to Martin Richards for this point), though the ideology of science would certainly lead us to suppose that it could.

12 Witness, for example, the popularity, a few years ago, of the 'Teenage Mutant Ninja Turtles'.

References

Adorno, T. and Horkheimer, M. (1977) *Dialectics of Enlightenment*, London: Allen Lane.

Bauman, Z. (1990) *Modernity and Ambivalence*, Cambridge: Polity Press.

Beck, U. (1992) *Risk Society: Towards a New Modernity*, London: Sage.

Berman, M. (1983) *All That is Solid Melts into Air: The Experience of Modernity*, London: Verso.

Burman, E. (1994) *Deconstructing Developmental Psychology*, London: Routledge.

Craib, I. (1994) *The Importance of Disappointment*, London: Routledge.

Day Sclater, S. (1998) 'Creating the self: stories as transitional phenomena', *Auto/biography* 6: 85–92.

Elliott, A. (1996) *Subject to Ourselves: Social Theory, Psychoanalysis and Postmodernity*, Cambridge: Polity Press.

Elliott, A. and Frosh, S. (eds) (1995) *Psychoanalysis in Contexts*, London: Routledge

Featherstone, M. (1991) *Consumer Culture and Postmodernism*, London: Sage.

Foster, H. (ed.) (1987) *Postmodern Culture*, London: Pluto Press.

Frosh, S. (1991) *Identity Crisis: Modernity, Psychoanalysis and the Self*, London: Macmillan.

Giddens, A. (1991) *Modernity and Self Identity: Self and Society in the Late Modern Age*, Cambridge: Polity Press.

—— (1992) *The Transformation of Intimacy*, Cambridge: Polity Press.

—— (1999) The 1999 Reith Lectures, BBC Radio 4.

Hallowell, N. (1999) 'Doing the right thing: genetic risk and responsibility', *Sociology of Health and Illness* 21: 597–621.

Henriques, J., Hollway, W., Urwin, C., Venn, C. and Walkerdine, V. (1998) *Changing the Subject*, London: Routledge. First published 1984.

Lasch, C. (1991) *The Culture of Narcissism*, New York: Norton Paperbacks.

Lyotard, J.-F. (1984) *The Postmodern Condition: A Report on Knowledge*, Manchester: Manchester University Press.

Minsky, R. (1998) *Psychoanalysis and Culture*, London: Routledge.

Mitchell, J. (1996) 'Questioning the story', Centenary Public Lecture for The Squiggle Foundation, London, 7 December.

Nava, M. and O'Shea, A. (eds) (1996) *Modern Times; Reflections on a Century of English Modernity*, London: Routledge.

O'Shea, A. (1996) 'English subjects of modernity', in M. Nava and A. O'Shea (eds) *Modern Times: Reflections on a Century of English Modernity*, London: Routledge.

Parker, I. (1992) *Discourse Dynamics*, London: Routledge.

Phillips, A. (1988) *Winnicott*, London: Fontana Press.

—— (1995) *Terrors and Experts*, London: Faber & Faber.

Richards, B. (ed.) (1989) *Crises of the Self: Further Essays on Psychoanalysis and Politics*, London: Free Association Books.

Richards, V. (ed.) (1996) 'The person who is me: contemporary perspectives on the true and false self', *Winnicott Studies Monograph Series*, London: Karnac Books, for The Squiggle Foundation.

Riley, D. (1983) *War in the Nursery: Theories of the Child and Mother*, London: Virago.

Rosenwald, G. and Ochberg, R. (eds) (1992) *Storied Lives: The Cultural Politics of Self-Understanding*, London: Yale University Press.

Wieland, C. (1996) 'Matricide and destructiveness: infantile anxieties and technological culture', *British Journal of Psychotherapy* 12(3): 300–13.

Williams, R. (1993) *Culture and Society*, London: Hogarth Press. First published 1958.

Winnicott, D.W. (1951) 'Transitional objects and transitional phenomena', in D.W. Winnicott (ed. M. Khan and R. Masud) (1975) *Collected Papers: Through Paediatrics to Psychoanalysis*, London: Hogarth Press and the Institute of Psycho-Analysis.

—— (1953) 'Psychoses and child care', in D.W. Winnicott (ed. M. Khan and R. Masud) (1975) *Collected Papers: Through Paediatrics to Psychoanalysis*, London: Hogarth Press and the Institute of Psycho-Analysis.

—— (1960) 'Theory of the parent infant relationship', in D.W. Winnicott (1965) *The Maturation Processes and the Facilitating Environment*, London: Hogarth Press and the Institute of Psycho-Analysis.

—— (1965) *The Maturation Processes and the Facilitating Environment*. London: Hogarth Press and the Institute of Psycho-Analysis.

—— (1971) *Playing and Reality*, London: Routledge.

10 Culture and emotions: depression among Pakistanis

Rabia Malik

When we think of emotions we think of them in the first instance as powerful personal experiences or feelings which arise within the body. This highly internal conception of emotions is also evident in mainstream psychological theories, which construct emotions as 'natural' and universal. While it is acknowledged that culture may exert an external influence on the expression of emotions, this influence is usually relegated to a superficial effect. In this model, culture is the 'thin' layer concealing the 'thick' biological and psychological unity of humankind. Segal (Chapter 2, this volume) explores the recent resurgence of the most biological versions of this model. Cultural psychology, in contrast, argues for a social constructionist theorising of emotions in which the distinction between individual and culture is no longer possible (Shweder, 1991). The social constructionist perspective allows too for the possibility that emotions may work differently in different cultures. This is not to say, however, that culture dictates social and cultural practices, rather that culture on the one hand constructs and gives meaning to individual experience of emotions and on the other is constructed by individual emotional experiences.

In order to explicate the constructed nature of emotions, this chapter will look at the experience of the 'emotional' syndrome of depression among British Pakistanis. National mental hospital admission statistics suggest that the rate of depression in British Pakistanis, and Asians in general in the UK, is considerably lower than in the indigenous population (Cochrane, 1977; Cochrane and Bal, 1989). Whether these statistics reflect lower rates of distress in these groups, or are artefacts of different cultural meanings and constructions of distress, which go unrecognised by mainstream mental health services, is still debated. This more general debate on the incidence of mental disorders in minority ethnic groups highlights the contested and interactive nature of culture in societies where cultures coexist (Goldberger and Veroff, 1995).

On the basis of in-depth interviews with indigenous Pakistanis and first-generation British Pakistanis I argue that in order to understand the experience of depression, and more generally distress, in British Pakistanis, a wider understanding is required of cultural ideologies, including the construction of 'person' and 'emotions'. Before considering the Pakistani cultural construction of emotion, I shall first briefly outline traditional Euro-American theories of emotions, depression in particular, and the social constructionist challenge posed to them in light of cross-cultural research (Kleinman, 1986; Lutz, 1985, 1988; Schieffelin, 1985; Shweder, 1991).

Traditional psychological theorising of emotion

Western discourses on emotions, including psychological discourses, have tended to theorise emotions as internal essences. In the seventeenth century, before Descartes, these essences were thought to manifest as humours, which pervaded the body and were responsible for both physical and mental states. After Descartes' separation of mind and body, cognitive and affective processes came to be seen as distinct. Emotions were now clearly located in the body and thought in the mind. This western dualism was perpetuated in subsequent theories of emotions. For example, Darwin's theory constructed emotions as primitive states of arousal involving instinctual drives (Harre, 1986). Later psychological theories of emotions continued to focus on the 'inner subjective' physiological, or feeling, aspect of emotions (James, 1884), but further implicated the role of 'perception' or interpretation in giving emotional experiences meaning and expressive value (Schachter and Singer, 1962). These theories thus continued to separate emotion from thought and body from the mind.

This model of emotions also perpetuated a dualism between the individual and the social. As the 'feeling' and the interpretation of emotion were all postulated to occur within the private space of the individual, the individual was also separated from the external and sociocultural realms in these theories. In fact as Lutz (1988) argues, Euro-American pre-scientific and scientific explanations for emotions have always looked internally, to the spleen, soul, human nature or individual psychology, rather than externally to cultural processes.

Social constructionist theorising of emotions

Traditional psychological theories of emotions, then, have focused on the 'how' or 'feeling' aspect of emotions and not the meaning they hold. As soon as one takes the turn to meaning, a more social approach is required. Cross-cultural research from a social constructionist perspective has challenged the essentialist notion of emotions as internal to the person (Lutz, 1985; Schieffelin, 1985; Shweder, 1985). Such research has found considerable social and cultural variation in the content and interpretation of emotions. There are many emotions that cannot be translated across cultures, and different cultures think of emotions in different ways. For example, the Kaluli of Papua New Guinea do not internalise anger. Rather, blame over loss or misfortune is externalised and the self is seen as being wronged (Schieffelin, 1985). In Euro-American cultures, although theorists acknowledge that emotions are evoked in a social context, they tend to 'psychologise' them, presenting them as an index of a personal state, rather than of social relationships as in other cultures. This has led several researchers to suggest that concepts of emotions stem from more general implicit assumptions about the culturally constructed nature of the person (Lutz, 1985; Schieffelin, 1985).

The cultural construction of the person has been described in essentially two different ways, referred to by Mauss (1985) as 'personhood' and 'selfhood'. 'Personhood' refers to an individual's social role as a member of a collective. 'Selfhood', on the other hand, refers to the mental and physical awareness human beings have of their own individuality. Along similar lines, Shweder and Bourne (1991) and Gaines (1982) have proposed a continuum between a 'sociocentric', 'referential' and 'egocentric', 'indexical' self. The 'sociocentric' or 'referential' self is an unbounded, permeable self that is indexed in time, in place and in a particular set of social relationships. Behaviour, cognition and emotion are functions of particular self–other relations and are contextually located. The 'egocentric' or 'indexical' self is an individual, autonomous self, perceived to be the principal locus of thoughts, feelings and actions. Behaviour, cognition and emotion are generated from inside a three-dimensional space with firm boundaries (Lakoff and Johnson, 1980). Interpersonal and social problems are seen as a series of person-centric constructs (Kelly, 1955), and the individual is viewed as a unitary agent acting upon the natural world (Judhav, 1996). Once self and emotions are defined 'egocentrically', the major role of emotions is to inform oneself (mind) about oneself (body), as opposed to about relationships or events (Matsumoto, 1994). Emotions thus come to have enormous personal meaning in such societies.

The 'sociocentric' 'referential' self is usually associated with non-western cultures and the 'egocentric' 'indexical' self with western cultures. It should be noted, however, that these constructions of 'self' are not absolute (Kleinman and Becker, 1991). Although the 'social' aspect of self may be stressed in a particular culture, that is not to say that there is no individual or internal conception of self. In terms of emotions, however, the different constructions of the person predicate different conceptions of emotions.

Depression across cultures

Theories of depression can also be deconstructed to reveal how their history and meaning are embedded in western culture and epistemology. Psychoanalytic theories such as Freud's (1956) and Bowlby's (1980) regard depression as resulting from the unconscious emotional conflicts associated with unresolved grief and loss in childhood and a breakdown of rational defence mechanisms (Judhav, 1996). Cognitive theories such as Beck's (1979) and Seligman's (1975) see depression as resulting from self-defeating thought processes and a struggle between cognitive and emotional aspects of self. Both sets of theories rest on a bounded notion of the individual. Indeed, even social theories of depression (Brown and Harris, 1978), while acknowledging the impact of social context, social vulnerability and provoking factors, such as life events, socio-economic status and gender, comply to the notion of depression occurring within the person. Treatments of depression also work on the premise of its egocentric, internal construction. Cognitive treatments attempt to expose self-defeating thought processes and help cognition regain its check on emotions. Psychoanalytic treatments attempt to engage with the 'affected' self by working on key emotions as they are transferred from 'within' the analysand on to the analyst (Judhav, 1996). The concept of depression, its theories and treatments are thus embedded in Euro-American cultural systems and theories of emotions. This inevitably raises the question of the cross-cultural validity of the syndrome of depression.

Cross-cultural research has attested both to the universality of depression, claiming that there are few cultural differences in depression across cultures (O'Daniels, 1988; Sartorius *et al.*, 1983; Singer, 1975), and to the relativity of depression, arguing that the differences in experience of depression across cultures cast doubt on the universal validity of the concept (Good *et al.*, 1985; Kleinman, 1986; Obeyesekere, 1985). These differential findings are a result of different methodological orientations as well as of the multifarious aspects of depression. Even within Euro-American contexts, depression has numerous meanings and can either be regarded as a state, a symptom or a syndrome.

Ethnographic research focusing on the 'state' of depression has argued that the quintessential dysphoric mood element of depression has different cultural meanings and expressions in different societies (Kleinman, 1986). For example, Obeyesekere (1985) has argued that the generalisation of hopelessness, which underpins western depression theories – such as that of Brown and Harris (1986) – is valued and not pathologised in Buddhist cultures; pleasure from worldly things is considered the basis of all suffering and wilful dysphoria a step towards salvation. Along similar lines Good *et al.* (1985) have argued that the association of grief with religious experiences in Shi'ism has led to grief or dysphoria being considered markers of a person's depth rather than pathology. Research focusing on the 'symptomatology' of depression has generally reported a dominance of somatic symptoms (Bal, 1987) and a reduced frequency of psychological symptoms such as guilt feelings and suicidal thoughts in non-western cultures. Depression has also been associated with culture-specific bodily complaints, such as 'a sinking heart' in Punjabis (Krause, 1989) and a sensation of the 'heart being squeezed' in China (Kleinman, 1986). Finally, epidemiological research focusing on the 'syndrome' of depression has found differences in the prevalence and incidence figures of depression across cultures (Carstairs and Kapoor, 1976; Engelsman, 1980; Murphy, 1982; Murphy and Leighton, 1965; Shah *et al.*, 1980; Silverman, 1968; Singer, 1975) and within minority ethnic groups in the UK (Cochrane, 1977; Cochrane and Bal, 1989).

Together, these cross-cultural differences in depressive 'state' and 'symptoms', which serve as the criteria for depression in western psychiatry, cast doubt on the universality of the syndrome of depression. This is not to say that dysphoric affect or 'sadness' do not exist in all cultures, rather that dysphoric affect is interpreted and socially organised in different ways in different societies (Kleinman, 1986). As Lutz (1985) and Schieffelin (1985) have proposed, depression, or the experience of distress, is related to the particular cultural structure of the emotional system in which it appears.

In this chapter I will attempt to explain the subjective experience of depression for British Pakistanis – what it is caused by, how it is expressed, what symptoms it is associated with and how it is managed. In doing so, I aim to deconstruct the implicit theories of personhood and emotion on which the Pakistani experience of distress resides before considering its equivalence to the western conception of depression and why there appear to be lower rates of depression in British Pakistanis (Cochrane and Bal, 1989).

The cultural construction of depression in Pakistanis

Because there is no directly equivalent word for depression in Urdu and, even in those Pakistanis familiar with the English term, a western understanding of it cannot be assumed, a more universal starting point was required in this research (Fabrega, 1992). The more general concept of 'distress' was abstracted from the concept of depressions and the research was consequently introduced to respondents as being 'about their experience of distress'. To avoid making assumptions about knowledge of depression, the word 'depression' was not used unless it was first mentioned by the respondents themselves.

A vignette, constructed on the basis of a pilot study, depicting a man or woman (depending on the interviewee's gender) suffering from a number of symptoms of an unnamed condition, was used to elicit conversations around distress. In a series of open-ended questions respondents were then asked to name the condition and what they thought the causes, symptoms, consequences and cure were. Interviews were conducted in Urdu or Punjabi, the first language of indigenous Pakistanis and the language that all the first-generation British Pakistanis stated a preference for. English words and phrases were also used by both samples, but more frequently by British Pakistanis. The interviews lasted on average one and a half hours and were audio-recorded with respondents' permission and later transcribed and analysed.

One hundred and twenty respondents were interviewed. Sixty were indigenous to Pakistan and sixty were first-generation British Pakistanis. Half of the sample were male and half were female. The research was conducted over a period of three months in north-west London, England, and over four months in Karachi, Pakistan. Attempts at matching the sample for age, socio-economic status and ethnic origin were made. The age of the sample members was between 30 and 65 years, as the research was conducted with first-generation migrants who had mainly emigrated to Britain in the late 1960s and early 1970s. Some were more recent migrants through marriage to British citizens. The sample was made up of middle-class and working-class families from Punjabi and Muhajir ethnic groups.

Samples of indigenous Pakistanis and first-generation British Pakistanis were used to help gauge the interactive and dynamic nature of cultures, enabling a comparison of the experiences of people residing in a dominant majority culture (in Pakistan) and a subordinate minority culture (in Britain). It was also hoped that by using a comparative methodology light might be shed on the contested low rates of depression in Asians in the UK reported by Cochrane (1977) and Cochrane and Bal (1989).

The naming of distress

All the respondents recognised the vignette as a description of someone suffering distress. The three predominant names given to the condition in the vignette were distress (*parishani*), depression and mental tension (*zahni daboa*). Of the three terms, 'depression' was always stated in English and had no Urdu equivalent. Forty-five per cent of the British Pakistani respondents referred to the condition as 'depression' compared with 15 per cent of the indigenous Pakistani respondents. The vast majority of respondents claimed they had heard of someone who had suffered, or had themselves suffered, from the kind of distress described in the vignette.

The respondents' descriptions of what they tended to refer to as distress or depression drew on cultural themes that made the experiences of distress meaningful on a personal and social level. These were in line with the 'holism' and 'ecology' of the South Asian indigenous theories of Unani Tibb and Ayurveda (Kakar, 1982; Zimmermann, 1987), which characteristically interconnect the affective, somatic, personal, social environmental and moral realms. A brief description of the natural theory of Unani Tibb[1] helps to explain the interplay of these realms of human experience and subsequently the construction of emotions and depression in Pakistanis.

Unani Tibb

Unani Tibb or Greco-Islamic medicine originates from the system of medicine that was developed in Arab civilisation during the early spread of Islam, dating back to AD 661 (Said, 1983). Concepts of health and illness in this medical system are inextricably woven into the general body of Islam and Islamic practices, with a stress on the ethical and the holistic (Khan, 1986). In Islam the human being is viewed in the context of a larger cosmos, with which it is perceived to share elemental properties. In Unani Tibb the macrocosm of the universe is symbolically linked with a perfectly reflected microcosm, the human being (Good and Good, 1992), and thus the cosmos is perceived to be subject to the principle of *Thawid* – the oneness and unity of all creation. The origin, nature and purpose of human beings is to live and function harmoniously within themselves and their surroundings in a dynamic condition of balance.

The psychological[2] component of Unani Tibb resides on the concept of *Nafs* – the self, which in its desirable state should be in a state of unconditional tranquillity – *Sakoon*. The essence of the *Nafs* is the heart, which is the point of union between the soma, psyche and spirit. The heart on the one hand distinguishes humans from other created beings,[3] and on the other symbolises the whole human being in relation to the world. The heart is thus considered the seat of the mind and the reservoir for emotional processes (Obeyesekere, 1976), which makes it the medium for the perception and interpretation of reality. The functions of the heart are enabled by the *vital force*, which transcends corporeal reality and is considered the guiding principle within the human organism. It is believed that the quantity and quality of vital force can be modified with appropriate nutrition, medication and psycho-emotional factors.

The physiological component of Unani Tibb conceptualises the universe in terms of *Quwa* (energy), which is delineated by four primary qualities: hot, cold, wet and dry, symbolically corresponding to fire, air, water and earth. The entire cosmos – minerals, plants, animals and human beings – is constituted through an interplay of these four elements. These elements and their properties also analogously constitute the *Akhlaat* (humours): yellow bile, black bile, phlegm and blood. In order to understand the concept of body in Unani Tibb, it is crucial to appreciate that humours are not just substances located within the body. As Langford elaborates, 'they are principles that are linked through an elaborate system of correspondences not only to somatic processes but to processes in the natural environment' (1995: 336).

This fundamental link between organisms and their environment can be clarified through an understanding of the concept of *Mizaj*. Every being is regarded as having an inherent but dynamic predisposition or temperament (*Mizaj*), resulting from the interaction of the elemental qualities. While to some extent *Mizaj* is inherited, it is also determined by climate, flora, fauna and diet, all of which have their own characteristic distribution of elements. *Mizaj* is also thought to be affected by factors such as age and gender. Disorder, then, can be caused by ecological, dietary, physiological, mental and/or emotional factors (Khan, 1986). Treatment adopts natural substances, which are endowed with their own natural temperament and can thereby modify and treat the internal balance of the individual. As a consequence the internal and external worlds are closely interlinked (Khan, 1986).

This characteristic convolution of the emotional, the body and the social (Zimmermann, 1987) was evident in many respondents' descriptions of distress. In order to explicate these connections, we need first to focus on the social level and its connection with the affective, then the connection of the affective with the somatic and finally the somatic with the social. This line of argument is not, however, indicative of a linear relationship. Rather, it conveys a more circular and diffuse relationship, in which the conceptualisation of 'person' is not bounded simply by a physical body, and mind cannot be separated from soma or body from environment.

Causality of distress

Both Pakistanis' and British Pakistanis' descriptions of causes of distress were marked by plurality. Typically, informants viewed a number of overlapping interactive factors as causes. These were categorised into circumstantial, relational (kinship), personality and supernatural causes. The predominant causes cited, however, were circumstances and relationships, which are external to the body.

Both Zimmermann (1987) and Kakar (1982) have attested to this external aspect of distress in Ayurveda and Unani Tibb, where the symbolic correspondence between the macrocosm of universe and the microcosm of the body means that the body and the person are fluid and permeable, engaged in a continuous interchange between the internal and external environment, including the influence of others.

This construction accords with the 'sociocentric' or 'referential' 'self', in which emotions are contextually located and believed to be a function of particular self–other relations. Laungani (1992) and Kakar (1982) argue that South Asian society cannot be seen in terms other than familial and communal. When a problem arises it is seldom regarded as personal or private. As one male respondent said:[4]

> Everyone's mental distress is different. For me it is from my children because I want them to do as I say. For someone else it may be to do with their husband or according to their circumstances.

Thus distress functions as a 'signifier' overlying a particular conceptualisation of self and society. By evoking the social in distress's causality, respondents in this study were simultaneously expressing their relationship to the social world (Herzlich and Pierret, 1986). Marsella (1980) has suggested that the cultural values of a 'sociocentric' self and a focus on kin group may influence the process of self-identification with dysphoric affect and bodily states.

The language of distress

Drawing on the philosophy of Wittgenstein, Harré (1983, 1989) argues that subjective experience of selfhood is implicitly structured by the beliefs about 'person' that are inherent in our language. This structuring can be illustrated by Phillips' (1993) chapter 'Worrying and its discontents'. Phillips describes how the Old English word *wyrgan*, meaning to kill by strangulation, was originally a hunting term used to describe what dogs did to their prey. 'Worrying' in this sense was something that was done to you; that is, a person was the object of worry, and so one could say, 'I have worries'. However, during the mid-nineteenth century there was a distinct change in the use of the word: a person could now be the subject of worry; that is, one could say, 'I am worried'. This subtle transformation of the use of the term from the external to the internal reflects the western epistemological split between mind and body and the notion of an intentional mind ruling over an unintentional body. The current English use of the term 'depression', as in 'I am depressed', similarly renders the person the subject of depression.

In contrast to the English use, Pakistani respondents in this study typically used the terms *distress* and *depression* in object-relational ways. For example, they frequently used such phrases as 'my distresses', 'depression happens', 'depression stays', 'became prey to depression'. The externality of these phrases seems to correspond with contextualised thinking connected with a sociocentric self which is the object rather than the subject of 'depression'. Although in Urdu it is grammatically possible to construct a sentence which would make the 'self' the subject of depression, it was seldom done by respondents.

Respondents also seldom used *mai* or 'I' in conjunction with distress or depression, but while first-person pronouns were little used, the heart was frequently implicated, reflecting the Unani conceptualisation of heart being the site of the self or *Nafs*. The heart (*dil*) is a common word for 'I', and connotes feelings of the person. A person's heart is in this sense the person, as in the common phrases 'heart doesn't feel like doing anything' – '*dil nahi chahtha koch karnai ko*' – or 'my heart doesn't want to talk to anyone' – '*dil nahi chahtha kisee sai bath karnai ko*'. In the mediation of emotion through the heart, the Pakistani 'I', in contrast to the western 'I', connects with mind and body, as well as spirit. The heart consequently serves to distance the 'individual self' from emotion. In this context the use of the pronoun *mai*/'I' and a focus on internal feelings can connote self-centredness. The use of language, as well as particular terminology, is thus indicative of deeper cognitions and conceptualisation of 'self'.

'The self' in distress

This discussion of the 'sociocentric' construction of 'self' is in no way intended to imply that Pakistanis do not have a sense of individual self. From the content analysis, it was evident that Pakistanis identified internal personality or *thabiyath* factors in the causation of mental distress/depression. These were, however, structured as secondary to and dependent on environmental factors. As a female British Pakistani respondent said:

> The biggest cause is the mercy of circumstances and the atmosphere at home. What else can it be? You feel you can't come out of the situation. Some people's heart is strong and they try to come out of the situation but you can't come out of it, if it is not created by you. You end up feeling depression.

The notion of 'self' for these Pakistanis does not reside in the mind alone and is not characterised by a mind/body split. The interconnection between mind/body and social world is, once again, depicted in Unani Tibb's polysemous symbol of the heart. This diffuse 'self' has important implications for the symptomatology of distress and depression.

Symptomatology of distress

The symptoms described by respondents were also pluralistic: affective, somatic and socio-behavioural. For example, one woman described how

> Sleep doesn't come. There is no tranquillity (*sakoon*). A weight will stay in the heart and a lot of illness can happen. They will stay quiet. If there is no recognition (of it) then there won't be any care about the family or the children – there isn't any care about anything apart from about (your) self. (Your) heart won't feel like doing the housework. Crying comes again and again, there is a pain in the head, pain in the body, sweating and anxiety.

Affective symptoms

Affective or emotional symptoms of distress and depression were described by 32 per cent of the indigenous Pakistani sample and 31 per cent of the British Pakistani sample, and were typically expressed in relationship to others and social roles, again in line with a sociocentric or relational construction of self. Emotions were thus placed in a mediatory position between events, relationships and individuals (Lutz, 1985). As one man described the relational effects of depression:

> you can't spend your life properly and you can't do anything. It affects the whole family and children. They stay in tension and worried about him. All of the attention is diverted to him. You keep other people depressed to release your own depression.

This pattern lends credence to Schieffelin's (1985) argument that emotions extend beyond the internal personality and should be seen as socio-behavioural systems.

Somatic symptoms

Somatic symptoms were also frequently cited – by 29 per cent of indigenous Pakistanis and 26 per cent of British Pakistanis. The somatic expression of distress can be understood through Leder's (1984) notion of a 'lived body', or an 'emotional body', suggested by Ots in relation to Chinese medicine (1990). These terms refer to a phenomenological body of perceived experiences that transcends the western dichotomy of psyche and soma. The conceptualisation accords well with the key role of the heart in Unani Tibb. Clearly, the connection of psyche and soma is reiterated in many languages, in idioms for distress. Ots' study of the meaning of bodily perceptions in the discourse of Chinese medicine showed how many somatic symptoms – the 'angry liver', the 'anxious heart' and the 'melancholy spleen' – relate to emotions. This connection has, however, been frequently misinterpreted and the anatomical correspondence between organs and emotions used as an argument for 'somatisation', propagating the notion of the somatic as a metaphor for the psychological. In fact, as Porket (1974) argues, terms such as 'heart' or 'liver' do not directly refer to anatomical substrate, rather to a certain pattern of functions. The heart, therefore, or any other such symbol, cannot simply be taken as metaphoric; rather it is a highly polysemous symbol simultaneously referring to the physical, the psychological and the social.

The link between affective and somatic was further explicated in interviewees' responses to what the 'consequences of such a condition may be', which were cited as physical, mental and social. A large number of respondents considered distress and depression to have a major effect on the body, in particular the heart, as well as on the wider social network, especially the family, hence linking the 'emotional' or 'lived body' to the environment and social relationships.

The cure for distress and the role of religion

The cures advocated by Pakistanis and British Pakistanis were split into the categories of worship or seeking the help of a spiritual healer, self-initiated cure, family intervention and support, professional medical help, and the belief that only a change in circumstances, situation or environment would cure the person. The most frequently cited cure was self-help, through a variety of strategies, such as religious faith, keeping oneself busy, going out and meeting people, not thinking too much or thinking positively. These Pakistanis, therefore, had a clear notion of 'selfhood' and the role this can play in managing distress and depression.

Many respondents, however, regarded depression as a 'signifier' of spiritual weakness in the 'self'. In line with Unani Tibb they placed humans in a larger moral order, over which the 'self' is regarded as having limited reign, and discussed the importance of faith and worship in providing balance to the body and helping to achieve a state of *sakoon* (unconditional tranquillity), as illustrated by a male respondent:

> A person can only treat depression themselves. Doctors can't help you. It is in your hands – how you take it, how you face it. If you have tried your best and something still goes wrong it is from God. Trying is a necessity, if a person gives up trying his life is virtually finished. But if a person has sincerely tried and made the right type of effort and still that thing doesn't get done, according to our faith – that is fate. But God will only put such difficulties on you that we can bear. Happiness is from God and distress is from him too.

The role of Islam in distress can be related to Obeyesekere's (1985) discussion of Buddhism in Sri Lankan culture. By drawing on the psychoanalytic notion of the 'work of culture' (as Day Sclater and Yates similarly do in this volume when they investigate the emotional valency of a particular cultural object, or more generally Apfelbaum does in her discussion of the affective dimensions of various forms of uprootedness), Obeyesekere argues that the 'work' of a religious culture can transform a constellation of symptoms in a different direction as compared with a western cultural context. He suggests that in non-western cultures symptoms are defined in existential terms rather than illness terms. Unpleasant affects are expressed and resolved through meanings provided by the religious orientation of that culture. For Pakistanis in this study, religion thus played a central role in resolving unpleasant affects, and many respondents claimed that if one's faith was strong, distress or depression should not happen in the first place.

Religious beliefs do not, however, as we have seen, fatalistically preclude the use of 'self' or other in cure. A large number of respondents, in line with an external causal conceptualisation of distress and depression, also advocated family support, and thought that the only lasting cure was an external one that involved a change in circumstances or a solution to the problem. Interestingly, only 10 per cent of Pakistanis and 13 per cent of British Pakistanis advocated seeking professional medical advice from a doctor, psychologist, psychiatrist or counsellor. This was mainly explained by either the doctors' lack of cultural understanding, or their powerlessness to change domestic situations which respondents did not feel comfortable disclosing to non-kin.

> Doctors can't do anything. It is just your family atmosphere. Look my Doctor, he is just seeing it physically. I am telling him (I) am tired, (I) can't do anything, (I) sleep a lot. Everyone knows a sign of depression is exhaustion, but he isn't understanding. If my husband was good with me my depression would not stay. But what can the doctor do?

From distress to depression

In summary, then, for the Pakistanis in this study, 'depression', and distress in general, was externally instigated and was located in concrete situations and relationships rather than within the individual. Their construction of a permeable unbounded 'self' is in accordance with Shweder and Bourne's (1984, 1991) and Gaines' (1982) description of a 'sociocentric' or 'referential' 'self'. The objective rather than subjective experience of distress was also clearly evident in respondents' language, which constructed depression/distress as 'happening to' them as opposed to 'within' them. Moreover, the personal experience of both distress and depression for the respondents was associated not simply with the mind but also with the 'emotional body', resulting in highly interconnected affective, somatic and socio-behavioural symptoms. This 'holistic' construction of distress corresponds with the indigenous theories of Unani Tibb, which contextualises the microcosm of human being in the interconnected macrocosm of the universe and also places human beings in the natural moral order of Islam. Within this order, events happen for ethical purposes and are considered part and parcel of life, not necessarily indicative of illness. Distress serves an ontological purpose, while communicating and confirming important ideas about the real world also reconstitutes and reconfirms cultural beliefs (Young, 1976).

Whether these Pakistani respondents' experience is synonymous with the western construction of depression is highly questionable. At the level of state or mood, the 'feeling' of depression and its subsequent expression is psychological and somatic, as opposed to primarily psychological. It is thought to be primarily instigated through relationships and events, and the feelings imply information about important kinship ties rather than about the individual person. It is thought that such depression should be managed within these relationships or through one's faith, rather than through individual-centred therapy or treatment.

A sociocentric construction of personhood and the notion of an 'emotional body' transcend the mind/body dualism of the western construction of self, and construct a different experience of depression, and emotions in general. This is not to say that emotions are fixed practices. Cultures are interactive, and, as would be expected, British Pakistanis in this study more frequently referred to their experience of distress using the English term 'depression' than did indigenous Pakistanis. However, differences in cultural meaning, as predicted by Kleinman (1986), did seem to affect the experience of depressed mood and symptoms for all interviewees. These differences in meaning may account for health professionals' lack of recognition of experiences of distress reported by many British Pakistani respondents, and for statistically lower rates of depression in British Pakistanis compared to the indigenous population. Such a view of 'culture', however, remains contested. It contrasts with other views of 'culture' in the debate on 'the mental health of ethnic minorities' which suggest, for example, that the lower rate of depression in British Pakistanis is due to lack of psychological sophistication in Asians or a preference for 'keeping things in the family'. These latter views of 'culture' place the onus for differential rates of mental disorder on subordinate minority ethnic groups and contribute to constructing them as 'other'.

The challenge to western theories of emotions posed by some cultural psychology has shown those notions to be Eurocentric. By undermining the universalism of emotions, the challenge allows for an alternative construction of emotions, predicated on alternative constructions of personhood. Emotions are argued on the one hand to create reality, and on the other, to be negotiated aspects of social reality which are frequently manipulated, misunderstood or reconstructed (Lutz, 1988). The cultural constructionist account of emotions, then, suggests, as in this study, that emotions, and syndromes such as depression, are not innate or universal, but rather they are shaped by a cultural system of learned meaning, which gives them both personal and social value.

Notes

1   Unani Tibb is particularly tied to Islam, the dominant religion of Pakistan. During the course of the description reference will also be made to Ayurveda and the relatively larger body of research associated with it. This is justified by the similarities and close coexistence of these two humoral paradigms in the Indo-Pakistani subcontinent (Khan, 1986). The concepts of both are therefore inherent in Pakistani culture.
2   Although this description is structured in terms of psychological and physiological components it is in no way intended to be divisive and to detract from the holism of the paradigm. The interconnection of the two will become apparent during the course of the chapter.
3   This is in contrast to the western view that rationality distinguishes humans from other beings.
4   The quotations given in this chapter are translations of the Urdu version. In these translations emphasis was placed on the conceptual essence of what the respondents were saying.

References

Bal, S.S. (1987) 'Psychological symptomatology and health beliefs of Asian patients', in H. Dent (ed.) *Clinical Psychology: Research and Development*, London: Croom Helm.
Beck, A. (1979) *Depression: Clinical, Experimental and Theoretical Aspects*, New York: Harper & Row.

Bowlby, J. (1980) *Attachment and Loss*, Volume 3, New York: Basic Books.

Brown, G.W. and Harris, T. (1978) *Social Origins of Depression: A Study of Psychiatric Disorder in Women*, London: Tavistock.

—— (1986) 'Stressors, vulnerability and depression: a question of replication', *Psychological Medicine* 16: 39–44.

Carstairs, G.M. and Kapoor, R.L. (1976) *The Great Universe of Kota: Stress Change and Mental Disorder in an Indian Village*, London: Hogarth Press.

Cochrane, R. (1977) 'Mental illness in immigrants to England and Wales: an analysis of mental hospital admissions, 1971', *Social Psychiatry* 12: 25–35.

Cochrane, R. and Bal, S.S. (1989) 'Mental hospital admission rates of immigrants to England: a comparison of 1971 and 1981', *Social Psychology and Psychiatric Epidemiology* 24: 2–12.

Engelsman, F. (1980) 'Culture and depression', in I. Al-Issa (ed.) *Culture and Psychopathology*, Baltimore, MD: University Park Press.

Fabrega, H.J. (1992) 'The role of culture in a theory of psychiatric illness', *Social Science and Medicine* 35(1): 91–103.

Freud, S. (1956) 'Mourning and melancholia', in S. Freud (ed. J.A. Strachey) *Collected Works of Sigmund Freud*, London: Hogarth Press.

Gaines, A.D. (1982) 'Cultural definitions, behaviour and the person in American psychiatry', in A.J. Marsella and G. White (eds) *Cultural Conceptions of Mental Health and Therapy*, Dordrecht: Reidel.

Goldberger, N. and Veroff, J. (1995) *The Culture and Psychology Reader*, New York: New York University Press.

Good, B.J. and Good, M.J.D. (1992) 'The comparative study of Greco-Islamic medicine: the integration of medical knowledge into local symbolic contexts', in C. Leslie and A. Young (eds) *Paths to Asian Medical Knowledge*, Berkeley: University of California Press.

Good, B.J., Good, M.J.D. and Moradi, R. (1985) 'The interpretation of Iranian depressive illness and dysphonic affect', in A. Kleinman and B. Good (eds) *Culture and Depression*, Berkeley: University of California Press.

Harré, R. (1983) *Personal Being: A Theory for Individual Psychology*, Oxford: Blackwell.

—— (ed.) (1986) *The Social Construction of Emotion*, Oxford: Blackwell.

—— (1989) 'Language, games and the texts of identity', in J. Shotter and K.G. Gergen (eds) *Texts of Identity*, London: Sage.

Herzlich, C. and Pierret, P. (1986) 'Illness: from causes to meaning', in C. Currer and M. Stacey (eds) *Concepts of Health, Illness and Disease: A Comparative Perspective*, Leamington Spa: Berg.

James, W. (1884) 'What is an emotion?', *Mind* 9: 188–205.

Judhav, S. (1996) 'The cultural origins of western depression', *International Journal of Social Psychiatry* 42: 269–86.

Kakar, S. (1982) *Shamans, Mystics and Doctors: A Psychological Inquiry into India and its Healing Traditions*, New York: Knopf.

Kelly, G. (1955) *The Psychology of Personal Constructs*, New York: Norton.

Khan, M.S. (1986) *Islamic Medicine*, London: Routledge & Kegan Paul.

Kleinman, A. (1977) 'Depression, somatisation and the "new cross-cultural psychiatry"', *Social Science and Medicine* 11: 3–10.

—— (1980) *Patients and Healers in the Context of Culture*, Berkeley: University of California Press.

—— (1986) *Social Origins of Distress and Disease: Depression, Neurasthenia in Modern China*, New Haven, CT: Yale University Press.

—— (1988) *Rethinking Psychiatry: From Cultural Category to Personal Experience*, New York: The Free Press.

Kleinman, A. and Becker, J. (1991) *Psychological Aspects of Depression*, New York: Lawrence Erlbaum Associates.

Kleinman, A. and Good, B. (1985) *Culture and Depression*, Berkeley: University of California Press.

Kleinman, A. and Kleinman, J. (1985) 'Somatisation', in A. Kleinman and B. Good (eds) *Culture and Depression*, Berkeley: University of California Press.

Krause, I.B. (1989) 'The sinking heart: a Punjabi communication of distress', *Social Science and Medicine* 29: 563–75.

Lakoff, G. and Johnson, M. (1980) *Metaphors We Live By*, Chicago, IL: University of Chicago Press.

Langford, J. (1995) 'Ayurvedic interiors: person, space and episteme in three medical practices', *Cultural Anthropology* 10(3): 330–66.

Laungani, P. (1992) 'Cultural variations in the understanding and treatment of psychiatric disorders: India and England', *Counselling Psychology Quarterly* 5(3): 231–44.

Leder, D. (1984) 'Medicine and paradigms of embodiment', *Journal of Medicine and Philosophy* 9(1): 29–44.

Lutz, C. (1985) 'Depression and the translation of emotional worlds', in A. Kleinman and B. Good (eds) *Culture and Depression*, Berkeley: University of California Press.

—— (1988) *Unnatural Emotions: Everyday Sentiments in a Micronesian Atoll and their Challenge to Western Theory*, Chicago, IL: University of Chicago Press.

Marsella, A.J. (1980) 'Depressive experience and disorder across cultures: a review of the literature', in H. Triandis and J. Draguns (eds) *Handbook of Cross-Cultural Psychology*, Volume 5: *Culture and Psychopathology*, Boston: Allyn & Bacon.

Matsumoto, D. (ed.) (1994) *People: Psychology from a Cultural Perspective*, Monterey, CA: Brooks/Cole.

Mauss, M. (1985) 'A category of the human mind: the notion of personhood; the notion of self', in M. Carrithers, S. Collins and S. Lukes (eds) *The Category of the Person*, Cambridge: Cambridge University Press.

Murphy, H.B.M. (1982) *Comparative Psychiatry: The International and Intercultural Distribution of Mental Illness*, New York: Springer-Verlag.

Murphy, J.M. and Leighton, A.H. (1965) *Approaches to Cross-Cultural Psychiatry*, Ithaca, NY: Cornell University Press.

Obeyesekere, G. (1976) 'The impact of Ayurvedic ideas on the culture and the individual in Sri Lanka', in C. Leslie (ed.) *Asian Medical Systems: A Comparative Study*, Berkeley: University of California Press.

—— (1985) 'Buddhism and the work of culture in Sri Lanka', in A. Kleinman and B. Good (eds) *Culture and Depression*, Berkeley: University of California Press.

O'Daniels, P. (1988) 'Cultural influences and psychiatric disorders', *Current Opinions in Psychiatry* 1: 212–16.

Ots, T. (1990) 'The angry liver, the anxious heart and the melancholy spleen: the phenomenology of perceptions in Chinese culture', *Culture, Medicine and Psychiatry* 14: 21–38.

Phillips, A. (1993) 'Worrying and its discontents', in A. Phillips (ed.) *On Kissing, Tickling and being Bored*, London: Faber & Faber.

Porket, M. (1974) *Theoretical Foundations of Chinese Medicine*, Cambridge, MA: MIT Press.

Said, H.M. (1983) 'The Unani system of health and medicine', in R.H. Bannerman, J. Burton and C. Wen-Chieh (eds) *Traditional Medicine and Health Care*, Geneva: World Health Organization.

Sartorius, N., Davidian, H., Ernberg, G., Fenton, F.R., Fujii, I., Gastpar, W., Jablensky, A., Kielholz, P., Lehmann, H.E., Narghari, M., Shimizu, M., Shinfuku, N. and Takahashi, R. (1983) *Depressive Disorders in Different Cultures*, Geneva: World Health Organization.

Schachter, S. and Singer, J.E. (1962) 'Cognitive, social and psychological determinants of emotional state', *Psychological Review* 69: 379–99.

Schieffelin, E.L. (1985) 'Cultural analysis of depression affect: an example from New Guinea', in A. Kleinman and B. Good (eds) *Culture and Depression*, Berkeley: University of California Press.

Seligman, M.E.P. (1975) *Helplessness: On Depression, Development and Death*, San Francisco, CA: W.H. Freeman.

Shah, A.V., Goswami, U.A., Maniar, R.C., Hajariwal, D.C. and Sinha, B.K. (1980) 'Prevalence of psychiatric disorders in Ahmedabad: an epidemiological study', *Indian Journal of Psychiatry* 22: 376.

Shweder, R.A. (1985) 'Menstrual pollution, soul loss and the comparative study of emotions', in A. Kleinman and B. Good (eds) *Culture and Depression*, Berkeley: University of California Press.

—— (1991) *Thinking Through Cultures: Expeditions in Cultural Psychology*, Boston, MA: Harvard University Press.

Shweder, R.A. and Bourne, E.J. (1984) 'Does the concept of the person vary cross-culturally?', in A.J. Marsella and G.M. White (eds) *Cultural Conceptions of Mental Health and Therapy*, Dordrecht: Reidel.

—— (1991) 'Does the concept of the person vary cross-culturally?', in R.A. Shweder (ed.) *Thinking Through Cultures: Expeditions in Cultural Psychology*, Boston, MA: Harvard University Press.

Silverman, D. (1968) *The Epidemiology of Depression*, Baltimore, MD: Johns Hopkins Press.

Singer, K. (1975) 'Depressive disorders from a transcultural perspective', *Social Science and Medicine* 9: 289.

Young, A. (1976) 'Some implications of medical beliefs and practices for social anthropology', *American Anthropologist* 78: 5–24.

Zimmermann, F. (1987) *The Jungle and the Aroma of Meats: An Ecological Theme in Hindu Medicine*, Berkeley: University of California Press.

—— (1992) 'Gentle purge: the flower power of Ayuerveda', in C. Leslie and A. Young (eds) *Paths to Asian Medical Knowledge*, Berkeley: University of California Press.

11 The impact of culture in the face of genocide

Struggling between a silenced home culture and a foreign host culture

Erika Apfelbaum

For who can live without antecedents, without officially acknowledged dead ancestors? (Car qui peut vivre sans antécédents, sans morts reconnus?)

(Piralian, 1994: 17)

In this chapter I will be examining the difficulties faced by those who experience some form of uprootedness from their social and historical linkages. I shall look at some of the mechanisms by which people cope after they have been summarily cut off from their cultural roots, forced to live away from what had been their ancestors' home for generations. Such cases can, in my view, shed some light upon the way in which cultural dimensions contribute to the construction of individual and social identities. Culture refers here to the traditions and values, the social codes and norms, the official accounts of historical events shared by a given collectivity or society, and is therefore that society's various social representations and idiosyncratic components which contribute to 'regulate its collective life, set its specific goals and define its identity' (Mauss, 1969: 210–11). Culture also shapes the individual identity of each member of the society. This notion of culture resonates with the concept of the social imaginaries (*imaginaires sociaux*) introduced by the Polish political scientist Bronislaw Baczko to refer to the symbolic system through which a collectivity determines its identity and boundaries as well as the places, status and social identity of its members (1984: 32–3).

The individual's identity is closely determined by the framework of his/her multiple social encounters and experiences, as Maurice Halbwachs (1952) has shown in his 1925 ground-breaking exploration 'The social framework for memory'. Halbwachs analyses extensively how individual experiences are constructed, stored in memory and recollected through social interchanges within various social institutions – first mainly within the realm of the family, then later in educational and religious contexts as well as in the various other institutional systems of any given state. He insists on the need for one's personal experiences and private recollections to be couched in, or voiced within, a collective, public chronicle: the collectivity's historical accounts provide the legitimising foundation for individuals to make sense of their personal experiences and therefore for constructing their identity.

Living away from 'home', uprooted people have become part of a society – the host society – whose idiosyncratic cultural features may well be at odds with their family's former home culture. Elements of the earlier home culture continue to circulate and be transmitted from generation to generation by the family's saga and its distinct social rules. Such cultural discrepancies between former home and current host cultures embody the reality of the uprooting. They are a daily inescapable reminder of the earlier dislocation of the family and of the socio-political reality which led to emigration. The implications of such cultural tensions which are part of the day-to-day experiences of uprooted people and their children will be the central focus of this chapter. How do the tensions affect the sense of belonging? How are they played out in the development of personal and social identity even across generations and what does it mean, in such a context of cultural tension, to say 'I' or to say 'we'?

I will rely largely on autobiographical statements from interviews I have conducted or from published accounts. But I will also draw upon literary narratives (*le récit*). As the French historian of Greek mythology Jean-Pierre Vernant (*Droits d'auteurs*, Channel Arte, 10 October 1999) has recently stated, such narratives and/or mythical tales can help open up and give access to private experiences which otherwise are often described by those who have actually lived through them as being unspeakable, *indicible*. Through such fictional accounts, untellable tales can none the less be transmitted across generations in a way that family accounts often cannot. Furthermore, I would argue, the fictional writing process embodies and personalises collective realities and creates a distancing which allows the writer to expose facts in their crudest reality while not violating the personal privacy of real individuals. Valérie Cadet (1999) has used a similar argument in reviewing Robert Bober's (1999) recent 'fictional novel' retracing the children's lives in a home for those whose parents perished in the Holocaust. While Adorno argued that poetry was no longer possible after Auschwitz, I wonder whether poetry and fiction are not in fact the only vehicles today for speaking the unspeakable, in order to express and convey the horrific emotional content of traumatised life to the generations who follow. As psychologists, we have largely failed to integrate such emotional components in our theorising, and have not had much success in expressing them in our 'scientific' writings.

Cultural uprooting, uprootedness and social identity

Today the uprooting of a population and all the subsequent consequences experienced as uprootedness are fairly common sociopolitical realities. Increasingly, groups have been forced to flee their homeland for economic reasons or have been expelled as a result of political upheavals. In certain cases, as with genocides, people can no longer entertain any hopes of returning to their original homes and communities of family and friends. The idea that we live in a culturally homogeneous environment is today increasingly difficult to maintain – and the research by Frosh, Phoenix and Pattman (Chapter 3, in this volume) which explores the impact of 'cultural resources' upon the construction of masculinities, as well as

Marshall and Woollett's account (Chapter 8) of the self-presentation of a young Asian woman living in Britain, are illustrations of the cultural diversity of our societies. This diversity is seen by those who must deal concretely with the current worldwide humanitarian needs of populations uprooted for political or economic reasons. It is also evident to those who work politically towards the ongoing construction of a more unified Europe, a more unified world. Each asks: How does one cope, at the intra-personal, interpersonal and at the inter-group level, with the reality of coexistence or confrontation between diverse cultural communities, each with long-standing traditions and socio-historical claims?

In fact, the migration of a large number of populations is not just a recent phenomenon. During the nineteenth century, as a result of the industrial revolution, there were vast migrations of agrarian population towards urban settings. Those displacements and the reshuffling of populations into mass agglomerations produced major disruptions of the traditional social fabric and a number of social problems (*la question sociale*) which became a starting point for the development of the social sciences (Apfelbaum, 1986). Today, however, the questions tend to be more focused on finding modes of coexistence of groups from different backgrounds in a culturally diversified society (see Apfelbaum, 1999).

Although in this chapter I generally refer to uprootings and the sense of uprootedness associated with geographic, territorial displacement, there is a much broader range of situations in which these terms are equally relevant. The cultural unease associated with technological change is one example (Yates and Day Sclater, Chapter 9, this volume); another is the anxiety, hostility and possibility resulting from recent displacements in self-presentations and realities of gender (e.g. Gill *et al.*, Chapter 7, this volume). When women break away from 'home places', leave traditional roles and enter spaces which have long been the exclusive territory of men, such as the world of politics, they can equally be described as socially uprooted. The ways in which women in leadership positions cope with their marginality is directly relevant here; the differences in the socio-historical contexts between Norway and France (Apfelbaum, 1993) offer an additional cultural dimension which affects the way in which women cope with gendered uprooting.

Cultural uprooting, cultural conflicts and social identity

If we refocus our attention on geographic uprootings, my own question, within the limits of this chapter, is this: For people who leave one place for another, how do their multiple, often competing cultural histories impact upon the construction of the person's identity?

At first sight, as is argued by proponents of multicultural societies, for example Canada, it seems plausible to believe that the presence of multiple cultural references should represent an additional richness, a valued resource which provides a diversity of experiences and outlooks, from which to construct a broad and diversified self. However, at certain stages of the development of this identity, such richness may instead become a factor in estrangement or alienation, and may even appear to the person as a marked disadvantage. This may be particularly true during times when finding one's stable social niche appears vitally urgent, as during the crisis of adolescence or, for the purposes of this chapter, during the process of adaptation following immigration, to which I shall return shortly.

Let me cite an example of a double cultural tie, lived conflictually. In Andreï Makine's (1996) more or less autobiographical novel *Le Testament français*, the Russian hero describes at great length how his grandmother, who is of French origin, teaches him French throughout his childhood. But she does much more than that: the accounts of her Parisian youth represent a direct heritage which anchors his personal history, his own life, as a member of French society because of the close genealogical bond which exists between them. These accounts also ground him in the pre-revolutionary history of Russia where French culture was the ultimate sign of education among the upper classes. The grandmother's tales provide specific ways of imagining and approaching the world which come to have for the narrator the same reality, legitimacy and importance as the teachings from the context of his Russian upbringing. He is fascinated by the exoticism and uniqueness that his grandmother introduces into his life until he realises just what a burdensome legacy it can be. During adolescence, when the need for conformity with the peer group is the strongest, and existentially most important, the co-existence of two divergent mirrors becomes a burden: this 'other' way of seeing highlights the narrowness and parochialism of his Russian friends and is an obstacle to his becoming a member of their group without reservation.

Similarly, in a recent interview, Doris Lessing stresses the particular sensitivity to the world resulting from her own history of uprootedness. She migrated as a child to South Africa; this gave her a sharpened, de-centred perception of the world together with a permanent sense of 'insecurity'. But these are, she claims, necessary conditions to enhancing awareness, being creative, and in her case to becoming a writer. It is probably not accidental that Andreï Makine also became a writer.

To a certain extent, one can say of Andreï Makine or Doris Lessing (1997) that the way in which they speak of themselves makes them outsiders to the world. Similarly, being outsiders to the world was the status of a number of Jews following the period of their emancipation in Germany, at least for those who were unable or unwilling to fully assimilate into German society. Because they were neither in tune with the culture of their origins, nor fully part of the German society in which they lived, Hannah Arendt (1987) defines them as 'pariah', a concept she borrows in part from Max Weber but in the meaning which Bernard Lazare (1996) gave it at the end of the nineteeth century. The pariah does not feel at home in the world because he 'opposes passionately his Jewish as well as non-Jewish environment' (p. 177, my translation), unlike the 'parvenu' who tries to assimilate and vanish into the host culture. In Arendt's analyses the feeling of insecurity that goes with the status of pariah is productive of creativity and originality in art, as with Heine or Kafka, or in politics, Bernard Lazare (1987: 194–218).

Eva Hoffman's (1989) autobiographical account, *Lost in Translation*, is another example of the disturbing, destructuring consequences of uprooting. She was born in Poland of parents who survived the Nazi genocide of the Jews and went to Canada with them when she was a teenager. Reflecting on the insurmountable gap between the past and the present, the home culture and the host culture, Hoffman writes:

> I exist in the stasis of a perpetual present, that other side of 'living in the present', which is not eternity but a prison. I can't throw a bridge between the present and the past, and therefore I can't make time move.
>
> (1989: 116–17)

In this no man's land, language is indeed one of the key elements, the touchstone which reveals this painful adaptation process.

> We want to be able to give voice accurately and fully to ourselves and our sense of the world. . . . Linguistic dispossession is . . . close to the dispossession of one's self. Rage that has no words is helpless rage.
>
> (Hoffman, 1989: 123)

In other words, not being at home in our own tongue deprives us of both self-assurance and a sense of control. Joseph Conrad illustrates this point when he claims that the writing process had always been extremely painful and that he had constantly to struggle in search of the proper word: 'It might well be that his dread was provoked by the language which he had adopted (Conrad, who was of Polish origin, fluent in French, had chosen to write in English) and within which he produced an immense and admirable body of work, without ever having known the spontaneity of indigeneity' (Bianchotti, 1997: 7, my translation) as would someone writing in their own mother tongue. The linguistic behaviour of one of my close friends is a case in point. Never using any colloquial or slang expressions has been his way of coping in a situation where he felt linguistically homeless. Born and raised in a working-class suburb, he was such a brilliant student that, as a teenager, he was sent to a prestigious high school in Paris in a very bourgeois neighbourhood where he felt totally alienated from his schoolmates. Elegant and refined speech soon became his protective shield against the painful awareness of not belonging socially.

Hannah Arendt, who had to flee her homeland, Germany, because of the rise of Nazism, also insists on the major importance the mother tongue has for her. She reclaims the tongue, refusing to let herself be dispossessed (Arendt, 1987: 247). She notes how language bonds one to a culture and history: 'In language, the past has its inalienable place, and it is in the face of language that all the attempts to rid oneself of the past finally fail' (Arendt, 1974).

As a counterpoint to Arendt's victorious linguistic tenacity, Eva Hoffman (1989) reports the deep sense of distress she felt after she was given a diary notebook as a present: In what language was she to address herself? The gift brought to the foreground the gloomy, painful reality of her uprootedness, which continues to haunt her in many obscure ways.

Writing in Polish at this point would be a little like resorting to Latin or ancient Greek – an eccentric thing to do in a diary, in which you're supposed to set down your most immediate experience . . . in the most unmediated language. Polish is becoming a dead language, the language *of the untranslatable past*.

(1989: 120, emphasis added)

Ultimately she chooses to write in English, 'the language of the present, even if it's not the language of the self' (p. 121), but remains incapable of saying 'I' in English, nor can she speak of herself as 'she'; so she resigns herself to addressing a fictitious interlocutor. She also describes the sense of estrangement, familiar to all those who live 'away from home', even if only temporarily, that she experiences when she tries to tell stories relating to her life before her arrival in Canada. These accounts, highly meaningful to her, none the less miss their targets (pp. 117–18) with her listeners, who can understand neither the events nor the way in which she recounts them because they have different implicit cultural references.

Overcoming the inherent difficulties of bridging different socio-historical and cultural contexts is at the very core of all translation work, and this is precisely what makes translation a truly creative writing process. The adequacy of translation is equally at stake when concepts travel cross-culturally, migrating from one epistemological context to another. Thus, for example, 'French feminism', as it is known in Anglo-Saxon contexts, has little to do with what feminist theory refers to in France:

In my own attempt to bridge different traditions of thought between the North American and the European continents, concepts keep betraying me. They lose their socio-historical complexity and density; they change meaning during the journey within the diplomatic pouch. . . . In breaking away from the historical tradition and political preoccupations in which they first emerged, concepts take up a life of their own and tend to fertilize other grounds in unexpected ways.

(Apfelbaum, 1995: 56; see also Pheterson, 1995; Varikas,1995; Walkerdine, 1995)

Radical uprootedness and genocides: the obligation of silence and the obligation to live

In the remainder of this chapter I focus more specifically on genocides, the most radical and traumatic of uprootings. This focus may help us understand the centrality of cultural factors both for the development of social identity and for our existence as social human beings in this world. There are an increasing number of publications devoted to the long-term repercussions of genocidal events on the children of survivors, the inheritors of these genocides. In France, Jeanine Altounian (1990) and Hélène Piralian (1994), both children of survivors of the Armenian massacres, have extensively analysed, largely from a psychoanalytical perspective, the burden connected with an obligation which proves to be an impossible task – that of integrating oneself and blending into the host culture. Piralian insists on the fact that genocides, beyond the primary goal of physically annihilating a social group in its entirety, are ultimately geared towards eradicating the very cultural roots by which this group has historically established and maintained its identity. An example is the Armenian massacre by the Turks between 1890 and 1915. More recently, the extermination of entire eastern European Jewish communities has at the same time almost completely destroyed Yiddish culture at its very life-source.

Genocides, I will claim, as the ultimate and most radical forms of uprooting, are paradigmatic cases. The way in which first the survivors of genocide and later their children cope with this irreversible loss of their cultural groundings, with the reality of vanished and therefore unreacheable forebears, offers a relevant terrain for observations. Because they have disappeared, they are not living, nor are they dead. Recently, I met a woman, well over 60, who had 'lost' both her parents during the Nazi genocide. She 'had known' that they had never come back from deportation but had engaged in no search to find out details of their fate. As it turns out, they were both listed in Serge Klarsfeld's (1978) compilation of the names of all the Jews who were deported in the series of transports which left France for the death camps between March 1942 and August 1944. When I sent her this document, which specifies the date and convoy of deportation but gives no details about the exact circumstances of people's death, she wrote:

> I have of course found the names of my parents on the list. It is impossible for me to thank you . . . yet, uncanny as it may seem, to see them be there, among the others, bestows upon them a reality. They must in fact have existed since they have died.
>
> (1996, personal communication, my translation)

Violently and definitively disconnected from their original home base, exiles or survivors of genocides have lost part of their social identity, because their traditional and familiar ways of being in the world are no longer anchored in any tangible territorial and social reality. In describing her own status as a refugee, Hannah Arendt says:

> We have lost our home, that is to say the familiarity of our daily life. We have lost our profession, that is to say, the assurance of being of some service in the world. We have lost our maternal language, that is to say, our natural reactions, the simplicity of gestures and the spontaneous expression of our feelings.
>
> (1987: 58, my translation)

Elsewhere, she insists on the central role which friends play for exiles: 'they replace the lost Heimat for we the refugees' (Arendt, 1945, in Lebovici, 1996). Friends help to cope with the eerie sense of isolation and uprootedness and restore the cosiness of a familiar environment.

The host country generally remains silent about the historical events which brought about the present status of uprootedness of the survivors. The survivors evolve in a no person's land in which the memories of the past receive no legitimation by collective public recognition in the host country. Thus recollecting, remembering and re-elaborating those memories remains an exclusively private affair. Yet, as Halbwachs (1952) long ago demonstrated, the possibility of *making sense* of one's uprooted and disrupted personal history depends on the content of public collective discourses. The experience of estrangement is directly related to society's official representations and interpretations of the events surrounding one's family's uprooting. It will depend upon the prevailing 'social framework for memory' (p. vi), to use Halbwachs' terminology. But this framework alters over time because the representations of past history are subordinated to changing political and ideological purposes. Therefore, the construction of personal identity, and attempts to reconstruct shattered or broken identities, depend in part on societal and political fluctuations.

Silence, and even more so the official silence of the state, is harmful because it delegitimises private personal history. The lack of official references in the host country makes it impossible 'to translate the survivors' experiences' (Altounian, 1990). Altounian insists that the silence of the state is rarely challenged by the survivors because of the respect they owe to their hosts, who could be shattered by the obscenity of the horrors experienced by the survivors or their families and community. There is a need, she claims, to respect minimal codes for the '*bienséance*' of the social link. There are many other reasons for neglecting the place of genocides in the history accounts of a given state . . . but this is outside the scope of this chapter (see Apfelbaum, 1999).

The disconnection with past history is even more devastating for the children of survivors of genocide because they have had no direct access to the cultural roots of their parents. 'My parents tell me little about their prewar life . . . as if the war erased not only the literal world in which they lived but also its relevance to their new conditions', recalls Eva Hoffman (1989: 8). Parents' silence about their early history and past traumatic events is a way to protect the children from this burdensome past as well as an attempt to provide the pacific environment favourable for successful integration. But in keeping silence, the parents also increase the rift: in not ensuring the transmission of the family's saga, genealogical continuity is broken. The result is to create generations of children born out of any genealogy, so that children of survivors can truly be considered as 'cultural orphans' with no other alternative than integrating into the host country. The inheritors, the second generation, thus become strangers to themselves, 'having to face an eclipse of their origins . . . a human being without "a shadow"', suggests Altounian (1990: 204).

Although little research in France has systematically addressed such issues, several studies have looked at the difficulties of integration into the school system, as well as into adult professional life, faced by the children of migrant workers of North African, Portuguese or Spanish origin whose families came to France. These studies consistently indicate that the children of immigrants succeed better in their professional adult life in the host country when the parents help maintain a continuity between past and present, between what was then and what is now (Delcroix, 1998). And children tend to do better in school whenever their teachers take an interest in the origins and cultural background of their students and express, in a variety of ways, their appreciation towards the distinctive, culturally specific background of the children's parents. In Eva Hoffman's terms, it is helpful when teachers and parents 'throw a bridge between the present and the past'.

In order to be faithful to their parents' desire to protect their future lives, children of survivors feel obliged to integrate into the host culture, claims Altounian (1990), and have to learn its language and master its culture, its codes of behaviour and their application. But this second generation has to do so with an initial disadvantage: they have no family legacy to reclaim, no genealogical roots of which to be proud, and no possibility of bridging their current cultural context to that of their past ancestry.

The children of genocide survivors are in a paradoxical position. Given their impossibility of bonding with the past, they may reproduce symbolically the scenario of the genocidal process experienced by the previous generations. They themselves may re-enact the radical rift which the genocide has installed between the past and present, this radical rift which is both the condition for and the barrier to developing a sense of belonging. There is a basic impossibility: the children of survivors cannot be fully grounded in a society which does not share their experiences of persecution. But they themselves have only a vicarious knowledge of those persecutions, being raised in a family which can only speak of past events by means of euphemisms (Altounian, 1990: 203). There are moments in their lives when these incompatibilities come to the foreground, when they may become cruelly aware of how different they are, how much they do not fit; and these are moments of great pain and shame. To give just one example, Altounian (1990) very eloquently describes these feelings when she takes her father to meet the principal of the exclusive school at which she has just been accepted and is faced with the normative discourse of the principal's secretary, which is obviously totally irrelevant to her father's values. She is ashamed both of her father *and* of her wish at that particular moment to disavow any bond with her father. The feelings of alienation, of lowered self-esteem, and problems with establishing a strong and grounded social and personal identity are very similar to those that appear in accounts from socially upwardly mobile working-class British women. Such women who, through their education, break away from their family's social background also experience uprooting and have to cope with a sense of betrayal which is equally at work in the case of the children of Maghrebian workers and immigrants in France.

In the work which Valerie Walkerdine has done with women from working-class British backgrounds and portrayed in her film *Didn't She Do Well* (1992), she describes at length the pain experienced by the women, who no longer feel at home in their childhood environment or in the world in which they have been educated and work. These emotions are determinant in our sense of belonging, of legitimacy, and thus in our ways of being in the world.

The demands on children of immigrants, especially those of Muslim origin, are somewhat different, yet not necessarily easier, when the parents insist on remaining strictly faithful to their home traditions. Such is the case for a number of North African children of the second generation: '*les beurs*', who are born and schooled in France from parents who immigrated from North Africa. They find themselves caught between two contradictory sets of behavioural codes and customs, torn between their attempt to assimilate into French culture with a strong secular ideology and the obligation to keep to traditional Muslim teachings and codes of ethics. Thus each time Muslim girls have worn the chador in a state school, it has raised heated debates widely echoed by the press (Jamous, 1996).

Some theoretical implications

One final word about the epistemological implications of the analysis which I have, within the limits of this chapter, only briefly outlined. Such a perspective implies, I would claim, a major and radical shift in our ways of theorising. Well before psychologists started to become truly concerned with the cultural dimensions of their field, Hannah Arendt insisted on the fact that we do not evolve in a vacuum and that it is impossible to ignore our inscription in the world. This inscription occurs in various ways. On the one hand, it happens through our filiation, our genealogical link. It is not just accidental that adopted children may express a need to find, at some point in their lives, the trace of their biological parents, as part of the broader family history. The silence and the 'unspoken' ('*le non-dit*') in this matter can be destabilising, painful, and ultimately detrimental to the child's social and personal identity. On the other hand, the inscription occurs because we are part of a given society at a given moment of its history. These contextual dimensions are indispensable in order to understand the way in which men and women construct their lives, their identity and their rapport with others. But those original givens which are often seen to carry right from birth (sex, social or ethnic origin, and so on) acquire their particular meaning and are shaped within a specific socio-historical context. Each subject *replays them in his/her own unique way* (Arendt, 1974). Thus being born a woman or an Armenian or a black person does not reveal any essence which must confine the person to a given location or culture. Each life represents a unique narrative which reveals how we cope with and combine, within specific cultural and socio-historical circumstances, the components of our personal and collective history, how we build our personal and social identities, and how we make use of the *freedom* the socio-historical environment leaves us. This approach provides a very different, conception of humankind, one less deterministic than the traditional models of social psychology.

Furthermore, such a perspective takes the *diversity* of humankind as a starting point rather than focusing on an abstract universal man: in this respect the study by Malik (Chapter 10, this volume) is a relevant illustration of the way in which acknowledging the diversity of experiences of emotions in different cultural settings not only undermines the universalistic conception of emotions but opens the way for a different theoretical conceptualisation. But for all that, it does not mean that one cannot reach the universal and must go along with the perspective of relativism as it is presently developing. Quite the contrary; here again I refer to Hannah Arendt (1974). The singularity of experience offers one of the possible ways to confront the universal; for as we question certain men and women about the fashion in which they have each lived their life, in which they have evolved on the world's stage, we take the measure of a whole epoch and we illuminate what is common to everyone.

Acknowledgements

I thank Ian Lubek for his helpful comments and revision of the English version of this chapter. I am also grateful to Corinne Squire for her thoughtful editorial suggestions.

References

Altounian, J. (1990) *Ouvrez-moi seulement les chemins d'Arménie. Un génocide aux déserts de l'inconscient*, Paris: Les Belles Lettres.

Apfelbaum, E. (1984) 'La mémoire à éclipses et la mémoire volée', *Traces* 9–10. Judaïsme, judaïcités: récits, narrations, actes du langage: 281–9.

—— (1986) 'Prolegomena for a history of social psychology: some hypotheses concerning its emergence in the twentieth century and its raison d'être', in K. Larsen (ed.) *Psychology and Ideology*, New York: Ablex.

—— (1993) 'Norwegian and French women in high leadership positions: the importance of cultural contexts upon gendered relations', *Psychology of Women Quarterly* 17(4): 409–29.

—— (1995) 'Cross-cultural issues in social theorization: the case of feminism', in I. Lubek, R. van Hezewijk, G. Pheterson and C.W. Tolman (eds) *Trends and Issues in Theoretical Psychology*, New York: Springer-Verlag.

—— (1999) '"And now what, after such tribulations?" The importance of legacy and the obligation of remembrance', the 1999 Lynn Weiss Lecture. An APA Foundation Lecture presented to the Society for the Psychological Study of Social Issues, at the Annual Meeting of the American Psychological Association, Boston, 20–24 August.

Arendt, H. (1974) 'Walter Benjamin', in H. Arendt (ed.) *Vies politiques*, Paris: Gallimard. First published 1971.

—— (1987) *La Tradition cachée*, Paris: Bourgeois Trad française. First published 1948.

Baczko, B. (1984) *Les Imaginaires sociaux*, Paris: Payot.

Bianchotti, H. (1997) 'A propos de Conrad', *Le Monde des Livres*, 23 May.

Bober, R. (1999) *Berg et Beck*, Paris: POL.

Cadet, V. (1999) 'Sur Bober', *Le Monde des Livres*, 8 October.

Delcroix, C. (1998) 'Que transmettent les pères à leurs filles et à leurs fils sur le travail?' Journée sur 'Des hommes et des femmes face à la précarisation. Quelles dynamiques biographiques?' GEDISST Seminar, Paris, Iresco, 6 April.

Halbwachs, M. (1952) *Les Cadres sociaux de la mémoire*, Paris: PUF. First published 1925.

Hoffman, E. (1989) *Lost in Translation*, New York: Penguin.

Jamous, H. (1996) 'Les jeunes filles au foulard', *L'Homme et la Société* 120: 17–23.

Klarsfeld, S. (1978) *Le Mémorial de la déportation des Juifs de France*, Paris: Edité par Beate et Serge Klarsfeld, BP 137–16.

Lazare, B. (1996) *Le Fumier de Job*, Paris: Circé. First published 1928.

Lebovici, H. (1996) *Hannah Arendt: expérience, Juive, boutique et histoire*. Thèse pour le Doctorat de Sociologie, Université de Paris VII – Denis Diderot.

Lessing, D. (1997) Interview, *Le Monde des Livres*, February.

Makine, A. (1996) *Le Testament français*, Paris: Poche.

Mauss, M. (1969) *Oeuvres*, Paris: PUF.

Pheterson, G. (1995) 'Group identity and social relations: divergent theoretical conceptions in the United States, the Netherlands, and France', in I. Lubek, R. van Hezewijk, G. Pheterson and C.W. Tolman (eds) *Trends and Issues in Theoretical Psychology*, New York: Springer-Verlag.

Piralian, H. (1994) *Génocide et transmission*, Paris: l'Harmattan.

Varikas, E. (1995) 'Traveling concepts: feminist theory in cross-cultural perspective', in I. Lubek, R. van Hezewijk, G. Pheterson and C.W. Tolman (eds) *Trends and Issues in Theoretical Psychology*, New York: Springer-Verlag.

Vernant, J.-P. (1999) *Droit d'auteurs*, Channel Arte, 10 October.

Walkerdine, V. (1995) 'French feminism and British francophilia: some preliminary thoughts', in I. Lubek, R. van Hezewijk, G. Pheterson and C.W. Tolman (eds) *Trends and Issues in Theoretical Psychology*, New York: Springer-Verlag.

Conclusion

Valerie Walkerdine

For many years, scientists and the general public have attempted to take sides in a debate about cultural influences on psychology, from disputes about what part of intelligence is nature and what nurture, to controversies over the suggestibility and violence of crowds such as those on football terraces, in political demonstrations, or performing 'ethnic cleansing'. Argument still rages as to whether culture or some failure in child rearing is to blame for the most horrific acts. After the murder in Britain of the toddler James Bulger by two older boys and the recent high school killings in the USA, for instance, the question of whether the killers had watched violent television films or played violent video and computer games surfaced again and again. It seems as though there can be only one kind of explanation: either evolution or culture, or an additive mixture of both. As all the authors in this volume attest, such simplistic distinctions do not do justice to the crucial and complex issue of the relationship between cultural forms and practices and the production of subjectivity.

Perhaps the most important contribution to current understandings of the significance of culture has come from cultural studies. This field developed as an attempt to make sense of contemporary culture. It has always been concerned with Otherness, especially, in the beginning, class, commencing as it did in the aftermath of the western New Left and activists and academics' turn to studies of ideology, particularly through the work of Gramsci and Althusser. In addition, work in post-structuralist and postmodernist anthropology (Clifford and Marcus, 1986) and cultural geography (Pile and Thrift, 1995) has developed the theme of the cultural aspects of subjectivity. This work, together with postcolonial theory in literary studies (Bhabha, 1994; Spivak, 1987), has remained largely outside the reference of most psychologists. Lynne Segal (Chapter 2) points to the way in which the resort to a psychobiology that invokes Darwin comes after disappointment with a number of other 'turns' to modernist theories, notably those of Marx, Keynes and Freud. Postmodern cultural, and cultural and literary criticism also stemmed from a critique of what modernist anthropology, sociology and literary theory had to offer. However, this work has been characterised by a love/hate relationship with the psychological, far more ambivalent than evolutionary psychology's straightforward claim that the psychological is inscribed within biology. For much of the more textually based cultural theory makes reference to postmodern psychoanalysis stemming from the work of Lacan, while more ethnographically based work, for instance in the British cultural studies tradition, has tended forcefully to oppose this move (see, for example, Morley, 1992).

The chapters in this book might be understood as representative of a new, hybrid endeavour, which takes arguments from cultural studies and remakes them, producing a third space, a constructive blend of the psychological and the cultural which neither psychology nor cultural studies can afford to do without. In moving forward from psychology's arguments about culture and cultural-studies arguments about the psychological, the book finds a set of new phenomena, and creates novel and exciting discourses and modes of enquiry through which to read them. Many of the chapters deal with hybrid forms of subjectivity, especially in relation to 'race', ethnicity and gender, and hybrid methods through which culturally specific subjectivities may be understood. They are a model of how a new kind of psycho-cultural work could be accomplished.

One of the distinguishing marks of the chapters in this book is that they move away from the obsession with resistance which has typified British cultural studies, particularly in its engagements with youth research. Coping, surviving, living in post-Holocaust cultures or within urban multiculturalism are not the stuff of romantic proto-revolutionary masculinity with which this cultural studies tradition has been preoccupied. They are, rather, examples of the production of subjectivity. I believe that this work is ground-breaking in its attempts to understand the making of subjectivity within the cultural transformations that have characterised the past hundred years. Engaging with the psychological aspects of cultural, political and technological change, like those associated with genetic modification, is long overdue. There is a tradition of such engagement in quantitative psychological studies, and in some psychoanalytic work (Hanna Segal's writing on nuclear war, for instance). The difference in the work presented here is that it does not distance itself methodologically, as in the first case, from the subjective living-out of culture; nor, as in both traditions, does it offer a fundamentally psychological reading of cultural and political phenomena. Instead, it attempts to understand subjectivity as culturally produced. That is, it works in the third space that does not reduce the psychological to the cultural or the cultural to the psychological.

The difference is vital. This is the moment neither of Lacan nor of the Frankfurt School, and still less of psycho-history. Some of the chapters use psychoanalysis, but it is important to recognise that psychoanalysis is deployed and understood here as part of a wider cultural project. The 1970s promise of Lacanianism was, for many, that it allowed a cultural reading of psychoanalysis that went beyond Freud's essentialism. However, Lacanianism's concern with a universalised and insurmountable patriarchy did not easily allow engagement with new and heterogeneous forms of subjectivity, and psychoanalysis in general continues to pay surprisingly little attention to such subjectivities. At the same time, it is difficult to envisage a way of working with these complex subjectivities without considering patterns of defence, of relations between social, cultural and unconscious fantasies.

All the chapters could be identified as part of the movement known as critical psychology. Although as yet very diverse in its orientation, this movement is critical of mainstream psychology's failure to engage with the social, political and cultural conjuncture in which we live, and tries to find new and more adequate ways to address the subjectivities that characterise the beginning of the second millennium. It is to be hoped that this critical work in psychology can stray beyond the limit-conditions which have marked the discipline, to become that hybrid form which I am advocating.

When I first came to discuss some of the chapters in this volume at a conference in Dublin where they were presented, I was struck by something that happened on the way. I had been to the west of Ireland with my partner, an Australian of Irish descent, to look for his grandfather's birthplace and any living relatives. While engaged in this endeavour, interesting in itself, we discovered that Ireland was littered with people from the New World who were trying to trace their relatives and ancestors. People put ads in newspapers, sometimes only knowing that a relative had lived in a particular county or even 'the West' of Ireland. Here, despite contemporary postmodern concerns with surface, moves away from depth, and the schizophrenic waning of affect that Jameson (1992) describes, was living testimony of a longing for connection and for a past denied by twentieth-century diaspora. In the midst of a celebration of new, hybrid spaces was a longing for wholeness that seemed to be their antithesis. But as we know, there is no simple 'going back', just as there is no return to the certainties of place, gender and class that structured the socialities of the now largely disappeared manufacturing base. Economic rationalism has ended such certainties of identity, though they still haunt the uncertain, hybrid, post-diasporic identifications that inhabit the cosmopolitan spaces of the present. Erika Apfelbaum writes of the importance of being recognised for your authentic origins and cultural roots and of being able to speak about them (Chapter 11). And while I acknowledge the aching intensity of that desire, I wonder what those origins and roots are, in the midst of the huge transformations now occurring and their production of fragmentary, uncertain identities.

It is ironic that psychologists influenced by postmodern theory have, like many literary and cultural theorists, tended to celebrate fragmented subjectivity as a critique of the rational, unitary, Cartesian subject (Henriques *et al.*, 1998). For while that critique is central to critical approaches within psychology, the much greater challenge is to develop it in order to understand just what 'fragmentation' means and how it is lived by people in the complex post-industrial and diasporic world of the twenty-first century. The authors of this volume take up the challenge. The world is pitting nature against culture in new ways, as Segal's and Yates and Day Sclater's chapters on evolutionary psychology and genetic modification make clear. Campaigns against genetically modified foods project the longing for a known wholeness on to a 'nature' which big business has not mutated, at a time when genetic technology is exploring the limits of biological 'hybridity' through surrogacy, gene insertion and cloning. Genetic modification serves as a metaphor for a mixed-up world peopled by those who no longer know or trust who or what they are, or who fall outside existing categories. White boys who envy black boys, Asian girls who love Madonna.

It is in this context that psycho-cultural work is absolutely vital in attempting to understand the complex production of the new subjectivities. The consequences of global changes are not easily understood by either traditional social psychology or traditional cultural studies. I suspect that as many people feel lost and in pain as feel celebratory of the new possibilities afforded by global monetarism and economic rationalism. The 'new' world contains as many of those who look back with undiminished anguish as of those who look forward with eager anticipation. This social and cultural constellation demands subtle, sensitive and complicated psychological work, which does not simplify cultural meanings and practices, and which understands psychology itself as culturally and socially produced. The work presented here testifies to the diversity and vibrancy of that endeavour. It is work that has never been more vital.

References

Bhabha, H. (1994) *The Location of Culture*, London: Routledge.

Clifford, J. and Marcus, G. (eds) (1986) *Writing Culture*, Berkeley: University of California Press.

Henriques, J., Hollway, W., Urwin, C., Venn, C. and Walkerdine, V. (1998) *Changing the Subject*, London: Routledge. First published 1984.

Jameson, F. (1992) *Postmodernism, or, the Cultural Logic of Late Capitalism*, London: Verso.

Morley, D. (1992) *Television, Audiences and Cultural Studies*, London: Routledge.

Pile, S. and Thrift, N. (eds) (1995) *Mapping the Subject: Geographies of Cultural Transformation*, London: Routledge.

Spivak, G. (1987) *In Other Worlds*, London: Routledge.

Index